What Women Watched

Book Ten
Louann Atkins Temple Women & Culture Series

What Women Watched

Daytime Television in the 1950s

✦ ✦ ✦

Marsha F. Cassidy

University of Texas Press
Austin

3-15-2006
WW
 # 21.95

The Louann Atkins Temple Women & Culture Series is supported by Allison, Doug, Taylor, and Andy Bacon; Margaret, Lawrence, Will, John, and Annie Temple; Larry Temple; the Temple-Inland Foundation; and the National Endowment for the Humanities.

∞ The paper used in this book meets the minimum requirements of ANSI/NISO Z39.48-1992 (R1997) (Permanence of Paper).

Library of Congress Cataloging-in-Publication Data

Cassidy, Marsha Francis, 1946–
What women watched : daytime television in the 1950s / Marsha F. Cassidy.
    p.   cm. — (Louann Atkins Temple women & culture series ; bk. 10)
Includes bibliographical references and index.
ISBN 0-292-70626-x (cloth : alk. paper) — ISBN 0-292-70627-8 (pbk. : alk. paper)
1. Television programs for women—United States—History. 2. Television and women—United States—History. I. Title. II. Series.
            PN1992.8.w65c37   2005
        791.45'6—dc22   2004019568

For Robert, Heather, Gwen, and Michael, with love

Contents

Acknowledgments

The research for this book began in 1996 at Northwestern University, where I was privileged to study with Larry Lichty, James Schwoch, and Mimi White, all of whose ideas contributed significantly to the development of this project. Larry's emphasis on historical detail, Jim's refined judgment and vision, and Mimi's theoretical acumen and gift for collaboration are among the many models of scholarship for which I am grateful.

I want to thank especially my longtime friend and mentor at the University of Illinois at Chicago, Virginia Wright Wexman, who has supported my career in every possible way. Conversations about popular culture with Virginia, John Huntington, Chris Messenger, Jerry Graff, and many other UIC colleagues have added new dimensions to my work. I value their original insights, which have always kept standards of discourse high and ideas fresh. Several stipends helped support my research travels, and I am grateful to Jerry Graff, Walter Benn Michaels, and Tom Hall for their support. Tom Hall deserves additional mention for the dozens of ways, both big and small, he has facilitated the completion of this project.

I owe thanks to Susan Ohmer and other members of the Chicago Film Seminar for their exceptional insights and suggestions that significantly improved earlier drafts of this book, and I am deeply indebted to the two peer reviewers the University of Texas Press asked to critique the manuscript, both of whom were thorough, discerning, and encouraging. While one reviewer remains anonymous, I want to thank Louise Spence by name for her extraordinary insights. Gratitude goes to my editor Jim Burr as well, who was able to provide exactly the right measure of practicality and wisdom. Bob Fullilove copyedited the manuscript with precision and insight; for his excellent contributions and for the diligence of Lynne Chapman and the entire staff at the University of Texas Press, I am sincerely grateful.

For their help finding rare archival material, kinescopes, and photographs, I want to thank J. Fred MacDonald for access to his collection; Dorinda Hartmann and Maxine Ducey at the Wisconsin Center for Film and Theater Research; Harry Miller and Lisa Hinzman at the

Wisconsin Historical Society; Julie Graham and Lauren Buisson at the UCLA Arts Library Special Collections; Sean Noel and J. C. Johnson at Boston University's Howard Gotlieb Archival Research Center; Mickey Fisher at WLWT in Cincinnati; and the staffs at the Cincinnati Historical Society Library, UCLA's Film and Television Archive, the Museum of Television and Radio in Beverly Hills, the Museum of Broadcast Communications in Chicago, and the Harold Washington Library in Chicago. The cooperation of Peter Gabel, Phyllis Adams Jenkins, Susan Speckels, Art Linkletter, Mickey Fisher, and Sue Chadwick has added a personal dimension to the research that I value greatly.

Finally, I wish to thank my family: my son, Michael, whose growing independence aided my efforts to write and made me increasingly proud, and who graciously tolerated my frequent use of his scanner; my daughter, Gwen, who is a feminist in her own right but who never balked at doing the dishes to help me complete the book; and my husband, Robert, whose advice, research skills, and editorial contributions were invaluable and whose cheerful support of the project never faltered.

What Women Watched

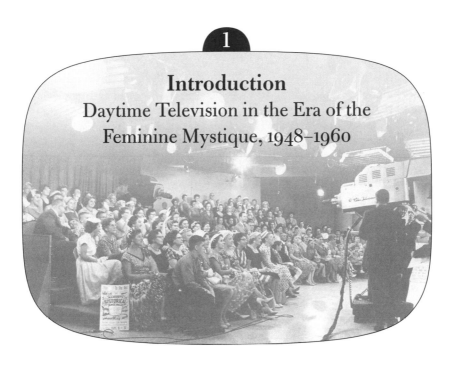

Introduction
Daytime Television in the Era of the Feminine Mystique, 1948–1960

The rise of daytime television in the United States coincided with a monumental period in American culture that reshaped the image of the ideal woman. As the country's new iridescent screen began flickering to life during the day and a nascent industry searched for ways to entice women to their sets before dinnertime, broadcasters beamed home hesitant answers to the question, What is the nature of this new femininity? Throughout the 1950s, the simulated realm of daytime broadcasting continued to inquire, Who is this new woman, and what is her place in postwar America?

The industry's quest for daytime viewers within the private world of the home also confronted the homemaker's uneasy relation to television and its promise of leisure. This book explores the modes and genres of early daytime television that encouraged women to incorporate the small screen into their daily lives and does so within the framework of gender studies. Its purpose is to contemplate the ways in which contested representations of postwar womanhood, broadcast on television in a variety of genres, mediated the home viewer's earliest bond with the new medium.

In 1948, 94.2 percent of homes owned a radio, while television ownership that year stood at a bare 0.4 percent, accounting for only 172,000 households.[1] At the dawn of television, viewers often congregated in public spaces, with taverns demarcated as a significant locus for men, as Anna McCarthy has noted.[2] Even for those few women who had access to TV sets at home in 1948, there was little to watch during the day—afternoon sports for the tavern crowd an occasional exception.[3] With fewer than 50 television stations in operation across the country,[4] radio remained the media outlet most U.S. homemakers tuned in. According to A. C. Nielsen, during the week of 15 February 1948, each of the 15 top-rated programs on daytime radio attracted listeners in some 4 million homes, representing 10–12 percent of the total possible radio audience.[5]

Yet 1948 proved to be a watershed year for television expansion, as new programming stimulated domestic adoption and fostered a pattern of television growth that pulled viewership away from public spaces like the tavern and into the home.[6] Although the government's freeze on new station licenses that took effect on 29 September 1948, was not lifted until April 1952, the television industry multiplied its reach significantly during this period, as William Boddy has documented.[7] Moreover, as Chapter 2 explains in more detail, regulatory and economic factors profoundly influenced the daytime ventures of ABC, CBS, Dumont, Mutual, and NBC during these seminal years.

Between 1948 and 1960, viewers were drawn to the television screen in staggering numbers. Television ownership skyrocketed to 87.1 percent of households by the end of the 1950s—a remarkable 45,750,000 homes[8]— and the number of commercial stations grew tenfold, from 50 to 515.[9] Daytime viewership also leaped from virtually zero in 1948 to 7.61 million homes tuned in *every minute*, on average, between 10:00 a.m. and 5:00 p.m. in 1958. That same year, 10.6 percent of the nation's total TV homes were already viewing television at 10:00 a.m. (per minute average), and the percentage of homes turning on their TV sets as the day progressed rose steadily, reaching 23.3 percent between 4 and 5:00 p.m.[10]

What initially attracted so many women to their television sets during the day is the focus of this book. This volume traces an array of modes and genres that first negotiated television's entry into domestic isolation, situates these programs within the economic and regulatory context of the industry's formative years, and critiques the most significant of these examples in light of the decade's historic reinvention of femininity— what Betty Friedan enshrined in the phrase "the feminine mystique." Friedan argued that American homemakers experienced a "sense of dissatisfaction" during the 1950s—even a "schizophrenic split"—because the postwar model of womanhood equated femininity solely with domestic fulfillment.[11] While this book acknowledges the driving influence of the era's gender expectations, it also recognizes (as Friedan did) the conflicts these expectations stirred. The chapters ahead thus reject a feminist history that merely catalogues the years 1945 to 1960 as a period of universal stagnancy.[12] Instead, the epoch of the feminine mystique is reclaimed as a noteworthy stage that connects first-wave feminism (the women's suffrage movement and the early struggle for equal rights) to feminism's second wave (the renewed political activism that began in the 1960s).[13] Within this framework, the programs reviewed in succeeding chapters are shown to express the tensions and contradictions that lay beneath the surface of a transitional period.

The Legacy of Soap Opera and Daytime's Earliest Modes

In March 1948, all but one of the 15 top-rated daytime shows on radio were soap operas,[14] but serial dramas on television did not achieve their unstoppable growth toward dominance until well into the 1960s. Because TV soap opera's fullest propagation was more than two decades away,[15] a variegated tapestry of daytime modes originally fascinated women audiences, with serial drama but one thread among many. Although soap opera and the extensive feminist scholarship about it remain crucial to the understanding of daytime's inaugural years, the chapters ahead single out for analysis prominent examples of other noteworthy genres, recognizing that television's combined array of foundational categories outnumbered soap opera by more than 7 to 1 during the 1950s.[16]

While soap opera remained a vital factor in programming, its infiltration of television's daytime schedule proceeded unevenly across the decade. Measured in quarter hours of programming aimed at women, the standard 15-minute serial provided only 4 percent of daytime fare in 1951, rising to 15.8 percent by 1954, and reaching a decade-high 23 percent in 1955. This fresh influx mid-decade may have seemed a "prodigious" rate of increase to critic Gilbert Seldes, who foresaw a new TV era of soap opera supremacy, but his timing was off by more than ten years.[17] Serial programming dipped back to 11.5 percent in 1956, then remained steady at approximately 16 percent for the rest of the decade.[18] As Robert Allen explains, it was not until the 1960s that the soap sponsors' flight to television began in earnest and programming of serial drama gained swift momentum.[19]

According to Allen, this late conversion was based in part on economics. Because daytime serials generated such enormous profits for the radio networks—profits necessary to sustain television's substantial start-up costs for these same companies—industry executives were reluctant to risk shifting soaps from radio to television too soon. Radio serials were cheap to produce, generated huge ratings, and brought in millions of dollars in sponsorships. The low number of TV viewers, combined with the double or triple monetary outlay for the requirements of a visual medium, delayed soap opera's transfer to the small screen.[20]

But profits were not the only factor. Concerns over audience reception in the home also hindered a rapid shift from radio to television. In September 1948, Irna Phillips, radio's dean of daytime serials, expressed qualms about the promise of television adaptations "unless a technique could be evolved whereby the auditory could be followed without the constant attention to the visual."[21] She was convinced that busy housewives had no time to sit down and pay attention to the screen. In February 1949, Phillips tested this hypothesis when she telecast *These Are My Children* from the NBC studios in Chicago. Phillips instructed her crew to frame the action performed behind a proscenium arch in an unobtrusive and static long shot.[22] *Variety* panned the attempt, concluding that the program failed because there was "no visual interest."[23]

Uneasy about serial drama's chance for success on daytime television, other networks approached its production with caution too. In February 1949, DuMont aired its only soap opera, *A Woman to Remember*, between 3 and 3:15 weekdays on WABD in New York City. After two months on daytime television, the series was shifted to weeknights, then summarily canceled in July, its imaginative premise depicting the behind-the-scenes adventures of a radio soap opera troupe insufficient to sustain it.[24]

On 4 December 1950, CBS premiered *The First Hundred Years*, network television's only soap opera that year. Although it enjoyed modest success, the program, which aired daily from 2:30 to 2:45, was canceled in June 1952,[25] prompting Seldes to quip that the show's title overestimated "its appeal exactly fifty times."[26] Soon thereafter, Phillips's enormously popular soap *The Guiding Light* premiered as the first radio serial rebroadcast on television. To protect its radio franchise, CBS aired the radio version at 1:45 p.m. and broadcast a television enactment of the same episode at 2:30.[27] Phillips initially requested that directors employ the same static style she had endorsed earlier, but before long *The Guiding Light* had adopted camera work befitting new televisual practices.

As the 1950s unfolded, CBS developed the largest number of soap operas of any television network, and its serials attracted strong ratings and coveted sponsors like Procter & Gamble. Yet CBS's other daytime programs also delivered impressive statistics. The yearly average audience for *Search for Tomorrow* in 1951–1952 was 10.2, while *Strike It Rich* rated 10.6.[28] In April 1956, four serials on CBS ranked among the top five multiweekly shows, scoring between 9.9 and 12.1, but both *Arthur Godfrey Time* and *The Big Payoff* followed close behind, with 9.7 and 9.3, respectively.[29]

The paradigm of serial drama was a vibrant force in daytime programming, as Chapter 7 recounts more fully, and 15-minute interludes of melodrama rippled across the flow of television. Yet in the decade's schedule of programs, serial drama formed but one vital tributary. On one March day in 1955 (the decade's apex year for serials), CBS offered Chicago women four different 15-minute serials in a row from 11:00 to noon, followed by two more at 3:00. Yet *The Garry Moore Show, Arthur Godfrey Time,* and *Strike It Rich* flowed directly into the morning serials, while *Art Linkletter's House Party, The Big Payoff,* and *The Bob Crosby Show,* totaling 90 minutes, launched the final half hour of afternoon soaps.[30]

With soap opera's dominance years away, an assortment of other genres aimed at women gained primacy during television's first decade. Beginning in 1948, programmers at the local, regional, and national levels experimented with a wide range of program types during the hours before 5:00 p.m. Significant among them were homemaking shows, shopping shows, variety-vaudeville combinations the industry called "vaudeo," live anthology drama, feature films edited for television, and dozens of popular programs the broadcast industry broadly categorized as "audience participation shows," a catchall phrase that embraced quiz shows, game shows, stunt shows, human interest shows, and so-called misery shows.[31] The industry's programming pioneers experimented with a variety of strategies, stealing good ideas from evening television, copying innovative schemes that were succeeding in diverse television markets across the country, borrowing an array of tried-and-true formats from radio—and even inventing what seem today to be strange or improbable texts.

Appealing to a predominantly female audience became the prime directive for all these experiments. To this end, women hosts began appearing in local daytime programs across the country within weeks, even hours, of a station's start-up. In Cleveland, six weeks after WEWS-TV signed on, Alice Weston became the city's first female television personality, hosting a one-hour magazine show entitled *Distaff* (debuting on 14

February 1948).[32] A few months later, in Chicago, Barbara Barkley and her cooking program premiered 30 minutes after WGN began broadcasting its first regularly scheduled day.[33]

At the regional and national level, more famous women stars tested the appeal of their television images in untried regions. Local radio celebrities like Cincinnati's Ruth Lyons, whose program was broadcast on the full NBC network in 1951,[34] as well as national icons like Kate Smith, Arlene Francis, and Bess Myerson assisted regional and national networks in the colonization of the daytime airwaves.

A long line of daytime male hosts, men fondly labeled "the charm boys" by *Time* magazine in 1954, also capably arbitrated the place of daytime television in the lives of women, skillfully directing their charisma at studio participants, while simultaneously wooing the unseen thousands of women watching from home. Across the 1950s, television's charm boys were called upon to mediate postwar gender relations with deference, seduction, and a brand of chauvinism that preserved the definitive power of male speech.

While this study attends to the gendered appeal of daytime's most renowned celebrities, men and women alike, it also honors television's unheralded stars, the everyday women who populated the airwaves as studio audience members and program participants. On the popular audience participation programs discussed in full below, hundreds of inexperienced and unrehearsed viewers became onscreen celebrities every day, crowding the studios of live broadcasts and starring as contestants in quizzes, interviews, and games. The voices and bodies of these "average" women occupied a central place in television's new daytime sphere. Each day, the significations of a newborn femininity were transmitted onscreen in the retold fragments of women's life stories, in daily images of fresh hairstyles and up-to-date fashions, and in the sum of feminine expressivity, which swung precipitously from laughter to embarrassment, from confession to silent tears. In the abundance of these participation programs, and in the multiple social subjectivities apparent in them, television beamed across the nation both the promises and the limitations of postwar womanhood.

Lessons from Soap Opera

As Charlotte Brunsdon demonstrates in *The Feminist, the Housewife, and the Soap Opera*, many of the central tenets feminist scholars bring to their study of women and television were generated within the soap opera criticism of the past 25 years.[35] Three of these broadly influential constructs have been deepened and elaborated in recent feminist thinking and are especially pertinent to the study of the other women's genres central to this book.

The first fundamental precept under review here is the notion that women working in the home view television in a distracted state. In support of this idea, scholars have documented early television's introduction of fragmented formats women could watch in spurts as they completed chores, imitating the practices of radio listening. This book reconsiders the question of "just watching" and explores the decade's evolving promotion of television as a new form of leisure, both for women in the domestic sphere and for the hundreds of visitors who assembled daily in the public space of the television studios.

The second key construct that informs this book is the feminist recognition that daytime broadcasting has long been regarded as a subaltern feminine sphere with a debased status in the culture. As later chapters confirm, an attitude of critical condescension during the 1950s gave rise to a clamorous debate over the quality of television programming offered homemakers. To clarify the terms of this debate, this study examines postwar popular discourse that ranked hierarchies of taste as "highbrow," "middlebrow," and "lowbrow" and discusses the ways in which these divisions, considered absolutes at the time, were deployed to differentiate "quality" programs, like *Home* and *Matinee Theater*, from those deemed culturally inferior by critics, such as *Strike It Rich*, *Glamour Girl*, and *Queen for a Day*.

A third perspective at work in this book draws upon feminist scholarship that has widened its specific discussion of soap opera to discover melodrama's prevalence across television flow and to relate melodrama's emphasis on "full expressivity"[36] to other "confessional" modes on TV.[37] Application of ideas from this research suggests that the newly acquired power of postwar women to be seen and heard in television's daytime sphere raised familiar contradictions about femininity's relationship to appearing and speaking in public.

On the one hand, early daytime television fostered exacting new standards for women's physical appearance, urging viewers to leave wartime plainness behind and to embrace glamour. Postwar ideologies heralded what Christian Dior labeled a "New Look" for the "dolls" of the 1950s, and sumptuous clothing, highly crafted makeup, and all the accessories of ornate glamour once again signaled womanhood. With a brand-new category of fashion attire and beauty products to sell after the war, women viewers were interpolated as premier consumers, sustaining a crucial sector of the American economy.[38]

Yet the resurgence of female attractiveness and its spectacle on television screens was counterbalanced by the omnipresence of the speaking female subject. Female hosts and everyday women alike spoke millions of words on early daytime television, and this book confronts the consequent disjuncture between a woman's narrative agency and her presence as a mere image on the screen, sometimes cast as a figure silenced by strong emotion, at other times as the glamorous object of male desire.

These three overarching tenets borrowed from the study of soap opera serve to illuminate the programs reviewed in this volume. Yet each of these ideas must first be framed within the historical context of the postwar era, when wide-reaching economic and societal changes sent women home, redefined their femininity, and steered the future of daytime television.

Daytime Television and Leisure: A Lumpa on the Sofa

As the decade's new domesticated entertainment apparatus, television was ideally positioned to offer women companionate pleasure during the day as an antidote to isolation. Although postwar women were promised "psychic and social satisfaction" as homemakers and consumers within the private sphere, as Mary Beth Haralovich has noted,[39] their lived experiences frequently clashed with these visionary expectations. Elaine Tyler May found that "women in Levittown [the prototypical postwar suburb] often complained about feeling trapped and isolated . . . For them suburban life was not a life of fun and leisure but of exhausting work and isolation."[40] In 1953, daytime celebrity Garry Moore viewed the mission of his TV program in exactly these terms; he believed his task was "to ease the loneliness of women while their husbands and children are away." "I'm convinced," he told *Time* magazine, that housewives "want to hear the sounds of merriment while they work."[41]

Yet viewing television for fun and relaxation during the day threatened to lure housewives into an unseemly habit that could disrupt family life. As Lynn Spigel suggests, magazines of the decade "showed women that their subjective pleasure in watching television was at odds with their own status as efficient and visually attractive housewives."[42]

Broadcast historians have amply documented early television's consequent dedication to developing programs that complemented the busy housewife's daily routine of work. As Boddy explains, the industry's chief concern during the emergence of television's domestic paradigm was "integrating TV programming into the routines of the housewife's daily chores just as radio had done." To this end, television producers designed daytime programs they believed conformed to a homemaker's distracted state.[43]

Almost immediately, however, ambiguity emerged between the reception model inherited from radio, which accommodated a worker-in-motion, and a fresh paradigm that beguiled a more attentive viewing subject, who turned on television for repose and leisure. *The Bob Crosby Show* (1953–1957), a daytime variety program on CBS, broached this duality in 1953, when the cast sang the show's closing song (to the tune of "Sing a Song"):

> Sing a song, while you're workin' along,
> Hum a tune, while you're dustin' the room.
> While you're doin' dishes, make a million wishes,
> We know they're bound to come true . . .
> So tomorrow, listen to Bob
> And you'll find it's an easier job.
> Or be a lumpa, as you sit down on the sofa,
> As we sing, sing, sing you a song.[44]

While the tune accentuated a whistle-while-you-work pose for home viewers, the lyrics also called forth the ominous figure of an indolent lounger. Crosby's rhymes summed up a pivotal confusion over the kind of viewing subject early daytime television hailed: Was she a whirlwind of cleaning and scrubbing or a "lumpa" on the sofa?

The industry's ambivalence between promoting television as a companion to household chores or as a respite from them was further complicated by advertiser complaints that their TV customers were not attentive enough. Concerned that housewives were not watching the visual features of their sales pitches—the product "demonstrations" touted as so persuasive by the television industry itself—sponsors began to balk at television's advertising rates. Leo Bogart wrote in 1956, "There has remained a good deal of skepticism as to whether the housewife actually watches her set—even though it is operating—what with all the other demands on her attention during daylight hours."[45]

A series of studies during the 1950s further aroused industry concerns. One such study in 1957, commissioned by clients of Young & Rubicam, confirmed that there was "a dissipation of attention due to such factors as answering the telephone, the door bell, sewing, ironing, children's cries, etc. . . . which must be taken into consideration in evaluating the use of television and certainly in the pricing of it." One advertising executive concluded, "There is no reason, in our opinion, why we should pay television prices for radio listening."[46]

Studies like these, which were designed to measure inattention, also unearthed the compelling fact that one woman in three was stealing relaxation and pleasure from daytime viewing.[47] With these statistics in mind, the television industry was trapped between marketing the medium as a work companion for women during the day—and alarming advertisers—or furthering viewing habits that could be censured for promoting sloth and idleness in homemakers—by luring more women to the couch.

Despite these concerns about the negative impact of a homemaker's "matinee habit,"[48] directives delivered during the shows themselves often instructed women to keep their eyes on the set. As early as 1948, on DuMont's *Okay, Mother*, host Dennis James ordered viewers to abandon their labors every day between 1:00 and 1:30 and sit down and watch (see Chapter 2). An early radio-TV simulcast of *Arthur Godfrey Time* helped train radio listeners to switch their daytime allegiance to television. At the moment the televised segment was about to air, the radio announcer instructed, "All right, ladies, out of the kitchen, into the living room. Turn the TV set on now!"[49]

As the decade continued, commands to watch attentively became bolder and more consistent. Before each commercial break in 1956, host Bill Leyden told viewers of *It Could Be You*, "Maybe our next surprise will be for you. Stay beside that television."[50] The advertising strategy for NBC's *Matinee Theater* went even further, designating it as a "quality" series worthy of commanding a housewife's full attention, and viewers were encouraged to draw the blinds, sit down, and watch.[51] Yet behind the scenes, NBC executive Thomas E. Coffin acknowledged the conflict for viewers in this instruction, wondering if "the major deterrent to watching *Matinee Theater* is the feeling of guilt it arouses."[52]

The stigma attached to daytime viewing was especially pronounced in programs that could make no claim to quality. In 1958, for example, *Look* magazine complained that *Queen for a Day* was a "housewives' schedule wrecker," a "house-keeping interruption": "Mops are dropped and diapers are ditched from coast to coast" when *Queen* goes on the air.[53] Dismissed as lowbrow forms of feminine entertainment, *Queen for a Day* and other audience participation shows were not considered worthy of uninterrupted viewing, yet they elicited the discordant impulse to sit down and watch just as predictably as *Matinee Theater* did.

Daytime Television and Leisure: Fun for All in the Studio

In sharp contrast to the censure-laden ambiguities attached to home viewing, attendance at live broadcasts was celebrated as unequivocally pleasurable. On a daily basis, studio outings validated women's playful relation to TV away from home; at the same time, live television's ability to "collapse space" legitimated the parallel pleasures of synchronous home reception.

The vast majority of daytime television's first genres actively sought out live audiences, and many of the era's most popular programs, notably the vast array of audience participation shows, integrated "plain people" centrally into the text. Of all the major programs under review in this book, only NBC's *Home* show and (ironically) *Matinee Theater* were not performed before live studio audiences. By 1954, the *New York Times Magazine* had concluded, "networks, sponsors and performers all consider a good audience a strong asset for a show."[54] The presence of a live and predominantly female audience, gathered together daily in a celebratory public space, defied the culture's harsher and more contradictory proscriptions for homebound viewing and opened the way for TV pleasure at home.

Writing for the *New York Times* in 1956, TV critic Jack Gould lauded live television for its capacity to unite "the individual at home with the event afar."[55] While Gould's admiration of this spatial synthesis was directed at the era's much-praised teleplays (Gould scorned most of daytime television), a similar conflation made communities of women intrinsically aware of each other's presence every day, energizing what Boddy calls "a metaphysic of presence."[56]

Daytime television's earliest formats exploited its live nature to connect viewers and studio visitors in synchronous time, establishing an interspatial community of women that was mobile as well as virtual.[57] Programs with live audiences announced a female subject who could freely traverse the home's threshold—materially and electronically—to engross herself in the amusements made possible by television.

The daytime audience represented in this emergent community read feminine and furthered the proposition that homemakers were linked via television to an imaginary social space that promulgated "girl talk," what Mary Ellen Brown has called "feminine discourse." She explains

*Every weekday in Cincinnati, studio visitors assembled from across the Ohio region to attend a live broadcast of **The Fifty-Fifty Club**, hosted by the legendary personality Ruth Lyons. Lyons regularly integrated members of the audience into her improvised performances. Photo courtesy Ruth Lyons Papers, WLWT-TV, Cincinnati, OH.*

that feminine discourse is "a way of talking and acting among feminine subjects . . . in which they acknowledge their position of subordination within patriarchal society" but are empowered by the comfort of validation.[58] During the long hours of daytime isolation, the homemaker could find solace in a fabricated community of like-minded sisters.

Live studio broadcasts drew women together from all walks of life and were reminiscent of the old nickelodeon, whose open accessibility during the day drew diverse audiences to what Miriam Hansen has called "a space apart and a space in between."[59] This social diversity in the TV studio was not only apparent visually, as cameras panned across a collection of disparate faces, but was even more discernible during individual interviews. While there were certainly women who identified themselves as the wives of bankers or army officers, many audience members came from more needy backgrounds, especially on the misery shows, where it was not uncommon to meet women who were too poor to own a washing machine or who were holding down a job while raising seven children alone. Occasionally, minority women also appeared on camera. On an episode of *It Could Be You*, a Cherokee contestant was honored for her missionary work and was awarded an organ to provide music on her home reservation, although not without first having to endure an offensive joke about the time she "couldn't get the flap in her wigwam open."[60] Afforded greater respect, Loretta Williams, a "full-blooded Pima Indian," competed on *Queen for a Day* in March 1956, while a Mexican American contestant, a widow with three young children, was voted "queen" on 24 February 1956. *Strike It Rich* especially welcomed a full range of participants, from the African American winner, Loretta Danny, whose victory in the summer of 1952 is discussed in Chapter 5, to a steady stream of persons with disabilities. Men who had been wounded in battle and the women who loved them, or women and children who were ill or disabled, appeared almost daily on these shows.

The diverse social collectivity of women gathered in the national television studios also demonstrated a geographic variety. In contrast to the local studios that attracted resident audiences in communities around the country (in Cincinnati, Chicago, Washington, DC, Los Angeles, and St. Louis, to name a few), the network television theaters were anchored in the entertainment capitals of America, and participants from around the country made pilgrimages to these media meccas. Daytime programs prided themselves on the geographically heterogeneous crowds that assembled daily. Art Linkletter explained that tickets for *House Party* were distributed all over Los Angeles three or four days before a broadcast but were concentrated in locations where tourists congregated.[61] If interviewed, participants were asked to declare their town of origin. Although the composition of audiences shifted from day to day—at times two-thirds local residents and at other times three-fourths out-of-towners[62]—producers in New York and Hollywood routinely preferred featuring "people from far-off places,"[63] a production strategy that further joined television pleasures to far-flung travel. In just three episodes of *It Could Be You*, home and studio participants represented San Diego, Los Angeles, Cincinnati, St. Louis, Grand Rapids, Omaha, Columbus, Dubuque, St. Paul, and a small town in Pennsylvania.[64] This new form of commercialized leisure, which attracted feminine celebrants from diverse classes, ages, backgrounds, abilities, and localities, built an atmosphere of sisterhood and sociability that seemed freely accessible to any woman.

As an emergent mode for women's leisure, daytime participation shows of the 1950s deployed an electronic circularity that conjoined two parallel but mismatched realms—studio space and domestic space—and in linking them devised an imaginary sphere dedicated to women's enjoyment.

By taking into account both the public space of the television theater and the private space of the home—and considering how these two spaces are mutually inflected—this books follows Anna McCarthy's rejection of an uncomplicated "privatization thesis" that sees television as "an apparatus which merely domesticates public life."[65] Daytime TV's earliest and most prosperous formats invited women into the television studio to join a "public collective engagement" that promised nonstop entertainment. When television projected images of these same engagements into the domestic arena in synchronous time, the prospect of TV pleasure during the day was extended to home viewers and thus served to reposition television's place in everyday leisure.[66]

Mediocrity and the Feminine

Daytime television's earliest programming was measured against a system of taste values that ranked the quality of texts against a scale that was held to be immutable. Dwight Macdonald, whose writing about cultural anxieties took shape in 1944 and was expressed in the harshest possible terms by 1953, articulated the trend to classify and judge popular texts that soon encompassed television within its critical glare.[67] Macdonald roundly berated "Mass Culture" and its capitalist aims, and bemoaned a rapidly emerging "homogenized culture" that "destroys all values."[68] For Macdonald, and for the many cultural elitists whose thinking caught the public's attention during the 1950s, the popular media corrupted and vulgarized High Culture. "There is slowly emerging a tepid, flaccid Middlebrow Culture," Macdonald lamented, "that threatens to engulf everything in its spreading ooze."[69]

In February 1949, when television's place within these cultural strata was still unclear, social critic Russell Lynes published an essay in *Harper's* magazine that suggested the class structure of the United States was no longer pinned to wealth and family birth but to intellectualism and its tastes,[70] what Pierre Bourdieu would later call "cultural capital." The article specified a hierarchy of four levels of taste in American society—highbrow, upper middlebrow, lower middlebrow, and lowbrow.

To Lynes, the highbrow was a self-avowed intellectual who fought to protect the arts from the "culture-mongers" and philistines (20–21). He divided the middlebrows into two camps. The upper middlebrows encompassed the "natural gamblers in the commodities of culture" (23). Composed of publishers in the popular press, movie producers, editors, and the like, they served as the "purveyors" of highbrow ideas and the creators of those cultural products that were offered for consumption to the rapidly expanding mass of lower middlebrows. Caught "between the muses and the masses," the upper middlebrows "straddle[d] the fence between highbrow and middlebrow" and "enjoy[ed] their equivocal position" (25).

The true philistines, according to Lynes, were the lower middlebrows, who were perpetually unsure about what they liked and were forever the target of advertisers (27). It was their taste that the "Lords of kitsch" were always pandering to, Macdonald mused later, and their cultural gauge tended "always downward toward cheapness" and "standardization."[71] The lowbrows, who remained closest to "folk culture" and expressed their art in an authentic "vernacular," were not philistines, in Lynes's view. Because the lowbrow "knows what he likes and he doesn't care why he likes it," he remained a friend to the highbrow.[72]

By April, in consultation with Lynes, *Life* magazine popularized the *Harper's* essay in a playful mass-market translation, presented as a cartoon grid.[73] Accompanying the Lynes summary was a harsher essay by *Life*'s senior writer Winthrop Sargeant, a self-proclaimed highbrow. Sargeant lamented that "[b]eneath the upper middle-brow there yawns an awful chasm," peopled by cultural oafs who make up some 90 percent of the population. He deplored the fact that profit motives pressed the media industries to pander to the oafish classes and to produce for their enjoyment an "overwhelming flood of cultural sewage."[74]

As television appeared on the cultural horizon in the late 1940s, social critics were thus apprehensive—uncertain if Lynes's upper-middlebrow purveyors of culture would use the new medium to "upclass" Americans' tastes or if "downclassing" to the masses was inevitable. On the one hand, in accordance with what Macdonald later called "the democratic-liberal proposal" (which Macdonald ridiculed),[75] television carried the potential to enlighten the masses by offering elite culture to everyone; on the other hand, television threatened to propagate the dreaded lower-middlebrow culture many feared would further vulgarize the nation.

It was within this context that the country's earliest television producers and critics assessed program value. Sylvester "Pat" Weaver, the legendary NBC program chief, advanced the first potential in what he called "Operation Frontal Lobes," an agenda of uplift whose metaphor was not based on "brow height" but brain anatomy. Elite New York critics joined this chorus when they supported the cultural products of television that furthered a set of aesthetic principles they endorsed; TV's "golden age" dramas, for example, brought legitimate theater, an upper-middlebrow favorite, to the small screen, and these plays were further praised for exploiting artistically the new medium's qualities of liveness, intimacy, and immediacy.[76] In Bourdieu's terms, Weaver and New York's like-minded coterie of critics and producers were "cultural intermediaries," who surrounded "themselves with all the institutional signs of cultural authority" and offered "guarantees of quality" to the masses.[77] Within this perspective, programs extolled for their quality during the 1950s were organized "to give the impression of bringing legitimate culture within the reach of all."[78]

Conversely, television's penchant for "vulgarity" shocked and offended these same taste-protectors. For the defenders of High Culture, it was alarming that radio programs popular with the "masses," like quiz programs, misery shows, and giveaways, were transferring their mediocrity straight to television. Chapter 5 explains the depth of outrage critics directed at daytime's misery shows and the legal action eventually taken against them (on the technicality that they collected charity funds without a license). These programs seemed to offer proof that television was a grand debaser, dumping cultural sewage into American homes.

Both "democratic liberals" like Weaver, who esteemed television's utopian potential, and the cultural pessimists who foresaw in television an imminent degradation shared the common conviction that taste categories were distinct and immutable.

The application of these rigid cultural values during the 1950s was especially acute in the assessment of daytime television. Even though soap operas filled comparatively few daytime hours, the stigma attached to them tarnished the entire daytime realm; like daytime radio, daytime television was marked as feminine and thus debased. As Lynes proclaimed in 1949, "In matters of taste, the lower-middlebrow world is largely dominated by women."[79]

The contest over these competing taste cultures, articulated in 1957 by ABC's Leonard Goldenson in terms of "Woolworth's" versus "Tiffany's," reverberated across the 1950s.[80] Under Weaver's direction during the first part of the decade, NBC's daytime shows were associated with the Tiffany's approach. *The Kate Smith Hour*, *Home*, and *Matinee Theater* were all promoted and reviewed as big-budget prestige programs

*NBC program executive and network president Sylvester "Pat" Weaver promoted the concept that every television show should serve a purpose beyond diversion. He incorporated this philosophy into visionary plans for **The Kate Smith Hour**, **Home**, and **Matinee Theater**. Photo courtesy Wisconsin Historical Society (WHi-10798).*

that honored the intelligence of the American homemaker and contributed to the elevation of her taste. *Kate Smith*'s producer, Ted Collins, spurned the "froo-froo" he deplored in other daytime programs; *Home*, under the sophisticated eye of Arlene Francis, was widely praised for its urbane virtues; and *Matinee Theater*, produced by the visionary Albert McCleery, sought to broaden "the cultural tastes" of its viewers.[81]

In the Woolworth's category were the audience participation shows, vehemently dismissed by critics as middlebrow and lowbrow kitsch. Defenders of true culture leveled their most animated outrage against daytime's misery shows, with *Strike It Rich*, *Glamour Girl*, and *Queen for a Day* offered up as the worst offenders.

Predating a postmodern sensibility that treasured the collapse of the low into the high, 1950s America clung fast to hierarchical absolutes of taste and judged television accordingly. As Bourdieu suggests, however, taste distinctions that are used to demarcate social class are not immutable but time-bound and ever changing. In Bourdieu's reasoning, "what makes middle-brow culture is the middle-class relation to culture." Legitimate or authentic culture (high culture) is not made for the middle-class consumer, and "it ceases to be what it is as soon as he appropriates it."[82] For Bourdieu, taste for authentic culture is, by definition, "the sum of the refusals of all socially recognized tastes," especially middlebrow tastes.[83]

Approached from this perspective, it becomes clear that cultural mavens in the 1950s, like Weaver, McCleery, Francis, and their colleagues, were doomed from the start, for as soon as the middle class was introduced via television to the fine points of modernist staging, or the cameo shot, or Picasso's paintings, or the Eames chair, elite thinkers inverted television's cherished hierarchies to laud the TV commercial and to welcome a new postmodern era.[84]

As Boddy has documented, for political as well as economic reasons, the most powerful men in television were reciting the catechism of quality during the 1950s.[85] Upper-middle-class taste-mediators, comprising an elite in-crowd of critics, producers, politicians, and regulators who were centered in New York City and Washington, DC, dictated the aesthetic criteria against which the new medium would be judged. The chapters ahead, particularly Chapters 5, 6, and 7, unravel in more detail the ways in which the decade's pervading concepts of fixed taste values were imposed upon daytime programs.

Glamour and the New Femininity

The famous World War II poster of Rosie the Riveter declaring, "We can do it!"—her sleeve rolled up to display the strong flexed muscle in her arm, her dark hair flattened under a polka-dot bandana—gave way to a reshaped femininity after the war. At the same time that television promoted ideals of womanhood that celebrated a "new and improved" domesticity, the small screen also advanced a new vision for the female form—what Karal Ann Marling describes as a sensuous "molded, hourglass shape," clothed in the era's glamorous new contours.[86] If "all the Rosies who had riveted had to find something else to do" after the war, as Elaine Tyler May explains,[87] they also had to find something new to wear.

In this spirit of transformation, Christian Dior succeeded spectacularly when he introduced his "New Look" for the American woman. Marling observes that the New Look represented "a form of living sculpture . . . a kind of body engineering" that exuded the decade's "palpable optimism."[88] If the basic shape of fashion could change the "soldier woman" of the 1940s into a flower, as Dior desired,[89] then the human condition could change too, or "at the very least, the life of the lady in the son-of-Dior suit."[90] When station WBKB in Chicago premiered a local daytime series in April 1948, it surveyed 2,000 women who owned television sets in the viewing area to ascertain their interests. "Fashions" led the list.[91]

The cosmetics industry mirrored this fashion renaissance. During the war, the government had asked women to curtail their purchases of cosmetics, and manufacturing plants warned against glamour on the job. Once the war ended, sales of beauty products skyrocketed.[92] Kathy Peiss calls the postwar years "a rococo period" for the beauty industry, with the war's end serving as a "catalyst for [a] psychological interpretation of cosmetics," promoting the fantasy of feminine beauty as an antidote to the harsh transitions women endured in the shift from war to peace.[93] Consumers were now offered a limitless array of beauty products, and the two Titans of the cosmetics world, Hazel Bishop and Revlon, invested richly in television sponsorships.[94]

According to Marling, the beautification of American women demanded artful coordination and design.[95] Yoking femininity to the opulence of 1950s consumer products, television from the start devoted itself to beauty and fashion advice and to the quest for glamour. One of television's earliest primetime successes was *Fashions on Parade*, which debuted in April 1948 and aired every Thursday evening on DuMont's WABD-TV in New York City. Adelaide Hawley, representing Bonwit Teller, emceed the program, which showcased "a half hour of attractive girls and gowns," supported by Vincent Lopez at the piano and woven together by a wandering fantasy mannequin.[96]

By promoting glamour to the masses, television opened up a fresh category of consumer products it could advertise during the day—

everything from hair coloring and chic hats to Fifi hosiery and Trapeze sports shoes (see Chapter 8). To this end, glamour advice filled daytime television across the country, locally and nationally. In San Francisco, KPIX aired *Your Beauty Clinic* as one of its first women's shows;[97] Chicago's WGN-TV scheduled a 30-minute fashion consultation entitled *Individually Yours* beginning in March 1949. Sponsored by the Blair Corset Company, whose commercials boldly pictured girdles and bras in close-up, the program featured guests adorned in outmoded clothing who sought tips on how to accomplish stylish alterations.[98] In Washington, DC, Inga Rundvold, a former model and fashion columnist for the *Washington Times-Herald*, hosted *Inga's Angle* on WNBW; she conducted a regular "beauty school segment" that emphasized elements of cosmetology, charm school, and the beauty pageant, and featured on-air makeovers for selected women.[99]

Other formats also integrated glamour into their consumption message. Magazine formats like *Vanity Fair* (1948–1951), home shopping programs, NBC's *Home* show, and even *The Kate Smith Hour* directed the camera's eye at the decade's lush new beauty ideals in discrete fashion segments, while the defining structures of other programs—*Glamour Girl*, *Queen for a Day*, and the *Big Payoff*—centrally glorified the stylish makeover as redemptive.

Postwar television proffered the housewife a lavishness associated in earlier decades with Hollywood stars. Denise Mann calls this the "spectacularization" of the everyday, in which Hollywood's entry into the television industry evoked nostalgia for "an opulent world that existed outside the home."[100] In Mann's view, postwar beauty standards conflated "the star's wardrobe with that of the average suburban housewife" in a two-way leveling effect, which superficially homogenized class difference.[101] On a daily basis, daytime television propagated the fantasy that every woman could be as regal and glamorous as a Hollywood star. As host Jack Bailey exclaimed at the end of each episode of *Queen for a Day*, "We wish we could make every lady in America a queen for every single day!"[102] Routinely, ordinary women who appeared on television were permitted to intermingle with film celebrities or were pampered as one themselves. One winner on *Queen for a Day* earned a dance with Clark Gable;[103] a contestant on *It Could Be You* flirted onstage with George Raft (see Chapter 8);[104] and on *Glamour Girl*, contestants were treated to a makeover by Mary Webb Davis, beauty consultant to the stars (see Chapter 5).

Through its female celebrities as well, the "oomph" or "it" of Hollywood was self-consciously transplanted to the small screen. Projecting audience desires, the glamorous women of television recirculated the escalating promise of personal sumptuousness now available to everyone. By 1956, actual beauty queens even dazzled the airwaves as feminine paragons, including Mona Young (Miss Norway); Kathleen Crowley (Miss New Jersey); Anita Ekberg (Miss Sweden); Lee Ann Meriwether (Miss America, 1955); and, of course, Bess Myerson (Miss America, 1945).[105]

Yet the truly glamorous TV star exuded "zip and zoom" as well as beauty.[106] The viable feminine star on television was most emphatically required to radiate personality and charm as an integral part of her attractiveness. An early portrait of Bess Myerson in *TV Guide* summed up this winning combination: "Put together a striking amount of beauty and more than a dash of charm, and you have Bess Myerson, the girl who parlayed both into a TV career."[107]

Charm and the New Femininity

The era's "femcees"—a term reportedly coined by agent Martin Goodman to describe talented women hosts like his client Arlene Francis— were all "charm girls."[108] Like the many "charm boys" who beguiled women during daylight hours in the 1950s, TV's feminine emcees were also called upon to exude the traits of likability, magnetism, and amiability.[109]

Unlike the masculine version, however, feminine charm was an elusive quintessence linked to authentic loveliness, what Arlene Francis called in her 1960 book about charm "that certain something."[110] As a founding charm girl, Francis was asked to write *That Certain Something: The Magic of Charm* at the close of the decade, and her work encapsulates the cult of charm and its relationship to attractiveness that had helped define femininity in the postwar era.

For Francis, charm was inextricably connected to good grooming and outward attractiveness (16). Learning how to walk with an "uplifted carriage" (145) and a sense of grace ("don't pull your girdle down every time you get up") (16); smiling often (144); applying makeup artfully to enhance one's best features (149); wearing classic, comfortable clothing, selected for its elegant simplicity at an upscale store (148–149); and speaking in a "well-modulated, controlled and quiet voice" (150) all contributed to the attainment of a charming aura.

Yet Francis positioned this intangible essence within true-felt individuality and self-knowledge. Francis's certainty that being oneself was inherently charming linked "authentic charm" to therapeutic introspection and the Golden Rule (21). "Charm is self-deep," Francis mused (69), and one must actively develop "one's best self."[111]

These therapeutic precepts for all women applied especially to the person who appeared on television. "The TV camera has an X-ray attachment," Francis remarked in *TV Guide*. "It pierces, it penetrates, it peels away the veneer. It communicates the heart and mind of man, and makes crystal clear the fact that the only charm is genuine charm, the charm that emanates from a person who is completely true to himself."[112]

Francis accepted the cherished views of the era's most influential critics and writers that television unveiled "authenticity, depth, and truth" in performers[113] and was capable of separating genuine charm from the counterfeit variety, in both men and women alike (masculine pronouns notwithstanding). As Susan Murray observes in her study of Arthur Godfrey, if cinema fans were forever searching for the "real" identity of a star as revealed outside the media text, prevailing attitudes about television promised viewers that star identities generated within the television text were authentic.[114]

Yet early television personalities were required not only to project their best selves; they were also obligated to sell consumer products in direct appeals to viewers. In this role, a star's alignment with "averageness" enhanced his or her credibility for selling products. Murray notes that Arthur Godfrey, for example, served as a "stand-in" for the consumer,[115] and his remarkable sales record derived in part from his habitual deflation of prepared advertising copy and the interjection of improvised product endorsements drawn from his personal experience. While other TV salespeople were less obstreperous than Godfrey in their cynicism about advertising, many successful hosts allied themselves with the viewer by publicly avowing they never endorsed a product they had not used and liked. Arlene Francis, Ruth Lyons, Garry Moore, and Art Linkletter all asserted their full confidence in the products they sold.

The pressure to sell products thus shaped the image of female TV celebrities in a nuanced way. While women performers were expected to be attractive, the most endearing saleswomen also conveyed a wholesome naturalness that appealed to female consumers. According to audience research, viewers of the era resisted sales pitches from overly formal or supersophisticated women.[116] The portrayal of women hosts as glamorous spectacle was tempered during the 1950s by the simultaneous transmission of a charm that radiated grace and naturalness. In 1956, the industry's top saleswomen struck a balance between glamour and unpretentiousness. A *TV Guide* article entitled "Profits and Lassies" photographed six of the industry's best-paid "salesgirls"—Joanne Jordan, Julia Meade, Mary Costa, Barbara Britton, Betty Furness, and Bess Myerson—whose salaries ranged from $50,000 to $150,000 per year. The two-page spread captured the attributes of this ideal feminine peddler. She was model-perfect in her appearance, but each woman also projected an arresting and friendly gaze into the camera's eye, as if she had just drawn a breath and was ready to converse warmly, intimately, and persuasively with the viewer at home.[117]

These exacting new standards for feminine glamour and grace permeated the atmosphere of daytime television like a fragrance (to paraphrase Francis on charm). While femcees especially were measured against the emerging visions of the ideal woman, photographs and kinescopes from the period also record the lavish display of dressed-up 1950s femininity visible in the era's studio audiences. Lynn Swalbe remembered that she and her mother got "all dressed up to the nines, with hats, gloves, and suits, because they knew they'd be on TV" when they attended a *Queen for a Day* broadcast in 1954.[118] Crinoline skirts, pinched waistlines, tailored dresses, gloves, purses, and a sea of hats filled the daytime airwaves with femininity's new designs.

The New Femininity and the Speaking Subject

At the same time that TV focused its lens on the new adornments of womanhood, early programs also reverberated with the sound of women's voices, as speaking subjects related the details of their lives to interlocutors of every stripe. In these repetitive declarations, the misery shows and other "confessional" game shows of the 1950s that centered upon women's stories complied with a television mode Mimi White calls "therapeutic discourse." For White, who traces this form across multiple television genres of the 1980s and 1990s,[119] confession mediated through television is "repeatedly linked with consumer culture and social subjectivity." As she explains, "Self-identity and social recognition within familial and consumer networks hinge on participation in the process of mediated confession."[120] The programs under discussion in Chapter 5 and 8, while predating White's examples by many decades, affirm this confessional pattern. In varying degrees on each show, female subjects were required to reveal personal details about their lives in the presence of interlocutors,[121] and winning confessions merited restoration by means of money or consumer goods.

On postwar TV misery shows like *Strike It Rich*, *Glamour Girl*, and *Queen for a Day*, the quandary of the confessing female subject also resembled her dilemma in earlier film melodramas or on TV's soap operas,[122] in that overbearing narrative frames constrained her expressivity and thereby served to dramatize what Sarah Kozloff has called the "pressure between speech and silence."[123] On the misery shows, women were obligated to recite their personal stories, yet their narratives were continually interrupted and reworked so as to accent the hysterical gesture and scenarios of "tears and fainting."[124]

If the misery shows epitomized the repression of speech and its consequence in hysterical signs,[125] other confessional game shows that centered on an aura of cheerfulness—notably *Who Do You Trust?*, *It Could Be You*, and *The Big Payoff*—also furthered a female subject who was split between speaking and appearing (see Chapter 8). As Mary Ann Doane has noted, women who assume the agency of speech do so within well-controlled strictures of enunciation.[126] Programs that placed women's life experiences at their center to lighthearted ends reproduced the same tension between confession and its curtailment found in the misery shows. In each case, a privileged masculine voice suppressed and reframed the words of women.

Just as Thomas Elsaesser and others have interpreted 1950s Hollywood family melodramas as "critical social documents" whose falsely happy endings expose the powerlessness of women in patriarchy,[127] the confessional shows of the same decade lay bare the fault lines beneath the decade's dominant thinking about gender. The stories of women's distress on the misery shows and the record of their visible entrapment in a masculine web of speech on many other daytime participation programs continued ad infinitum, and this very seriality serves to spotlight the plight of women in postwar patriarchy.[128] The new daytime sphere devoted to the visibility and expressiveness of women could not escape the contradictions of its historical era.

Postwar Femininity on View

Although history fails to organize itself into neat thematic intervals, the chapters that follow are arranged in approximate chronological order, overlaps intact, to convey the dynamism of the past. Chapter 2 traces the complex mix of women's formats and programs that began to flourish in local markets across the country as early as 1948 and notes the temporary but significant impact of the era's also-ran networks—DuMont, ABC, and Mutual—on daytime's earliest history.

The siren call of daytime's women was irresistible to NBC and CBS as well, and the historic rivalry between these well-matched networks dominated daytime competition across the decade. In 1950, NBC premiered its first grand entry into daytime television, *The Kate Smith Hour* (1950–1954), a spectacular vaudeo program that integrated elements of "variety-vaudeville-comedy"[129] into a daytime mix. Chapter 3 explores the contested signification of Kate Smith and her program in the country's transition from war to peace and from radio to television, with special emphasis on her body and voice.

Variations and permutations of the supple audience participation format, so familiar from radio, also began to blossom on daytime television as the 1950s began. To demonstrate the format's mediating possibilities and its fusion of daytime television to visions of participation and gendered pleasure, Chapter 4 examines three of the country's original "charm boys"—Garry Moore, Arthur Godfrey, and Art Linkletter—and their successful programs on CBS. Chapter 5 turns to a converse example of audience participation—the misery show—and explains how *Strike It Rich* (CBS, 1951–1958) and *Glamour Girl* (NBC, 1953–1954) became lightning rods for public censure, caught in the decade's hierarchies of taste.

Chapter 6 singles out another familiar daytime format reworked by NBC. Re-creating the locally prosperous homemaking format on a grand scale, NBC introduced the *Home* show in 1954, starring the Manhattan sophisticate Arlene Francis. The inevitable clash between her upper-middlebrow persona and the country's emergent models for suburban domesticity is the subject of Chapter 6.

As Chapter 7 explains, television theater was an especially esteemed genre of the moment, and NBC turned to the prestige of live anthology drama when it developed the ambitious series *Matinee Theater* (1955–1958). Because the program positioned itself as antithetical to soap opera norms, this chapter examines the battle over taste dichotomies that structured late-decade thinking about daytime television and discovers in retrospect an unexpected affinity between NBC's "quality" series and the humble soaps.

The last chapter reviews four participation programs that were flourishing as the decade ended—*Queen for a Day* (NBC and ABC, 1956–1964), *Who Do You Trust?* (ABC, 1957–1963), *It Could Be You* (NBC,

1956–1961), and *The Big Payoff* (NBC and CBS, 1951–1959) and addresses the tension women on each program faced between speaking and appearing.[130]

The empire of daytime television arose during a momentous time for American women. Women's voices, women's bodies, and women's selves were transfigured by the decade's emergent gender ideologies, and television was complicit in this transfiguration. The evolution of daytime television paralleled and intersected the lived experience of 1950s women as cultural expectations shifted around them, and TV's earliest daytime modes deciphered and reinterpreted femininity's transformation. As this book will show, thousands of women populated daytime television's glowing screen. For the first time, the intimacy of the television camera permitted an unprecedented close-up look at postwar femininity, and millions of women around the nation tuned in to watch.

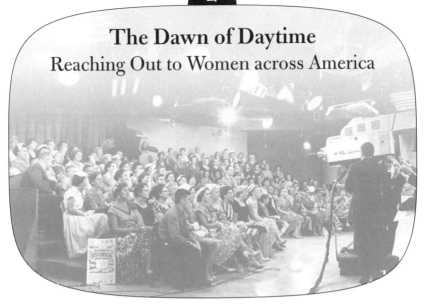

The Dawn of Daytime
Reaching Out to Women across America

From the first light of television, daytime programmers set their sights on women. Across the nation, producers at the local, regional, and national levels devised a curious assortment of programs calculated to attract the female spectator. During TV's earliest years, however, the power dynamics among the country's founding telecasters often operated erratically, making it difficult to forecast a program's chance for success. Yet in the ongoing contest for early daytime viewership, women spectators served as the industry's polestar.[1]

The historical overview presented in this chapter provides a necessary context for those that follow, as it highlights the complex competitive environment in which women's genres emerged. In pursuit of daytime viewers, television at its inception offered up multiple representations of postwar womanhood and tested in myriad ways the unknown dimensions of a new feminine sphere.

While NBC and CBS exerted enormous influence over daytime television history, the instability of early daytime programming and the volatile interplay of other industry powers competing for women viewers must also be acknowledged. During television's formative years, local and regional forces, as well as weaker national networks like DuMont, Mutual, and even ABC, remained for a time viable competitors against NBC and CBS. Each of these forces made its mark on the history of daytime television.[2]

This chapter begins by recognizing the influence of local programming on the course of early daytime broadcasting, a period when stations in the country's 63 television markets retained a degree of strength against centralization.[3] During the FCC's freeze on new license approvals (from September 1948 to April 1952), preapproved stations were scarce. This situation forced the major networks to compete furiously for affiliates.[4] Since FCC regulations prohibited exclusive contracts during these years, as William Boddy notes, local stations were free to affiliate with more than one network.[5] In the fall of 1948, for example, WTMJ in Milwaukee simultaneously held contracts with ABC, CBS, and NBC.[6] Even by 1952, only 36 percent of the country's stations were affiliated with a single network.[7] This meant that for a brief time before the freeze was lifted, stations around the country were able to select the network programming that suited them best or to refuse it in favor of locally produced fare.[8] In these years of relative independence, local stations were more at liberty to experiment with women's formats, and they invented a motley array of daytime programs, some stranger than others.

Local Stations, Local Women

At television's birth, locally produced women's programs made their appearance in every region of the United States, often within hours of a station's sign-on. WGN television in Chicago began broadcasting its first regular day of programming at 2:00 p.m. on Monday, 5 April 1948. A half hour later, *Chicago Cooks with Barbara Barkley* took to the airwaves, beaming its signal from a well-appointed kitchen set in the Goldblatts Department Store.[9] Later that month, rival WBKB launched a second weekday morning show called *Woman's World*, whose purpose, according to station director "Captain" Bill Eddy, was to test viewer interest in daytime viewing and to encourage the sale of television receivers.[10]

While Chicago was a particularly active television hub, the city's early attempts to program daytime sectors for women were being duplicated in stations around the country. Broadcasters soon discovered that formats with feminine appeal were both popular and profitable.

The most common of these formats was the homemaking show, which often garnered substantial profits from local sponsors.[11] Until Barbara Barkley left WGN in 1951, her hour-long program snagged the lucrative support of Kelvinator appliances and S.O.S. cleansing pads.[12] Homemaking programs were an early staple on WTNH-TV in New Haven, Connecticut, too. At its start-up, the station boasted only two studios—a

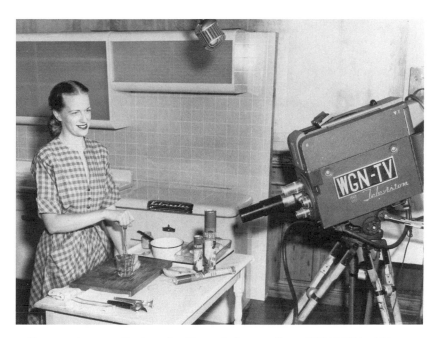

From 1948 to 1951, Barbara Barkley cooked up profits on WGN-TV in Chicago. One of television's earliest local homemakers, Barkley broadcast her show from a Chicago department store, where she found the recipe for success. Photo courtesy WGN-TV.

news set and a kitchen set—and its daytime schedule revolved around cooking: *Cooking with Roz, Cooking with Philameena,* and cooking with a family team called *The Bon Tempi's* that included Fedora the cook, Pino the accordionist, and a very large dog.[13] By 1952, a survey conducted at Iowa State College found that at least 72 of the country's 108 prefreeze television stations were producing homemaking programs, half of them running 30 minutes daily.[14]

While more than half the programs favored food topics, a nearly equal number covered an array of homemaking issues: "textiles and clothing, home furnishings, time management and work simplification, gardening, kitchen planning, child care, grooming, and family relations."[15] Beginning in 1949, KPIX in San Francisco devised a full lineup of women's shows dedicated to these themes: *Teleshopper*; *KPIX Kitchen*; *Stitches in Time*; *Design for Living*; *Flower Arrangement*; *Your Beauty Clinic*; *Gracious Living*; and *Let's Ask the Men.*[16]

As resident celebrities like Barkley and Roz incorporated an assortment of "feminine" interests into their daily programs, local broadcasters around the nation also experimented with the inventive use of fresh televisual formats. Programs like Chicago's *Women's Magazine of the Air*, Seattle's *Women's Page*, and New York's *Vanity Fair* were structured in the newly emerging "magazine format,"[17] while other daytime programs interwove women's issues with music, variety acts, comedy, and audience participation.

Across the country these early local endeavors often featured women hosts. In Washington, DC, Ruth Crane and Inga Rundvold pioneered a string of successful fashion and interview programs,[18] while in Boston, radio personality Louise Morgan transferred her midday conversations to television in 1949.[19] Out west, Monty Margetts hosted *Cooks Corner* in Los Angeles on KTLA,[20] while Betty White, not yet a network star, served as "girl Friday" to Al Jarvis on KLAC in Los Angeles, then hosted her own daily show as "the female Arthur Godfrey" for three years.[21]

Up north, Arle Haeberle anchored a late-afternoon interview program called *Around the Town* on WCCO-TV in Minneapolis,[22] while down south, Florida's first television station, WTVJ in Miami, featured two pioneering women: Judy Wallace, emcee of the morning show *Brunch with Judy*, and Helen Ruth, the host of a popular cooking show.[23] The Midwest provided especially fertile ground for local sweethearts. Alice Weston, Cleveland's "first lady of television," anchored a half-hour daily magazine show that was later syndicated on the "Ohio network";[24] Gretchen Colnick hosted a popular crafts show in Milwaukee;[25] Bea Johnson at KMBC-TV in Kansas City received *McCall's* Golden Mike Award for her outstanding international interviews;[26] comedian and host Charlotte Peters mixed spoofs, skits, and interviews on her daily afternoon program in St. Louis that was staged before a studio audience of 100 guests;[27] and Cincinnati's "first lady of broadcasting," Ruth Lyons, dubbed "Miss Ohio" for her popularity and influence on public opinion, earned huge profits for the Crosley chain of stations in a noontime show called *The Fifty Club* (later *The Fifty-Fifty Club*, when audience size doubled to 100), combining music, interviews, household tips, and lively participation from the studio audience.[28]

Dozens of women performers around the country established a daily rapport with viewers in their local markets. Building upon a sense of community cohesiveness, these attractive and personable women helped ease television into the everyday routine of local homemakers. Even decades later, their impact on women's viewing habits was still memorable. In 1996, the Cincinnati Historical Society asked visitors to write down their memories of Ruth Lyons, and many recollections documented the place Lyons's noontime program held in a viewer's daily agenda. "Mom would stand ironing all morning and gabbing with neighbor Rosie," recalled two sisters. "She would stop for lunch, make fried egg sandwiches—with mayonnaise—and we would watch Ruth! Every day!"[29]

The unprecedented success of *The Fifty Club* also attests to the strength locally produced fare could exhibit against network powers during these early years. In 1951, NBC became covetous of Lyons's remarkable ability to sell products and contracted to carry 30 minutes of *The Fifty Club* for one year on the full NBC network. At the end of the year, however, Lyons refused to move to New York City and resisted NBC's request to give her program more national allure. NBC withdrew its offer and was left to envy Lyons's dynasty from afar. *The Fifty-Fifty Club* outranked all competitors in its time slot in the growing chain of Crosley markets (Cincinnati, Dayton, Columbus, and Indianapolis) well into the 1960s, handily besting nationally supplied programs on rival stations.[30]

From coast to coast, women hosts and women's formats took to the local airwaves at the dawn of television. The quest for women viewers on all points of the compass was under way.

Local Surprises

While this accent on women viewers remained constant, the instability of a nascent industry meant that daytime hits were often unpredictable. As the case of *The Fifty Club* suggests, corporate strength and higher budgets did not necessarily guarantee daytime triumph. The unforeseeable fate of three Chicago programs that premiered in 1950—*Hi Ladies*, *Bob and Kay*, and the *Ransom Sherman Show*—highlights these power imbalances.

WGN-TV introduced *Hi Ladies* in March 1950, an audience participation program that aired three times a week from 4:00 to 4:30 p.m., with the engaging Tommy Bartlett as emcee.[31] Broadcast from a local soundstage, the program invited members of women's clubs to participate in games and interviews for "a few chuckles." Although *Variety* praised Bartlett for moving the program along at a good pace, the trade publication deemed the enterprise "productionless" and said its appeal was limited to those viewers tolerant of "handwaving housewives and a noisy studio audience."[32]

In July, ABC's owned-and-operated station (O&O) in Chicago, WENR, premiered a two-hour weekday strip designed "for casual viewing," called *Bob and Kay*. Airing between 11:00 a.m. and 1:00 p.m. Monday through Friday, the program's low-budget production was hosted by Bob Murphy and Kay Westfall and mixed interviews, fan mail, chat, and records. *Variety* described the program as "basically radio with sight added." During music time, the camera roamed the studio, capturing a view of the Loop and the lakefront from the 42nd floor, or focusing on the studio's pet animals, which included two rabbits, an owl, and a cageful of mice.[33]

On a grander scale, WNBQ, NBC's O&O in Chicago, premiered the *Ransom Sherman Show* in October 1950, an elaborate production to be fed live from Chicago to NBC's interconnected stations each weekday from 3:30 to 4:00 p.m. NBC's Central Division head Jules Herbuveaux, distinguished for his blue-ribbon contributions to an expanding repertoire of "Chicago school" programs, oversaw the ambitious variety show, which headlined singers, musicians, and the comedian Ransom Sherman. *Variety* liked Sherman's "low-geared whimsy,"[34] which excelled at lampooning the "how-to" segments central to other daytime programs. (When Sherman demonstrated how to repair a gas stove, he used a preposterous amount of equipment, and the skit ended in an explosion.)[35] *Variety* predicted the show would attract "a heavy hausfrau audience."[36]

The destiny of these three programs reveals the off-kilter dynamics of the daytime world in 1950s Chicago. Despite an impressive budget, the *Ransom Sherman Show* failed almost immediately and was canceled after three months.[37] *Bob and Kay*, its amateurish production values notwithstanding, drew respectable ratings on WENR and moved permanently to rival WNBQ in April 1953, where it achieved longevity. It occupied a weekday slot from 12:30 to 1:00[38] until February 1955, when WNBQ expanded the show to 75 minutes.[39]

The biggest surprise of all was *Hi Ladies*, which became Chicago's highest-rated afternoon program.[40] *Hi Ladies* was still going strong on WGN as late as 1954, airing at noon each weekday for 45 minutes under new host Mike Douglas, who offered audiences "guest stars, interviews, fun, and song."[41]

These three programs are also noteworthy because they each were hosted or cohosted by genial male performers. Like the new "femcee" appearing on screens across the nation, the male television host was fast becoming a key persona in daytime television. Tommy Bartlett, Bob Murphy, and Ransom Sherman foreshadowed a corps of men whose authoritative but friendly public personalities helped determine the outcome of daytime competition.

As the history of these programs suggests, daytime productions at the local level often followed an irregular path to viewer acceptance. Cancellations, revisions, and station reassignments were commonplace, and uncertainty was the norm. As local stations strove to prosper under these changeable conditions, the country's most influential networks complicated the daytime picture. ABC, CBS, NBC, DuMont, and Mutual soon initiated their own daytime programming and began their invasion of local markets.

National Networks and the Daytime Balance of Power

During most of the 1950s, the struggle for daytime domination at the network level was ultimately reduced to a two-way fight between NBC and CBS. Yet the influence of ABC, DuMont, and Mutual cannot be overlooked, for the programming strategies of each of these networks impacted the course of daytime television in unexpected but significant ways.

Television historians have amply documented the rising and falling fortunes of these five networks during the 1950s.[42] They note that in the long run, two factors were crucially important to network survival: first, network control over the programming of as many local stations as possible, both through contractual affiliations and the purchase of a full quota of owned-and-operated stations in key markets; and, second, competitive access to AT&T's coaxial cable, which could only carry the signal of two customers at a time. As William Boddy, James Schwoch, and Philip Auter and Douglas Boyd have documented, in both categories, economic and regulatory factors profoundly benefited the prosperity of CBS and NBC to the detriment of ABC, Mutual, and DuMont.[43]

These circumstances affected each network's entry into daytime competition in peculiar ways. In 1948, the three most prosperous radio networks were the three networks least eager to invest in daytime television. According to *Variety*, ABC, CBS, and NBC all approached daytime programming hesitantly at first, unwilling to erode the "lush enterprise" of their radio profits.[44] Determined to protect their "AM investment at all costs," the three radio giants argued that television audiences were not yet large enough for full profitability and that regular daytime viewing remained suspect because the housewife was "chained to her chores."[45]

For ABC, CBS, and NBC, daytime scheduling remained a low priority in 1948,[46] although some experimentation and spotty programming did occur. Early in the year, NBC relayed its first daytime program via microwave between New York and Boston. On 22 January 1948, at 2:00 p.m., *Boston USA* televised a fishing crew aboard a Boston trawler during a blinding snowstorm, detailing on camera for a full hour "dead fish in various stages of filleting." In its inimitable style, *Variety* deemed that, as entertainment, the show was "nsg" (not so good).[47]

On the fledgling CBS network, *This Is the Missus* aired from 1:30 to 2:00 on Wednesdays beginning in May 1948—a game, stunt, and quiz show set in New York City supermarkets and hosted by Bud Collyer.[48] The show was a revamp of *The Missus Goes A-Shopping*, one of the country's earliest daytime TV game shows, first broadcast locally on WCBS in August 1944.[49] In the fall, in addition to the magazine show *Vanity Fair*, CBS also launched *Ladies Day*, an early-afternoon variety program that incorporated audience participation and housewife stunts. Hosted by Warren Hull, soon to become the star of TV's *Strike It Rich*, the program only survived as a network offering until June 1949 (as *The Warren Hull Show*).[50]

When the coaxial cable first opened a link between the East Coast and Midwest regions in January 1949, CBS was the only network of the three radio giants to transmit daytime programming to its affiliated stations. NBC and ABC fed nothing over the cable between 10:00 a.m. and 5:00 p.m. ET.[51]

With no radio stations to protect, it was the DuMont network that was first to branch into a full daytime schedule. In September 1948 in New York City, DuMont premiered a local block of programs from 7:00 a.m. to 5:00 p.m. on its flagship station, WABD, planning to compete not against the other television stations, but against the city's AM radio stations. For cash-strapped DuMont, daytime television was a financial imperative. Mortimer Loewi, executive assistant to Dr. Allen B. DuMont (the network's founder and president), explained that WABD was unable to meet its costs through advertising generated during its evening programs alone (totaling 21 hours per week). To make up for this shortfall, DuMont's 19 new daytime programs would offer advertisers one-minute "demonstration spots" for $25 each, a price scheme low enough to bypass agency involvement and attract even the "smallest businessman in New York" to television advertising.[52]

The DuMont Network and Daytime Programming

The bold move to program daytime on WABD succeeded beyond DuMont's most optimistic hopes and helped shape the future direction of daytime broadcasting by profitably reproducing on television radio's feminine sphere. In *Variety*'s words, the schedule offered "little concession to any male viewer" and was adjudged "no worse" than the steady diet of radio deejays or soap operas on daytime radio. Unable to mount opulent visual productions, DuMont produced shows that could be enjoyed just as much from listening as from watching, each program telecast from the same set all day long. A "[n]ice, breezy informality is the keynote of the entire day," said *Variety*, sustained through ad-libbing, piano music, weather-temperature signals, and shots of 53rd Street from the studio window. Only Stan Shaw's noontime musical interlude came close to "straight entertainment."[53]

In January 1949, after making adjustments to its original WABD lineup, DuMont fed four and one-half hours of daytime programming Monday through Friday to its network stations in the East and Midwest over the newly completed coaxial cable:

10:00–10:30	*Johnny Olsen's Rumpus Room*
10:30–11:00	*Welcome, Neighbors*
11:00–12:00	*Stan Shaw* (musical interlude)
12:00–12:15	*Amanda* (hosted by an African American actress)
12:15–12:30	*Man in the Street*
12:30–12:45	*Camera Headlines*
12:45–1:00	*Fashions in Song*
1:00–1:30	*Okay, Mother* (hosted by Dennis James)
2:30–3:00	*Inside Photoplay*
3:00–3:15	*Needle Shop* (hosted by Alice Burrows)
3:15–3:30	*Vincent Lopez Speaking*[54]

Sensing a crucial advantage over its mightier rivals, DuMont enthusiastically promoted daytime programming at the network level during 1949. According to Mortimer Loewi, full daytime programming offered four advantages: increased public service; inexpensive buying opportunities for small advertisers; a boost in the sale of TV sets; and a decrease in idle cable time.[55] Humboldt Greig, assistant director of the DuMont Television Network in Chicago, further predicted that the television audience was "ready to be entertained during the day," optimistic that while daytime programs might lack "glamour and high ratings," they could sell products better by entering the family circle with personal endorsements.[56] A year ahead of network competitors, DuMont scored its most promising achievement when Sterling Products agreed to sponsor a full year of *Okay, Mother* on the DuMont network from 1:00 to 1:30 ET weekdays, beginning in December 1949.[57]

Okay, DuMont

As one of the country's first daytime programs carried live over a network, *Okay, Mother* serves as a rough-hewn but significant prototype for the scores of audience participation shows—hosted by men—that would soon inhabit the daytime airwaves (see chapters 4, 5, and 8). Under the exuberant guidance of host Dennis James, the daily festivities on *Okay, Mother* promulgated the liberating idea that daytime television viewing was meant to be fun. *Okay, Mother* offered women both at home and in the television studio a break from the daily grind of housework. At the same time, however, the domineering presence of Dennis James and the nature of his unpolished antics revealed all too clearly women's compromised position in this new world of leisure.

Casting aside the supposition that housewives merely glanced at their screens as they worked, *Okay, Mother* unashamedly instructed viewers to sit down and watch. On one particularly hot summer day, James clearly trumpeted the program as an oasis of repose for housewives. "All you girls at home, now take it easy and relax and settle back," he said, addressing the camera. "It's warm weather. Don't work between 1 and 1:30 every day . . . No dishes to do. No lunch to prepare. Just sit back, and all our entertainers here will entertain you."

The show's daily open also identified *Okay, Mother* as an interlude for women, a time when their ideas mattered and their need for midday diversion was recognized. The opening theme song was delivered each day a capella by male vocalists: "Okay, Mother, it's your time of day. Okay, Mother, time to have your say . . . So join in the fun, everyone, with laughs and problems and funny games. So Okay, Mother; Okay, Mother, we're presenting Dennis James!"

Following the song, James then engaged the studio audience in a call-and-response ritual:

> *James* (shouting): It's one o'clock, your time of day. Time you mothers have your say! OKAY, mother?
> *Audience* (loudly): OKAY, Dennis!

The audience's resounding "OKAY!"—repeated on a daily basis—assented to the program's mission of rest, entertainment, and fun, all enjoyed within a new feminine sphere mediated by television.

Furthering the program's theme to honor motherhood and mothers in an atmosphere of fun, James entertained the studio audience with rhyming games, riddles, skits, and improvised discussions about good parenting. Nonstop doggerel was the show's signature. In one contest, James recited rhyming riddles, called "mothergrams," to quiz studio guests. One typical mothergram stumped the audience: "Though at composing poetry, / This mother's boy excelled, / He couldn't stand the soldier's life / From West Point was expelled . . . Who is he?" (James later reveals the answer: Edgar Allan Poe.)

In another game called "line-and-rhyme," women in the studio challenged James by providing an opening line, which he then tried to complete as a couplet; those who foiled him won a box of hosiery, a compact, or a cigarette lighter.

No one in the audience seemed to mind that James's poetry was hardly up to Poe's standards. "I worked for the Air Force in Guam" inspired "That's the place from which I swum." To the line "The story is most unusual," James rejoined, "The story is most unusu-AL / That's all right because you're my PAL." Apparently unperturbed by James's complete lack of literary wit, participants during this segment clamored eagerly for James's attention and laughingly approved his stanzas.

Other customary segments of the show honored the opinions of the "average" woman. One such feature was the "problems playhouse," during which James and his assistant, the elegant model Julia Meade, performed skits that illustrated mothering dilemmas. One playlet depicted a child (played by James) who disobeyed his mother (played by Meade) on a hot day by running through the sprinkler wearing his best clothes. After the sketch, James posed the day's parenting quandary to the studio audience: "Should we spank and punish that child for going in front of the sprinkler?" After a spirited debate, James settled the issue by conducting a vote (12 to 9 in favor of spanking). In other segments of the program, James interviewed famous mothers or read letters from home viewers honoring nominees for "mother of the day."[58]

Yet in opposition to this tone of reverence for mothers and their wisdom, Dennis James came across as a bossy, at times abrasive host, who occasionally even upbraided his guests. When a woman proposed the line "My sister's name is Edna," James scowled and reprimanded her. "Oh, Honey," he scolded. "Every day we've had 'Edna' . . . We ask every day before the show to not use the words we had yesterday . . . [E]very time I get hit with the same words, every day, it stumps me, it stops me dead." Perceiving he had gone too far in his criticism, James then knelt before the woman, pleading, "You don't want to stop me, do you?" When she gave him a better line, he awarded her a box of hosiery and sprinted away.

James also conveyed a guardedly salacious attitude toward the women in the studio, freely hugging and kissing them and calling them endearing names. During one foray into the audience gallery, a woman asked James for his tie. He quickly removed it, draped it around her neck, used it to pull her toward him, and kissed her soundly on the cheek, to her apparent satisfaction. Later in the show, during the line-and-rhyme segment, a man in the audience supplied the tongue twister, "What is the best bread made?" When James's repetition of the line came out "What is the breast bed . . . ," he stopped short, laid his hand on his heart, and said, "I think I said something! I don't know what I said!" and the audience snickered gleefully.

With Meade, James was the most daring and chauvinistic, openly leering at her, wrapping his arm around her shoulders, or leaning inappropriately against her body. During a promotion for the Evans pocket lighter, James bent his head against her shoulder seductively (she was slightly taller than he), widened his eyes naughtily, and displayed the can of lighter fluid by propping it over her bosom. Later, when a woman in the audience provided the line "Have you ever been to Africa? (Afri-ker)," James pointed to Meade and teased, "I'd love to sit in the lap of her."

James reserved his most lecherous behavior for the parenting skit, which allowed him to use his role as Meade's young son to jump literally into her lap, a move that set off shrieks and giggles in the audience and appeared to startle Meade. The script reinforced this sexual innuendo, as Meade kept instructing her son to "take those wet trousers off," or inquired angrily offstage, "Are you out there without your pants on?" The punch line of the skit occurred when James reappeared wearing a moustache and a man's hat. No longer portraying a little boy, he replied to her question that of course he was wearing pants![59]

James's overt seduction of women in the studio and the liberties he took with Meade were toned down considerably in later network versions of male-hosted programs, but these suggestive behaviors never disappeared entirely. Part of the charm of the "charm boys" discussed in Chapter 4—Arthur Godfrey, Garry Moore, and Art Linkletter—derived from a flirtatious sexuality covered over by boyish naiveté. Likewise, the male hosts of later audience participation shows, described in detail in Chapter 8, continued to manipulate the speech and actions of women, albeit more deftly.

In its immature sexuality, combined with a boisterous commitment to daytime fun for women in the studio and at home, *Okay, Mother* served as a rudimentary archetype for future audience participation shows. The coolly chic Julia Meade foreshadowed the scores of glamorous women about to grace television screens everywhere, just as the brash Dennis James presaged the string of male hosts who would radiate a comparable but more subdued masculinity in the decade ahead. Most of all, the happy women in the studio signaled television's potential to provide a bridge of enjoyment for the housewife, even if her pleasure was compromised and her subjectivity laden with negations.

DuMont in Daytime History

DuMont's daytime lineup not only helped institute gendered programming during the day (its ambiguities for women fully visible) but also awakened DuMont's more powerful competitors to the potential for daytime profits. Between 1949 and 1951, DuMont's tactics stirred up aggressive countermoves at rival networks and rapidly altered the development and direction of daytime programming at both the local and the national level.

In response to DuMont's initial launch of its daytime schedule in January 1949, ABC, NBC, and CBS almost immediately expanded local daytime offerings on their New York City stations, albeit with mixed results. On 1 February 1949, WNBT (NBC's flagship station) premiered a 2:30–5:30 slot of programs pitched to housewives and modeled after DuMont's low-budget programs: *The Bess Johnson Club*, which featured fashion models and a discussion of fashion; *Armchair Wanderings*, a travel show, immediately replaced by *Want Adventure*; *The Three Flames*, an African American instrumental trio, whose "antics and rapid-tempoed music" elevated the program to evening-level quality, according to the trade press; *We're On*, an interview show hosted by Mr. and Mrs. Yul Brynner, who chatted with celebrities; and *Relaxerciser*, during which Claire Mann urged the home viewer to "[let] yourself go to music."[60] After only four months, however, WNBT dropped its daytime lineup when the shows "failed to pay off,"[61] in *Variety*'s words.

WJZ-TV (ABC's O&O in New York City) launched *Market Melodies* in mid-February 1949, a two-hour morning show for women, mixing homemaking tips with interviews and recorded music. By April, WCBS, vowing to do "a sounder job" in its programming than its rivals, was on the air in New York City starting at 12 noon.[62]

Within months, DuMont's competitors, flush with enough capital to remain flexible and adaptive,[63] began to raid DuMont's daytime schedule. CBS acquired *The Ted Steele Show* in June 1949, DuMont's one-man variety show that aired at noon, during which Steele, one of DuMont's most popular stars, chatted with viewers, read viewer mail, sang, held up photographs of child fans, and spoke to an anonymous "phantom voice" off-screen.[64] In March 1950, WNBT stole away WABD's *Television Shopper* with Kathi Norris, airing the program intact daily from 11:00 to noon beginning in May.[65] And in the fall of 1951, ABC grabbed up Dennis James to re-create *Okay, Mother* as *The Dennis James Show*, which aired over the fledgling ABC network weekdays from 11:30 to noon for a year.[66]

The DuMont Television Network was soon to fall, but its influence on daytime television's history was considerable. DuMont put into motion the national networks' initial drive into daytime scheduling, experimented with modes and genres designed to please women viewers, and provoked competition that stimulated the steady growth of daytime programming at all levels. After 1951—the year the DuMont Company reached its financial peak by grossing $75 million in sales of television sets[67]—the corporation suffered budget woes that could not be reversed. Without profits from radio stations to support the astronomical costs of national TV programming, DuMont was forced to air low-budget productions that paled beside the dazzling new shows being offered on NBC and CBS.[68] Failing to produce (or hold on to) hit shows, and further hampered by unequal access to AT&T's coaxial cable and an unsatisfactory corporate alliance with Paramount, the network spiraled ever downward.[69] On 10 October 1955, after years of devastating losses and a declining presence on the air, the DuMont Television Network ceased to exist.[70]

Not Even Queen for a Day: The Mutual Broadcasting Network

The Mutual Broadcasting System took itself out of the race to establish a national television network in 1948,[71] but in an odd turn of events, Mutual's influence on daytime programming, like DuMont's, was keenly felt well into the 1950s. Until 1956, Mutual held the rights to one of television's most notorious and profitable ventures, *Queen for a Day*.[72]

During the early 1940s, Mutual was a viable and competitive radio consortium with an impressive array of affiliates; and after World War II, Mutual stood poised to secure a television network. As James Schwoch has documented, however, the Mutual Television Network never got off the ground, even though key Mutual affiliates were already telecasting successfully in their respective markets.[73]

While Mutual "never broadcast a single nationwide television program," as Schwoch points out,[74] it did control a number of radio properties during the 1940s that swiftly made the shift to local or regional television, among them *Heart's Desire, Leave It to the Girls,* and *Queen for a Day.*[75] Because Mutual's stations were bound together in an arrangement that was cooperative rather than compulsory, Mutual had entered an alliance with the Don Lee corporation on the West Coast, an ad hoc "network" that included the experimental television station W6XAO in Los Angeles (soon to be KTSL). *Queen for a Day,* already a hit on Mutual's radio network, was first simulcast on W6XAO in May 1947, hosted by Jack Bailey. By 1948, *Queen for a Day* had become an enormously popular phenomenon in Los Angeles, and within two years, the program was successfully airing on seven sister stations up and down the West Coast.[76]

Recounting the story of *Queen for a Day* vividly highlights the decade's clash of unequal powers in the quest for daytime properties, as NBC aggressively battled to procure television rights to the program. Mutual's contractual agreement with the Raymond R. Morgan advertising agency, *Queen*'s producers in Los Angeles, stymied NBC's efforts for almost four years. The back-and-forth negotiations among Morgan, Mutual, and NBC between 1952 and 1956—well documented in NBC memoranda—demonstrate the ways in which a network that was virtually defunct managed to frustrate the aspirations of a monolithic corporation.

NBC first sought to acquire *Queen for a Day* in May 1952, when the show's rating in the Los Angeles market during the 3:00–3:30 slot averaged 11.9, making it the number one daytime television program by far. *Queen* (which had moved to KHJ-TV) attracted three times the daytime audience of the city's six other stations combined and twice the average nighttime rating of any single Los Angeles station.[77]

To NBC's annoyance, Morgan's contract granted Mutual not only exclusive radio rights to *Queen for a Day* but airtight television exclusivity in any and all local, regional, or national markets, even though a Mutual Television Network did not exist. While Morgan avidly sought to cut a deal with NBC that promised to be highly lucrative, Mutual steadfastly resisted, repeatedly demanding sizable royalties. When Mutual's Tom O'Neil insisted on the figure of $2,500 per week "now and forever,"[78] NBC declined.

It would take almost four full years of strenuous negotiations before NBC was able to overcome what executive Charles Barry termed Mutual's irksome contract "bugs."[79] Chapter 8 tells the story of this procure-

"Queen for a Day"

Raymond R. Morgan's advertising brochure promoted Mutual Broadcasting's popular radio version of **Queen for a Day** *long before NBC was able to acquire the television rights to the program. Private collection of Marsha Cassidy.*

ment in finer detail, but it is instructive to note here that the contested fate of this single program, often considered the era's most infamous runaway hit, may well have slanted the overall course of daytime television history. Had Mutual not blocked NBC's early acquisition of *Queen for a Day*, the program's unprecedented success and profitability on the NBC network may well have strengthened NBC against CBS and served to fund the big-budget daytime programs NBC cherished under Pat Weaver but could not sustain. Moreover, the exorbitant price tag placed on this misery show and the competition to possess it testify to the drawing power of daytime programs that reproduced a participatory feminine sphere, as *Okay, Mother* did, even when gender disparities remained in full view.

As this example further corroborates, during the formative years of daytime television, currents of power flowed in all directions. The demise of the Mutual Television Network even before its formation did not prevent Mutual from blocking the advancement of a much more powerful adversary. Even as a phantom network, Mutual thwarted a strong, shrewd opponent for four years and thereby skewed daytime television's overall competitive scene.

Not Even in Business: The ABC Television Network

ABC Television also faced the threat of extinction during the 1950s. Like DuMont and Mutual, ABC suffered from a shortage of TV affiliates[80] and encountered the same obstacles to accessing the coaxial longlines on a competitive basis that hamstrung DuMont and Mutual. As others have fully detailed, ABC survived because it reaped lucrative profits from its five wholly owned stations in the country's biggest markets, and because the FCC permitted the network to merge with United Paramount Theatres in 1953.[81]

At television's start-up, however, ABC "had trouble finding both daytime programs and sponsors," in the words of the network's former president, Leonard H. Goldenson. "ABC was considered a very risky buy," he recalled.[82] Peter Levathes, director of media and television at the advertising firm Young & Rubicam during the early 1950s, said that when he approached major advertisers like General Foods or Procter & Gamble to suggest buying shows on ABC, advertisers would counter, "They're not even in business."[83]

As NBC and CBS jumped into daytime competition with determination against DuMont (and to some extent against Mutual), ABC floundered. While the struggling network made several valiant attempts to program profitably during the day, nothing took hold. As Levathes expressed it, "the fatality rate" was very high.[84] Not until the inauguration of "Operation Daybreak" in 1958 did ABC find enduring success with *American Bandstand, The Mickey Mouse Club, Who Do You Trust?*, and

Beat the Clock.[85] (This period is discussed in more detail in Chapter 8.) The near absence of daytime programming on the ABC network during television's foundational years ultimately reduced the battle for women viewers to a well-matched duel between NBC and CBS. The failures and programming errors at ABC altered the outcome of TV history by eliminating yet another competitor.

The fate of *Don McNeill's Breakfast Club* as a television property highlights ABC's miscalculations. During the 1940s, McNeill's program was one of the network's top moneymakers on radio, broadcasting live each weekday morning from Chicago. The affable McNeill joked with audience members, played silly games, announced the time and weather, introduced performances by vocalists and a resident orchestra, and chatted with "Aunt Fanny," a caricatured gossip made memorable by Fran Allison.

A surviving kinescope of the radio show conveys the tenor of McNeill's pleasant but old-fashioned approach. A man in the audience had to "size up" a woman he had never met by guessing her age, her husband's profession, and other details about her; Mrs. Grauel of Indiana explained how she killed a skunk at 2:00 a.m.; a visiting Brownie troop marched to music around the studio ("I'm surrounded by Brownies!" McNeill giggled); and sidekick Sam Cowling described a "helicopter" as a "hecticopter" to avoid the semblance of foul language, much to McNeill's delight. On a more solemn note, singer John Desimone performed a musical tribute to a young boy killed in a car accident (written by the boy's father), and McNeill asked his listeners and studio guests to say a silent prayer together, "each in his own words, each in his own way, for a world united in peace."[86]

As early as 1946, ABC envisioned a television adaptation of the venerable show, simulcasting an episode locally that year on WBKB in Chicago. In May 1948, ABC "networked" an evening edition of the show over its Philadelphia, Washington, and Baltimore outlets (plus DuMont's WABD for one-time-only coverage in New York City). *Variety* called the radio simulcast "one of the most entertaining live shows ever seen in these parts over television." McNeill's "stage presence" and "glib ad-libness" added to the enjoyment, and *Variety* predicted the show's appeal would give a green light to "this type of program on a steady diet."[87] Yet ABC was unwilling to risk the transference of a valuable radio property to daytime television in precarious times, and the network chose instead to schedule only a weekly evening version, stalling even its premiere until 1950.[88] By the time ABC finally got around to simulcasting the morning show regularly on television beginning in February 1954, the well-established *Today* show offered stiff competition on NBC, and the television portion of the *Breakfast Club* survived for only a year.[89] In this way, ABC's inability to capitalize on a lucrative radio asset early in the decade led to gloomy consequences later.

ABC suffered two other costly fiascos in programming for women in 1951, when the network pinned its midday hopes on daytime offerings that appeared to hold the promise of success. The first, the aforementioned *Dennis James Show*, broadcast from 11:30 to 12:00 daily, closely imitated the format of DuMont's three-year hit and continued to costar Julia Meade, yet it only survived six months on ABC.[90]

The demise of the second show, a lavish hour-long variety extravaganza called *The Frances Langford–Don Ameche Show* that aired at noon, was just as quick but more spectacular. Langford and Ameche were already well known for their starring roles on the radio comedy *The Bickersons*, and ABC poured an estimated $40,000 a week into a show they touted as "The Biggest Show in Daytime Television."[91] Staged before a live audience in ABC's Little Theater on 44th Street ("a part of Broadway," as the announcer proclaimed), the segmented format swung from act to act in the new vaudeo mode, sewn together by Fran and Don. The lineup on 2 November 1951 offered the typical variety range: an opening song by Langford ("Hi, Neighbor"); light bantering between Fran and Don; sidekick Johnny Romano's guitar solo; the "artistry of dancing" by Richard and Flora Steward, who were bathed in chiaroscuro lighting as they twirled and flourished capes; two songs by Ameche (one sung standing beside an Ionic pedestal, one as Ameche's face was superimposed over a drum); and a comedic skit entitled "A Great Prison Drama," featuring guest Chester Morris, best known for his tough-guy role as Boston Blackie. Rounding out the hour, Ameche read a letter from viewer Joyce Mary Smith, who offered to adopt a little orphan girl who had appeared on an earlier show; Irene Hayes demonstrated flower arranging in honor of National Flower Week; and Morris returned to perform magic tricks with a rope.[92] Other episodes incorporated a quiz segment, a child ventriloquist, and tips for the housewife.[93]

Within six months, *The Frances Langford–Don Ameche Show* had lost close to a million dollars and was canceled.[94] ABC temporarily replaced it with *The Paul Dixon Show*, a half hour hosted by "Paul Baby" from Cincinnati, but when Dixon left ABC that fall,[95] midday programming on ABC disappeared entirely for six years.

As the decade unfolded, the void left by ABC's ill-fated daytime programs bolstered the fortunes of CBS and NBC. ABC skidded toward daytime oblivion, not offering a full daytime lineup for women until 1958. Even so, the erratic circumstances of early daytime programming led to one notable incongruity. In 1954, with so many daytime hours unfilled, the feeble ABC network opted to broadcast what developed into one of daytime television's most historic—and most-watched—events, the Army-McCarthy hearings.[96] For 36 days from April to June, ABC provided gavel-to-gavel coverage of all 187 hours, at a cost of $600,000. Recalling the event, Goldenson wrote that ABC could ill afford this "exercise in public service," but Goldenson believed live continuing coverage "was the greatest contribution we could have made at that time," since NBC and CBS were locked into extensive daytime schedules and were less willing to interrupt programming.[97]

Anomalies like this confirm the erratic nature of daytime's earliest years, as local, regional, and national powers all vied for supremacy. In the changeable environment of daytime's heady days, absolute hegemony was unattainable, and David-and-Goliath battles confounded predictable outcomes. Especially during the freeze, multilevel competition to produce and acquire lucrative daytime properties kept programming in a state of upheaval. As the 1950s rolled out, however, the chronic weakness of ABC during the day, combined with the steady disappearance of daytime programming on DuMont and Mutual's quick retreat from the national scene, enabled CBS and NBC to assemble vast daytime empires.

CBS and NBC: Clash of Empires

By 1950, daytime scheduling had emerged as television's next great profit frontier. In a lengthy report published by the BBDO advertising agency in the fall of 1950, the advice for advertisers was to enter daytime TV "now."[98]

According to the BBDO report, the perpetual motion machine of daytime television had been activated. Between the spring and fall of 1950, the number of stations broadcasting during the day rose from 75 to 89, and the hours programmed jumped from a total of 2,269 to 3,114, a 37 percent increase in only six months. Viewership figures rose concomitantly. A. C. Nielsen reported that the share of the total broadcast audience in the United States watching TV between 2:00 and 5:00 p.m. had almost doubled between January and June of 1950. Substantial gains in daytime viewing in key cities also occurred over the same six months:

in Chicago, up from 16 to 26 percent; in Boston, from 11 to 20 percent; and in Philadelphia, from 17 to 32 percent.[99] With aggregate audiences on the rise across the country, daytime programming was beginning to offer advertisers an affordable cost-per-thousand rate (the cost to reach 1,000 potential customers). BBDO persuasively outlined other benefits daytime television offered advertisers: twice the number of commercial minutes for the same length program (under daytime's less stringent advertising rules) and a greater ability to integrate live commercials into program content, often with a celebrity's personal endorsement.[100]

The strongest selling point for advertisers, however, was the growing evidence that daytime viewers were mostly women. According to an analysis by the American Research Bureau in 1950, 67 percent of the weekday audience watching TV between noon and 5:00 p.m. in New York was made up of women; moreover, TV audiences across the country increasingly represented a full range of economic levels, the vast middle class being especially prominent.[101] This meant that it was less expensive for sponsors to reach women shoppers of all economic levels during the day than in primetime.[102] As this magic formula was put to work, women more than ever became the axis on which the ever-rotating gyroscope of daytime competition spun.

Growth in television's daytime enterprise progressed unevenly across the decade, and with surprises, but the overall upsurge was dramatic. By 1956, a study commissioned by Lever Brothers determined that some 23 million unduplicated Nielsen homes watched adult programs between 10:00 a.m. and 5:00 p.m. in a week's time, and daytime television's cost-per-thousand at the network level had dipped to $1.25 (comparing favorably to daytime radio's $1.00 price tag). In that same year, 123 national network sponsors spent more money on daytime television advertising than on primetime.[103]

As daytime audiences grew, the enormous resources of CBS and NBC were brandished across the country. Once CBS obtained the O&O stations and affiliates necessary to reproduce the potency of its radio network, daytime triumph followed. As later chapters verify, CBS shrewdly transferred its most successful radio programs straight to the small screen, and thereby evolved an elegantly simple strategy to win over TV viewers. NBC's daytime ventures were equally aggressive but more turbulent. The history of *The Kate Smith Hour*, *Home*, and *Matinee Theater*, all produced under the guidance of NBC's best-known TV auteur, Sylvester "Pat" Weaver, describes a reach for "quality" entertainment on a grand scale that turned out to be decidedly risky.

In 1950, with TV's prospects for success still on the horizon, NBC, under the leadership of Weaver, envisioned a magnificent future for its daytime calendar, with *The Kate Smith Hour*, a variety program that pulled out all the stops, as its linchpin. Kate Smith was a vaudeville veteran, a stellar personality from radio, and a renowned vocalist whose recordings had sold millions of copies for decades. Because of her wartime contributions, she was also one of the country's most admired celebrities. NBC foresaw Smith's entry into daytime television as a spectacular coup that would secure affiliate loyalty, attract valued sponsors to late-afternoon television, and infuse NBC's nascent daytime lineup with prestige and character. Only a beloved celebrity like Kate Smith projected enough charisma to launch what NBC hoped would become daytime television's most majestic schedule.

Kate Smith
Remembering the Future

On 10 November 1938, Kate Smith announced on her midday radio program that she planned to introduce a special song on the eve of Armistice Day that would not only salute America's war heroes but also "emphasize just how much America means to each and every one of us." She had commissioned Irving Berlin, one of the nation's best-known composers, to write the song for her, asking him to create "a new hymn of praise and love and allegiance to America."[1] That evening, Smith sang "God Bless America" on radio for the first time, reprising it just before Thanksgiving in a slightly altered arrangement. Public reaction was overwhelming. In early 1939, as war clouds gathered, her recorded version became an instant hit coast-to-coast, and the song became her signature melody on radio.

During the darkest hours of World War II, Smith closed each of her public appearances across the country and on military bases with "God Bless America," and audiences rose to their feet, cheered, and wept. By the end of the war, her entire persona—voice, body, and song—had come to signify the nation itself in the popular mind. A 1949 Gallup poll of Americans found Smith to be the sixth most admired woman in the world, ranked below Eleanor Roosevelt and First Lady Bess Truman but higher than Senator Margaret Chase Smith and Princess Elizabeth of England.[2]

With the singer at the peak of her popularity, it is no wonder NBC viewed Kate Smith as destined to become the first lady of daytime television. Determined to colonize daylight hours as aggressively as possible, NBC signed the popular songstress to a five-year contract in 1950. For two seasons, *The Kate Smith Hour* exceeded all expectations. After only two weeks on the air, Smith's program surpassed in popularity many nighttime productions, reaching more homes per day than 28 sponsored evening shows.[3] Within two months, her ratings had more than doubled—measured by Nielsen at 18.5 in 31 markets[4]—and, a year later, that number climbed to an astonishing 25.9, as more than one-fourth of all TV households in America watched Smith in the afternoon.[5] The program also earned the prestige NBC sought for its daytime entries. In 1952, the *Motion Picture Daily*'s Poll of Television Critics named *The Kate Smith Hour* TV's "Best Daytime Program."[6] The network's chief programming executive, Sylvester "Pat" Weaver, declared *The Kate Smith Hour* to be "the most successful show in daytime television."[7]

In an unpredictable turnaround, however, Smith's ratings plummeted to 12.4 by the end of the 1952 season, and the program was canceled prematurely in 1954.[8] The unimaginable failure of *The Kate Smith Hour* opens up a crucial space for historical inquiry. A close study of her ill-fated program uncovers a complex web of historical forces that toppled *The Kate Smith Hour* and elucidates the pressures brought to bear on daytime broadcasting during its transition from radio to television and from wartime to postwar sensibilities. NBC's preference for entertainment modes borrowed from live theater and vaudeville strained to compete against rival formats that were more cost-effective and more televisual. *The Kate Smith Hour* also failed to meet advertisers' heightened demands for celebrities to personally endorse products, a practice Smith and her manager Ted Collins stubbornly resisted.

Most importantly to the undertaking of this book, the failure of *The Kate Smith Hour* underscores the cultural imperatives that were rapidly defining how American femininity would be constructed on the new medium. Because the 1950s promulgated a cult of glamour that overturned wartime images, Kate Smith was unable to represent woman as televised spectacle in the new decade. If her radio career tells the story of a large woman battling for control of her public persona, finally establishing herself as a patriotic idol, Smith's television career demonstrates the unavoidable devaluation of this image. As the United States entered the Eisenhower years, the nascent television industry ultimately cast aside wartime tropes for femininity and refashioned American womanhood according to the country's newly emerging postwar standards.

A Singer, Not Just a Big Girl

A series of women with slender silhouettes were officially crowned "Miss America" during the war years, but it was Kate Smith who achieved a singular kind of iconographic status as a symbol of the nation. As the war broke out in Europe, President Franklin Roosevelt reportedly introduced Smith to King George and Queen Mary of England with the words "This is Kate Smith; this is America!"[9]

Smith's status as an American icon cannot be separated from her physical dimensions. She learned early in her career how to survive in show business as a big woman by controlling the meaning of her size. Her 1938 memoirs, tellingly entitled *Living in a Great Big Way*, articulated her attempt to mitigate her body's "unruly" and transgressive excess, in Kathleen Rowe's vocabulary,[10] and to declare herself to be comfortable as a "fat woman." Eve Sedgwick explains in her work on the fat body that openly declaring what is already self-evident warns people that cultural responses that are "not fat-affirmative" will be interpreted as "assaultive and diminishing." Furthermore, coming out as a fat woman allows a person to renegotiate the "representational contract between one's body and one's world."[11] As Smith's career as a stage performer and radio star soared during the 1930s, she initially restructured the meaning of her hefty body through her voice. She was quickly dubbed "the Song Bird of the South," her image modeled in part after the operatic diva, whose extraordinary voice allowed for—indeed almost required—an extraordinary physical frame.[12] "I'm big, and I sing, and boy, when I sing, I sing all over," Smith said of herself.[13]

On radio, Smith openly denominated herself as overweight, joking about how much she liked ice cream or how much she ate. When petite actress Helen Hayes appeared on *The Kate Smith Hour* in 1939, Smith alluded to a previous meeting between them as "two ships that pass in the night: me the ocean liner and you the canoe."[14] As time went on, Smith's body size also became a metaphor for her other admirable traits. *Look* magazine celebrated Smith's "bounteous personality,"[15] and she enjoyed a reputation for having a big heart.

When Kate Smith's career began at the Knickerbocker Theater on Broadway in 1926, however, her large body was the object of ridicule.

Cast in the role of Tiny Little in the musical *Honeymoon Lane*, she played an overweight buffoonish figure who sat silently on stage until the play was almost over. In the finale on opening night, Smith sang three rousing songs and danced the Charleston with such gusto that she literally stopped the show. Playwright and actor Eddie Dowling, who had cast Smith as Tiny Little, rushed onto the stage to subdue the cheering audience, announcing, "A new and great talent has been born tonight . . . And the fat girl has got a contract."[16]

In her next stage hit, *Flying High,* in 1930, Bert Lahr insulted Smith even more ruthlessly, often calling her "Etna" under his breath during performances. Once again Smith played a comic character, Lahr's love interest, whose size was exploited for slapstick humor.[17] The *New York Times* noted in its review that her "proportions are mountainous," and Robert Littell in the *World Telegram* found the musical remarkable due in part to "a fat girl named Kate Smith."[18]

During her run in *Flying High,* Smith met Ted Collins, the man who would become her mentor, manager, and defender. In a pact sealed with a handshake, Smith and Collins embarked on a venture that would last 30 years. By all accounts, Collins became Smith's protector, and she deferred to him in all business matters. Collins reportedly promised her, "You do the singing and I'll fight the battles."[19]

Whatever else might be said about Collins, he foresaw the star power of Smith's voice in the nascent radio business and was perceptive enough to understand that Smith's public image required transformation. In 1931, he landed Smith a guest appearance on Rudy Vallee's *Fleishmann Sunshine Hour,* where she introduced what was to become her first trademark song, "When the Moon Comes over the Mountain."[20] As importantly, he implicitly showed Smith a way to recast the signification of her body. In her memoirs, Smith's description of their first encounter illuminates the cultural dilemma that Smith's size had evoked publicly, its cost to her inner self, and Collins's astute refusal of this stigma:

> Ted Collins was the first man I ever met in show-business who regarded me as a serious person, and who sympathized with my desire to become a success as a singer. Where others saw merely a fat girl to laugh at, this kindly Irish-American . . . looked upon me as an artist . . . Up to that time, I had been cast in parts designed to move my audiences to loud and hearty laughter. Cartoonists pictured me as a baby elephant; publicity men were continually writing yarns about my capacity for food . . . All this talk about capitalizing [on] my weight

made me boil with anger and weep by turns ... Ted Collins was the first man who regarded me as a singer, and didn't even seem to notice that I was a big girl.[21]

Under Collins's tutelage, Smith reworked the meaning of her size. She assumed the role of a popular diva during the 1930s—a big body for a big voice—but she was coached to be unpretentious and acceptable to the middle class. Her new image recirculated associations with fatness that were permissible, even if contradictory. Kate Smith became an affable prima donna, desexualized, middlebrow, and unsophisticated.[22] At the same time, her career choices minimized surveillance under society's gaze. Although she did not avoid public appearances, her overwhelming success depended upon phonograph recordings and radio programs, where her body was concealed.

The medium of radio allowed Smith to project a disembodied voice into the consciousness of America and to cast off fat-girl stereotypes.

Kate Smith said that her lifelong business partner and mentor, Ted Collins, was the first manager to look beyond her size and accept her seriously as an artist and singer. Photo courtesy Howard Gotlieb Archival Research Center, Boston University.

Concentrating on being heard rather than seen,[23] Smith recorded dozens of hit songs and attained radio stardom in primetime on the CBS network, anchoring *Kate Smith's A&P Bandwagon* from 1936 to 1937, then hosting the celebrated evening variety show, *The Kate Smith Hour*, from 1938 through the end of the war. She also entered daytime radio in 1939, addressing housewives from noon to 12:15 p.m. every day for the next eight years in a commentary called *Kate Smith Speaks*.[24]

Yet because Smith had acknowledged her size in public discourse, she did not hide behind the microphone. She ventured into public visibility during the 1930s, with predictable consequences. In 1932, she appeared in a four-minute cameo to sing "It Was So Beautiful" in the film *The Big Broadcast*, produced by Paramount Pictures to showcase its radio stars. After the success of *The Big Broadcast*, Smith was contracted to star in the film *Hello Everybody!* in which she played a heavy-set farm girl who falls in love with dashing businessman Hunt Blake (Randolph Scott). Released in 1933, the film once again highlighted Smith as a victimized fat girl, whose attractive sister Lily (Sally Blane) wins the businessman's heart. While the narrative respected Smith's vocal talent and dignified her character by arousing a sentimental sympathy for her self-sacrifice, it also offered the corollary that "nobody loves a fat girl," in the words of a *New York Times* review. Smith's corporeal presence on the screen inevitably aroused comments about her weight, even though her spunk in coming out in movies and her likable persona moderated assaultive responses. Reviews were tempered but fell short of full acceptance. The *New York Sun* judged Smith to be a "genial and excellent crooner" but still taunted her as "voluminous."[25]

In 1938, Smith confronted outright her experience as a stout woman in her best-selling autobiography, *Living in a Great Big Way*. Offering a primitive version of fat liberation, Smith devotes a whole chapter to "those who are not slender"[26] and declares she is "not the least self-conscious" about her size and has no plans to diet. She advises women "not to worry about weight, or feel inferior because you're stout" (173) and offers a set of guidelines to help the overweight woman look lovely (176–177), including active participation in sports and exercise (179–183).

Smith's confession that earlier in her career "[m]y whole heart—my entire life—revolved around the accomplishment of making everybody *listen*, rather than *look*" (174) accentuates her realization that the culture had promptly seized control of her appearance and its meaning. With effort, she reclaimed her body during the 1930s, adopting a discourse of fat awareness that allowed her to joke about eating two-pound ice

Throughout her career, Kate Smith extolled the pleasures and benefits of vigorous exercise and outdoor sports. Although full-figured, she was an avid swimmer, diver, golfer, tennis player, and ice-skater; her talent as a dancer was renowned. Photo courtesy Wisconsin Center for Film and Theater Research (WCFTR-10769).

cream sundaes.[27] But this self-deprecation also served to expose the cruel terms of fat oppression and worked to rebuff easy stereotyping. When war erupted and Smith was able to appeal to America's patriotism, her figure was revised yet again. For many, she came to represent the spirit of the country itself.

Visiting a U.S. submarine base in New London, Connecticut, Kate Smith autographed a wartime gift for Adolf Hitler. Her most memorable contribution to the war effort was a radio bond drive that raised an estimated $50 million. Photo courtesy Howard Gotlieb Archival Research Center, Boston University.

During World War II, Smith's career reinforced the spirit of "God Bless America" in word and deed. On radio, Smith strove to inspire and reassure her fellow Americans, especially women. The day after the attack on Pearl Harbor, Smith remarked on her midday show, "[O]ut of the tragedy of war the blessed spirit of unity is blossoming today ... [W]hile we women know we cannot go forth and achieve glory and greatness such as will be achieved by the men in our service ... never forget that we are the very backbone of this nation in keeping our morale at its highest pitch."[28] As the war progressed, Smith kindly but firmly scolded those on the home front to write letters to soldiers overseas with the catchphrase "If you don't write, you're wrong." On her nighttime program, she frequently dedicated songs to servicemen who wrote her with requests,[29] and she performed regularly for the Armed Forces Radio Service.[30] Her most memorable wartime achievement on radio was a series of war bond drives that sold such an astonishing sum, estimated at $50 million, that Robert K. Merton, one of the earliest media scholars at

Columbia University's Office of Radio Research, published an analysis of her tactics that has become a social science classic.[31]

Her public appearances during the war and press photographs that appeared everywhere reinforced the connection between her patriotic status and the bodily Smith. She traveled thousands of miles to entertain troops on the North American continent, supported the American National Red Cross around the country (for which she was awarded a Certificate of Honor for Distinguished Achievement in 1945), and continued to sing her patriotic and expressive ballads to cheering crowds. During one visit to the U.S. submarine base in New London, Connecticut, Smith was even photographed painting the words "To Hitler from Kate" on a torpedo headed for the European front.

Smith's large but well-corseted midriff; her height (close to six feet); her flawless complexion, softly curled brown hair, and dainty hands; her lightness on her feet when she danced—all effectively defined a wartime figure who was pretty, but sturdy and resolute. Her status as a single woman who led a solitary but meaningful life had already been accepted by fans. While Smith spoke longingly of marrying and raising children, the melancholy so admired when she sang her love ballads sprang from her position as a marginalized woman, one who "pours her heart out in her songs and lives vicariously in the happiness of others," as the *New York Times* declared.[32] The closing lyrics of her theme song, "When the Moon Comes over the Mountain," reverberated with new meaning during the war years, when millions of women were separated from lovers and husbands: "I'll see you in the morning sun / And when the night is new, / I'll be looking at the moon. / But I'll be seeing you."[33]

While certainly Smith conveyed the tenderness and prettiness of accepted femininity, her figure signified a robust strength fortified by genuineness. Feature articles often celebrated her athletic vigor and energetic pastimes; photographs caught her ice skating, skiing, swimming, playing tennis, golfing, horseback riding, speedboating, and driving around in sporty cars. Her commonplace vocabulary, which included identifying phrases such as "Hello, everybody!" "Thank you very, very much," and "Thanks for list'nin'," emphasized a femininity that was homespun but trustworthy. She came to represent a beloved overweight aunt—comely but asexual, a do-gooder, a stalwart American.

On 14 February 1949, the *Milwaukee Journal* ran a story entitled "Everybody Loves a Fat Girl, If She's Kate."[34] In a tone that at once praised and demeaned, the article called Smith America's "Number 1 'pitch lady'" for good causes, a woman who proves "a plump girl can get along in the world without counting her calories." Astutely, the story comprehends that Smith had realized "fully that her stoutness is a capital asset," and she had assumed the role of "the congenial, warmhearted, big sister of everybody in distress." That fall, Smith received an honorary Doctor of Humane Letters from John Marshall College. During the ceremony, she was lauded as a "Gracious Lady; Eminent Artist . . . whose voice has won its way in the hearts of mankind . . . [a] sterling American."[35] This was the popular image of Kate Smith in the late 1940s, just as the new medium of television was searching for prestigious talent.

Getting the Ladies Back Day after Day

It was exactly this legacy that sparked NBC-TV's excitement in 1950 about a daytime variety show hosted by Smith. A full year before the network's coaxial cable had reached the West Coast and other far-flung NBC stations, the network was committed to establishing a beachhead in daytime programming. Pat Weaver himself endorsed NBC's strategy to feed across the network Monday through Friday from 3:00 to 5:00 p.m. ET, new programs "naturally slanted considerably towards women." "[W]e have signed Kate Smith to spearhead our daytime network programming effort," Weaver wrote in an inaugural memo, and he envisioned her show as the anchor between 4:00 and 5:00 p.m.[36]

Weaver's two-page memo, whose phraseology and central ideas were echoed in all subsequent network promotions, set forth an ambitious design for Smith's show that typified the extravagance of NBC's early daytime efforts.[37] Weaver imagined Kate Smith's television studio to be "the center of the woman's world, connected by cable and radio to all parts of the country and the world." His grand vision called for a daily variety program that was staged in a television theater before a live audience. "It will not, however, be an out-and-out theatrical presentation such as the [Milton] Berle Show . . . Rather, we want to get the feeling that Kate Smith, one of the great women of her time, . . . invites the women of America to visit with her at her television program." Weaver hoped to balance the one-on-one intimacy Smith had achieved on radio with the New York–style theatrical presentation he so esteemed. "There is to be no phoney illusion that we are visiting at Kate Smith's home or her office or anything of the sort," he wrote. "She is putting on a television program offering entertainment, information and even inspiration to her fellow women."[38]

Weaver proposed for Smith the same fragmented format typical of the standard variety show, or vaudeo, that Milton Berle was perfecting to astonishing success at night, but with "information" and "service" segments added. "Kate Smith will, of course, sing. She will introduce variety acts. She will interview interesting people from all walks of life."[39] Tentative "jottings" from NBC coordinating producer Barry Wood outlined the mix of segments that ultimately became fundamentals on the show: the day's events from a woman's viewpoint; personality interviews; songs by Smith, with choreography; college and youth talent; fashions and makeup; news and commentary with Ted Collins; fan letters; drama presentations; outstanding acts selected each week from New York nightclubs; cooking advice from the "chef of the week"; a segment featuring household gadgets;[40] variety acts of all kinds; sports; and excerpts from Broadway shows.[41]

In NBC's first significant quest to control daytime programming, network planners perceived Smith as the ideal vehicle to introduce "bigtime shows in the daytime."[42] In the months before Smith's TV premiere, George H. Frey, director of television network sales, saturated prospective advertisers and agencies with impassioned letters and brochures. Several hundred telegrams were sent to presidents, sales managers, and advertising executives who Frey believed were likely sponsors.[43] *The Kate Smith Hour* was to cover 73 percent of all U.S. television homes in a lineup of 35 interconnected stations.[44] "We are getting daytime television off to a big start with one of the greatest personalities in show business," Frey wrote. "We are sparing no pains to make Kate Smith's entry into television as sensational as her radio career . . . [W]e are confident that this show will crack all daytime records in television for a large and continuing audience."[45]

After her first week on the air, Smith exclaimed at the close of her show, "I should like to have Howdy Doody's rating!"[46] Smith's hope was almost immediately exceeded, as her own numbers quickly set the standard at NBC. In the first weeks of its opening season in 1950, Smith attracted 9.1 percent of the audience, eight times the number of homes reached by the nearest competing show.[47] NBC sales executive Robert McFadyen boasted that by October, *The Kate Smith Hour* was attracting 86 percent of the sets in use, an "audience strangle-hold" that surpassed Milton Berle's.[48]

A start like this, which eventually translated into annual billings for NBC of $6.5 million, made *The Kate Smith Hour* NBC's "biggest property."[49] During its inaugural season, Smith appreciably outperformed not only the low-budget programs stacked against her but all other daytime programs scheduled earlier in the day as well, including those hosted by Garry Moore and Robert Q. Lewis.[50] Her drawing power continued during the first six months of 1951 too. The American Research Bureau (ARB) reported that her show outscored all other daytime programs, in any time slot, by more than two to one, reaching over 2 million homes per program.[51]

Within a single season, Smith appeared to be well on her way to earning the title "Miss NBC," but her success proved to be short lived. *The Kate Smith Evening Hour*, a Wednesday night version enthusiastically introduced in 1951–1952,[52] began to flounder almost immediately in competition with the *Arthur Godfrey Show*, a ratings blockbuster on CBS. NBC realized that Kate Smith was not ratings-proof, and the network began to worry in earnest when it was forced to cancel the evening program after only one season.

Although Weaver was quick to declare during the spring of 1952 that Smith's weekday program was still "the most profitable television operation on the NBC Network,"[53] the experience of her decline at night set off alarms. Only three months into the next season (1952–1953), Charles C. Barry, vice president of sales, wanted to know the termination details of the deal with Smith.[54] By March 1953, McFadyen expressed his growing concern about Smith's Nielsen numbers, which dropped from 16.2 to 12.4 in just one year. "This is not healthy," McFadyen warned.[55]

In the course of just three years, new daytime competition threatened Smith's ratings vitality, and NBC executives at the highest level were confronting the "profound negatives" in any decision to renew her contract. "The more I reflect on the [program's] . . . sales problems due to its high cost and falling ratings, the more I question the wisdom of the renewal," wrote Barry.[56] Due to a technicality in a contract agreement with Procter & Gamble,[57] NBC was forced to schedule Smith an hour earlier, against CBS's *The Big Payoff* from 3:00 to 3:30 and *The Bob Crosby Show* from 3:30 to 4:00. "Kate Smith's rating has seriously slipped over the past two years *without* program competition," Barry fretted. "When Kate is moved to three o'clock, a further rating loss must occur until she re-establishes herself in the new time and the added factor that she will meet 'Big Payoff' competition on CBS for the first half hour can cause *additional* rating loss."[58] The Trendex numbers reported on 26 October 1953 confirmed Barry's fears, with Smith drawing only a 4.5 rating during the first half of the show.[59]

The record-breaking statistics of Smith's first year vanished when the program faced serious challengers on CBS, and because these programs were much less expensive to produce, NBC's philosophy of opulence looked more and more like a miscalculation. Barry recognized that the expensive variety genre was not reaping the profits generated by CBS's audience participation programs and its few new soap operas, both tried-and-true daytime formats from radio. He remarked that at the time *Kate Smith* began:

> [N]o one knew how similar daytime viewing habits for television would be to daytime listening habits for radio. But now we do know and we can see that programs like "Strike It Rich," "Search for Tomorrow," "Big Payoff" and "Love of Life" can out-rate Kate at much lower cost and these programs are of the same genre as we programmed in daytime radio. True, the Kate Smith Show has Kate and Ted to hold it together but they don't seem to be strong enough to get the ladies back day after day . . . [I]t's a vaudeville show and viewers seem to be demonstrating that they can take it, or leave it.[60]

Barry's memo further underscores the extent of NBC's disaffection with *The Kate Smith Hour* by 1953. He dismisses any worry that Smith might turn up on a competing network and suggests that if she did, "I think we could program against her successfully." NBC had snooped out "authoritative prices" for sponsorship per quarter-hour on three of CBS's most popular daytime shows—Arthur Godfrey at $3,000 (including his radio simulcast); Garry Moore at $1,700; and Art Linkletter at $2,700 (also including radio).[61] As one of his staff put it to Barry: "It's pretty hard to justify a price of $4000 for a Packard (Kate Smith) when you can buy a Buick Roadmaster with horse-and-buggy trailer (Godfrey) for $3000."[62]

Kate, Ted, and the Sponsors

While unbridled production costs and the rapid rise of less expensive competition on CBS contributed to the ultimate failure of *The Kate Smith Hour*, another central obstacle to Smith's survival was NBC's escalating clash with Smith and Ted Collins over sponsor relations. Inger Stole attributes Smith's plummet from success in large part to the star's unwillingness to accommodate sponsors.[63] As *Variety* summed up the problem shortly after the program's cancellation in June 1954, NBC was unhappy that "Ted Collins . . . won't permit the star to personally identify herself with the clients' products." Weaver is quoted as saying,

"[W]e want a Kate Smith who, like all the other stars in tv, will refrain from holding herself aloof from her clients and will be willing to sell."[64]

Kate Smith was caught in a "seismic shift" in advertising policies that realigned sponsor transactions during the 1950s. TV's enormous production costs prohibited the single sponsorships that had governed radio, so networks turned to segmented selling, or the "magazine" approach; this method sold the sponsorship of smaller units of a program, typically 15-or 30-minute segments, for 13, 26, or 39 weeks, with production responsibilities shifted to the network—or, in the case of *Kate Smith,* to a subsidiary producer supervised by the network.[65] During the summer of 1950, NBC formulated an intricate selling plan for *Kate Smith* that pioneered this new "fragmentized" method.[66] The scheme sought to capture the bulk of daytime revenues for the network, forestalling other potential advertising arrangements that were gaining acceptance in the industry, like spot announcements aired locally.[67]

During this period of adjustment, sponsors especially valued compliant celebrities willing to utilize their popularity, charm, and credibility to endorse products. From the beginning, NBC extolled Smith's sales abilities to advertisers. "The important part of the Kate Smith show, obviously, is Kate Smith herself," read one promotion. "She is a woman of great sympathy and understanding. She is one of the leading women of her time, both as a performer and as a spokesman for the women of America. Women have complete confidence in Kate Smith and what she says. Her believability has made her one of the most effective salesmen of our time."[68] When Smith endorsed products on television, the results were impressive. A 1951 Hofstra-NBC study found, for example, that while the average daytime TV show produced only 15.6 potential customers per dollar, Kate Smith produced 38.8. Familiarity with a brand of home freezer advertised by Smith rose 146 percent after her 10-week endorsement.[69]

Yet a stack of NBC memoranda confirms the network sales staff's mounting frustration with Smith's reluctance to meet sponsor demands.[70] Under Collins's management, Smith almost immediately reneged on her agreement to participate in filmed commercials, and by April 1951, she had alienated two powerful sponsors. By May, Hunt Foods was "a very unhappy client," perturbed because Smith had refused to record a voice-over, and was threatening to jump to CBS. In the case of Jergens hand lotion, Collins believed cutting to a close-up of the product while Smith delivered the lead-in copy embarrassed and disgraced her. According to an advertising representative for Jergens,

Collins threatened to cancel the sponsorship without further discussion unless the close-up was eliminated. Jergens sent a letter to NBC complaining that Smith's handling of the spot "lacked enthusiasm right through." "It is bad enough we are so limited on direct testimonials by Kate Smith," the sponsor wrote, "and when she takes this attitude we are getting nothing."[71]

By the end of the first season, NBC executives began to harbor resentment against a celebrity they could ill afford to alienate. Fred Wile Jr. wrote a terse but telling memo to Pat Weaver in June 1951. "This is Kate's final week [of the season]," Wile explained, "Some day, therefore, I think you should drop over to fawn."[72]

Smith's aversion to lending her considerable prestige and credibility to the commercial endorsements newly demanded of the TV celebrity can be attributed in great part to Ted Collins. Her public status as a single woman outside the shelter of a patriarchal marriage necessitated a business partner who filled the role of protective father figure and husband, someone New York Times columnist Jack Gould considered practically her "alter-ego."[73]

Smith's unswerving loyalty to Collins until his death in 1964 suggests that her public reputation as an amiable, compliant, and cheerful celebrity required a contrary doppelgänger behind the scenes, a tough negotiator who was demanding, obstreperous, and inflexible. Smith told an interviewer after a year on television: "Honestly, I don't know what I'd do without Ted Collins. He's been more than a manager; he's been a close friend . . . All the problems, the worries, the constant details, and the pressing decisions are sifted through Ted's placid spirit. After 20 years with Ted, I've learned to trust his judgment implicitly."[74] Without compromise, Collins doggedly protected Smith's standing as a television superstar, and he fought hard to counter any requests that in his view demeaned or exploited her. In so doing, he failed to comprehend early television's reliance upon the sales quotient of stars. His reluctance to turn Smith from an "artist" into a saleswoman may have been meritorious in retrospect, but within the economic structures of the early 1950s, Collins's business dealings alienated both sponsors and network executives.

The historical record suggests that Smith alone experienced the placid side of Collins's personality. In the opinion of his business associates, Collins's behavior was consistently abrasive and uncooperative. By 1951, Collins had acquired a reputation at the network for hostility. In April of that year, Collins submitted a list of 21 complaints and demands to NBC producers regarding *Kate Smith*, from not enough nighttime plugs of Smith's show to dissatisfaction with the equipment on the set.[75] When Smith's Wednesday evening program flopped in the fall of 1951, Richard A. R. Pinkham openly blamed Collins for the fiasco in a damning memo to Pat Weaver, who had offered suggestions for the show's improvement. According to Pinkham, for the show's producers the problem could be summed up in two words: Ted Collins. "As you know, Ted is tough to deal with," Pinkham wrote Weaver. "He refuses to let Kate be properly integrated into the show, demands that he virtually spend as much time on the screen as she does, and insists upon heavy drama ... [Barry] ended by putting it mathematically: Ted Collins as a producer who can't produce, plus Ted Collins as a star with no talent, plus Kate Smith as a star of great talent equal 12.5 rating. Kate Smith as a star, plus NBC equal a 25 rating."[76]

By 1953, Smith's relationship with daytime sponsors had declined markedly, under Collins's jealous guardianship. In March, the NBC sales staff revolted. Thomas A. McAvity exclaimed, "The Sales Department is violently expressive in its collective opinion that the Kate Smith show cannot be sold next year at a higher cost than it was sold this year."[77] A week later, McFadyen summarized for Walter Scott "the impending sales problems faced by this show," ticking off eight trouble spots, including advertiser pressure for more commercial minutes (which Collins adamantly opposed) and more participation by Smith.[78] By the start of the 1953 season, half of Smith's commercial time slots were still unsold.[79]

NBC's reluctant agreement to grant production control to Collins when ratings soared reversed itself when profits were in jeopardy. By the spring of 1953, Barry Wood expressed his frustrations over budget excesses to Charles Barry in a memo marked "Confidential": "As you know, realistically, Ted has always had complete control of the Kate Smith Hour ... There is no doubt that we have a well produced show but we just don't have the money to do what he insists on ... [L]onger hours, heavier sets, more talent, etc. have been necessary to appease Ted." Wood continued, "[A]s long as control is not with NBC we are in trouble and will be in more trouble next year."[80] McAvity arrived at the same conclusion in a concurrent memo to Barry. "Ted will have to understand that a problem exists, that sacrifices have to be made, and that he must do things which will effect cost savings," he wrote.[81] A few weeks later, George H. Frey echoed NBC's assessment of Collins's impudence. He told John K. Herbert, "Tom [McAvity's] memo refers to the big problem as 'Ted' ... I believe if we are ever going to get KATE back to her rightful niche in daytime commercial programming, we will need Ted's cooperation, understanding, and a reasonable attitude to our clients and prospects in dealing with their individual problems."[82]

Under strong pressure from NBC to set up "a fair and realistic budget . . . immediately" and to alter rules governing commercials and selling techniques,[83] Collins resorted to a legalistic power play that raised the stakes. On 9 April 1953, Collins notified the network that NBC had breached Smith's 1950 contract, and the said agreement was therefore "terminated forthwith."[84]

Five days later, the bitterness of the sales staff reached the breaking point. John B. Lanigan, head of the Eastern Sales Division at NBC, expressed the ill will that had come to dominate relations with Collins (and, by extension, Smith):

> As a result of the constant irritations and impossible situations we are getting into with all our clients far too frequently in connection with the KATE SMITH show, because of the arbitrary attitude adopted by our friend, Mr. Collins, I heartily recommend that we drop the show completely and substitute something else in its place next fall.
>
> We have had three instances within the past week where Collins has either refused to see prospective buyers of the show or to render services for clients which are outlined in our commercial policy issued 2 September 1952.
>
> You may accept this as the firm and irrevocable recommendation of the Eastern Sales Division.[85]

Yet NBC was caught in a legal dilemma, and Collins knew it. Adrian Samish consulted with NBC lawyers about the fine points of the contract NBC had negotiated so optimistically in 1950. To his chagrin, he discovered that even if NBC canceled the program, the Smith-Collins production company was guaranteed $8,000 per week in 1953-54 and $9,000 per week in the final season. "In other words," Barry lamented, "if the Smith show is a flop, rating-wise and sales wise, . . . and we have to re-program because of CBS competition, it can cost us $570,500, plus the cost of sustaining new, more saleable vehicles in the time spot."[86] NBC had trapped itself in a half-million-dollar mess.

The decision-making process that ensued is not well documented in network correspondence, but it seems almost certain that NBC's renewal of the show for the 1953–1954 season was forced upon the network because cancellation would have been more expensive than continuation. After tense negotiations that summer at Lake Placid (where Smith and Collins owned adjacent vacation homes), *The Kate Smith Hour* was renewed for the fall of 1953.[87] Hostility lingered, however, and the network's commitment to the program had vanished.

Once the deal was set and Collins had finally acquiesced to add 30-second commercial lead-ins read by Smith herself,[88] John K. Herbert wrote Collins a conciliatory letter. "I think the 1953–1954 season will be most successful," he wrote, "and we hope we can continue to enjoy this very pleasant relationship between you, Miss Smith and the Advertising Department of NBC in the years to come."[89] This superficial civility belied the covert resolve of Adrian Samish to terminate the relationship once and for all. The day before Herbert wrote Collins, Samish assured Charles C. Barry, "I shall be thinking about a summer replacement for Kate Smith because, in my opinion, it's going to be a regular replacement,"[90] and the very day of the Herbert letter, Samish told Barry he was determined to do "some serious thinking about Kate Smith" and "some long range thinking and planning of the afternoon schedule, or we're going to be in for trouble . . ." Samish urged, "Let's get together and decide on a plan of action now, please."[91]

Surface manners aside, the network's perception of Collins as harsh and intractable was not easily undone. Collins's doggedness in protecting Smith from perceived exploitation, coupled with his aggressive business methods, further disgruntled both sponsors and NBC sales staff and clinched the network's decision to terminate *The Kate Smith Hour*. NBC's impatience with Collins and his defensive strategies hastened Smith's failure on daytime television. *The Kate Smith Hour* atrophied on NBC for another 39 weeks and aired for the last time on 18 June 1954, the network now apparently willing to cut its contractual losses.

The Smith/Collins rebuff of sponsors, combined with reinvigorated competition from CBS, were potent industry factors that helped bring down NBC's prized program. Equally powerful in the show's demise was the country's transition to a postwar sensibility that valued amended representations of womanhood and cast Kate Smith and her variety show in an atmosphere of patriotic nostalgia. On postwar television, *The Kate Smith Hour* began to appear outmoded, and its beloved star seemed a misfit. By 1950, Christian Dior and Mamie Eisenhower were dictating the era's "New Look," and American women were enchanted by the slim curves of the "new" haute couture.[92] Decades before any thoughts of a fat acceptance movement,[93] Kate Smith's television career confronted the country's revived aversion to overweight femininity.

"You're American, Kate"

In 1952, *Coronet* magazine acknowledged that Kate Smith was "no pin-up girl . . . she weighs 235 pounds and she has never denied it."[94] During the war years, Smith's public acceptance of her size had eased pejorative characterizations, and her ample figure had even served to represent, unite, and comfort the nation. A postwar return to pinched-waist glamour, endorsed by the new medium of television, ultimately excluded Smith from emerging significations.

Even in a review of the very first installment of *The Kate Smith Hour*, Jack Gould warned the show's director to be more careful with lighting, because several camera shots "were not exactly flattering."[95] In 1951, *Variety* found Smith's first-season triumph particularly noteworthy because her size had been "a running gag on radio" and she had entered a visual medium where "SA [sex appeal] and the low-cut neckline is considered the key to success."[96] Before long, as a younger generation of slim beauties began to vie for position in front of the camera, Smith was unable to represent "woman as spectacle" on television. The slender curves of Faye Emerson, Betty Furness, Ilka Chase, Bess Myerson, and dozens of other televised women cast Smith's proportions as atypically large.[97]

To compete against this standard, Smith revived her winning persona as an all-American icon, imbuing *The Kate Smith Hour* with the patriotic spirit that had characterized her wartime radio show. Film footage showing American mountain landscapes lush with trees opened each program as Smith was heard singing "God Bless America" in the background. In a lengthy promotional piece that appeared in *Variety* at the end of the program's outstanding first year, Ted Collins attributed Smith's appeal to exactly this patriotic reputation. In a mock letter addressed to Smith (part of a full-page ad), Collins wrote adoringly:

> There's something as basically American about you, Kate, as apple pie. I know. I stood in the doorways and among the crowds when thousands . . . clamored and still do to see you and hear you . . . That's what the people want, Kate, . . . [s]omebody who says, "This is a great land . . ." You're American, Kate, and they like you because they sense the realness of your programs.[98]

This time, however, Collins had misjudged the mood of the country. Smith's persona was growing outdated, rooted as it was in a wartime sentiment that no longer suited the broadcast milieu. After the war, the camera's relentless eye recorded a woman too large for the times.[99] And the fat jokes were back. In February 1952, Red Skelton told his Sunday night television audience a cruel joke about Smith marrying a midget, who is asked how the couple could possibly get along. Says the midget, "Well, I'm happy because I run up and down her back and I've got acres and acres of back and it's all mine." (The original punch line, cleaned up for television, used "ass" for "back.")[100]

As before, Smith fought to retain a measure of dignity and control over demeaning interpretations of her size. On her daytime show the Tuesday after the joke was aired, Smith soberly confronted what she described as Skelton's "switch on a very obscene joke." She said, "I'm very thankful to those of you who have become a bit irritated and annoyed at such bad manners. But I assure you that anything Mr. Skelton says or does is of no concern to me . . . [H]e certainly has the right to conduct himself as he sees fit . . . [H]e is the master of his own salvation . . . Thank you a lot and so much for Mr. Skelton."[101] Her brief dismissal of Skelton's poor taste could not hold back an inevitable reassessment of her image in postwar America. Although she slimmed down as she aged, Smith could not escape what was to become her enduring image— a stout woman and an unfaltering patriot.

Smith's old-fashioned persona was showcased within theatrical models Weaver was known to endorse but soon proved televisually prosaic. *Kate Smith* clung fast to the staging conventions of vaudeville and "legit" theater, preserving the proscenium arch, naturalistic stage sets, and a live but anonymous audience rarely seen on camera. Typically, the show opened with a medium shot of Smith planted in front of velvet stage curtains, crooning her first song. On 3 October 1950, for example, she sang "Maybe I'm Right, Maybe I'm Wrong" while a single camera slowly trucked out to a medium long shot and then gradually returned to end in close-up. The vaudeville-style entertainment booked on *Kate Smith* necessitated a reliance on static wide shots. When her guests the Upstars sang and danced their way through "Way Down Yonder" in the next segment, the camera sat idle in a long shot, the only change an occasional close-up of the lead singer. The "Acromaniacs," a team of energetic acrobats, also required a long view of the proscenium stage.[102]

During other segments as well, Kate Smith seemed to hold viewers at a distance. Smith's custom was to sit behind a large desk in her stage "office," the windows behind her simulating a view of Manhattan; from there, Smith introduced the program's succession of acts and chatted with viewers, her torso partially concealed behind a daily flower arrangement. In this setting, Smith was perpetually locked in a medium shot that placed the viewer on the subordinate side of the desk (and its flowers) and thereby diminished TV's potential for intimacy.[103]

A record-setting budget also permitted *Kate Smith* to mount short stage presentations in the Broadway style. These scenes seemed lavish for daytime television: a full living room set when Jack Gilford and Carl Reiner appeared in a comedy sketch that satirized how difficult it was to quit smoking; elaborate kitchen scenery when Arthur Lake as Dagwood prepared a Dagwood sandwich; and a general store presented in full detail for "The World of Mr. Sweeney," a regular feature during 1953.[104] More sets were required when Albert McCleery, the theatrical innovator who later helped mastermind NBC's *Matinee Theater* (see Chapter 7), began producing a series of vignettes for *Kate Smith* that aired once a week.[105] In a 1953 confidential memo about budget overages on *Kate Smith*, Barry Wood criticized Collins's preoccupation with excessive scenery, assigning Collins to "the 'Greenwich Village Follies' school," which believed the stage had to be "full of scenery at all times."[106]

The inclusion of these frequent live vignettes on *Kate Smith* served to add nighttime production values to a daytime show, reinforcing NBC's flair for the extraordinary, but it also signaled a reliance upon theatrical aesthetics rather than televisual ones. While camera work during these dramatic segments was more animated and varied than elsewhere on the show, technicians on *Kate Smith* did not incorporate the kinds of cutting-edge techniques that innovators like McCleery were developing.

In an interview conducted after her first year of telecasting, Smith stated she was warned about the risks of live television before her program premiered: "'Don't do it Kate,' [advisers] cried, 'TV's one big headache after another. One show a month is murder,' they said, 'and you want to do five a week?'" Smith claimed, however, that she was having more fun than she had had in 20 years of radio and theater, thanks to her staff—Ted Collins; her orchestra director Jack Miller; her "indispensable right-hand gal," Dorothy Day; and her crew of 105 members. "How can there be any TV headaches?" Smith asked. "I've spent almost 200 hours in television; I haven't taken an aspirin yet."[107] Yet *The Kate Smith Hour*, despite the crew's best efforts and Smith's self-satisfaction, never perfected a style suitable to television. From its inception, the program lacked electronic novelty and grace.

Weaver had noted in his preliminary memo that "[n]either Kate nor Collins have had any direct experience" with the medium of television,[108] and their amateurism surfaced in simplistic visual ideas, old-fashioned staging, and uncomfortable mix-ups in front of the camera. The visual concept for Smith's performance of "Don't Fence Me In" was to focus in close-up on a toy ranch with miniature cowboys, horses, and corrals, then pull out to show Smith playing with these toys as she sang. After the song, Smith described how much fun she had "foolin'" with the toy corral, but errant close-ups of Smith's hand descending on the "ranch," or Smith gazing playfully at a toy cowboy as she sang, bordered on the ludicrous. The show's title graphics were equally primitive, consisting of three rudimentary moon drawings, each bearing key credits.

Efforts to experiment imaginatively with an untested televisual style produced several attempts at innovation: fanciful superimpositions during a dance number that featured spirits conjured by a medium;[109] a two-shot that revealed a cameraman seated on his mobile dolly, Collins standing beside him; stark images of a trumpeter and trumpet in noir-style silhouette;[110] and a horizontal split screen in which Collins and Smith appeared to gaze down at a drama vignette.[111]

But two episodes that aired shortly after the premiere on 25 September 1950 offer a glimpse into the program's inability to meet the aesthetic challenges of the new medium, even when a well-equipped network brought its full resources to bear. During the program that aired 3 October, Collins promised makeup artist Eddie Sens that no untimely pulling of a curtain would be repeated, and when Smith introduced a "portable light pack" on the 20 November show, she fiddled with it awkwardly, and the camera was never able to frame the product in a tidy close-up.

Other inglorious moments haunted these early shows as well. During a fashion segment "for the small fry," featuring child models, Smith sat at her desk with fashion consultant Clare Butler as the children paraded on stage. Smith giggled with pleasure at the children's outfits ("Oh, what a cute little dress!" "Very, very sweet, indeed"), but she repeatedly gave instructions that confused both the children and the show's director: "Look at the camera!" or, "Let's move the camera right along!" To make matters worse, a flustered Butler rolled her eyes in exasperation at the end of the segment, unaware that she was still on camera.[112]

Another embarrassing moment occurred in the "Teenage Spot." Here six well-spoken young men and women gathered to debate teenage problems. When the discussion shifted to the question "Should sex education be taught in high school?" Collins hurried into the picture protesting, "The minute you mention sex, I gotta come over," and postponed any discussion to the next week's segment, admonishing, "At least let us know in advance how far you're gonna go with it." The two discussion leaders, both women columnists, struggled to smile and remain composed.

Although all of early television was plagued by mishaps, both Smith and Collins appeared ill at ease in front of the camera, a serious impediment in the new medium. Smith often readjusted her clothing self-consciously, touching her collar or smoothing her dress, and she persistently failed to establish easy eye contact with either the camera or her studio audience. All too often, the camera caught her staring down at her notes, apparently hurried or confused. After an almost operatic rendition of "The Best Thing for Me Is You," Smith achieved for a moment just the right eye contact with the camera during the grand finale, smiling warmly, yet she muffed the punchline. Instead of pointing into the camera and saying, "The best thing for me is YOU," she blurted out, "The best thing for YOU is . . . or rather . . ." and broke eye contact abruptly to search for Collins, who had sauntered onto the stage.[113] Even by 1953, interchanges between Collins and Smith appeared stiff and self-conscious, lacking the warm and easy spontaneity already the hallmark of CBS stars.[114]

Collins projected an aloof pomposity throughout the series. During one revelatory moment, Collins arrived on stage to end a makeup segment conducted by Eddie Sens, who had just demonstrated to Miss Ryan, a volunteer from the studio audience, how to reapply her lipstick in a more flattering way. At first, Collins ignored the seated woman altogether, peering over her head to speak directly to Sens. When Collins did finally address Ryan for a brief second before the curtains closed, he scarcely looked at her and his remarks conveyed a haughty reserve. The sharp contrast between Collins's hauteur toward Ryan and the easygoing charm directed at studio visitors by hosts like Art Linkletter, Garry Moore, or Bob Crosby on CBS, suggests that Collins was anything but a natural. He simply lacked the charisma that the new medium demanded.

Even Kate Smith's legendary appeal failed to translate well onto 1950s television. After three years on the air, Smith still appeared poorly rehearsed and uneasy before the cameras. During an "informal get-together" with the orchestra in March 1953, Smith took a step backward as she was preparing to sing and knocked over a music stand. "What was that?" she said to scattered and nervous laughter from the orchestra, "I thought I was shot!" Later on the same show, Smith introduced a crew member to discuss the program's video tricks, but she became unsure which of two cameras would cover their conversation. "Come on. Where are we?" she joked lamely, "Make up your mind. Is it gonna be here or over there? Oh, here we are!"[115]

Smith's old-fashioned magnetism languished in the dynamic post-war setting, and her stellar reputation could not compensate for the program's mounting negatives. In the rapidly changing production environment of daytime network television, her program's dependence upon vaudeville acts and theatrical staging quickly began to look obsolete. Banal segments demonstrating "amazing things with balloons," or Smith's girlish giggles when little dogs performing on stage broke script, may have been charming in a bygone era, but failed to keep up with television's forward momentum. During "Request Time" one day in 1953, as Smith was about to sing nostalgic tunes selected by viewers, she observed that old songs "are like old hats and old shoes." "They may be out of style," she explained, "but they're so personal and so comfortable, you just can't bear to part with them."[116] Similarly, *The Kate Smith Hour* and Smith's television persona itself, while reassuringly familiar, grew ever more antiquated as the years went by.

Most of all, Smith's body, representing as it once did the nation's wartime vigor, was disproportionate to the new age. Her daily visibility presented a figure that clashed with the new fantasies for women seen elsewhere on daytime television—Julia Meade's pencil-thin elegance on *Okay, Mother* or the youthful gorgeousness of the first official Miss America to reign after the war, Bess Myerson, cohost of *The Big Payoff*, which ran against Smith at 3:00 p.m. and outrated her. Understated efforts to conceal her body behind her stage desk or NBC's use of Smith's face alone on brochures for advertisers[117] could not obliterate the image of an oversized woman not entirely comfortable on camera.

Long before television, Smith had discovered that "excess weight doesn't mean one has to go through life looking untidy and frumpish" (in her words). She purchased expensive dresses from the finest modistes in New York, had them carefully fitted, wore fine undergarments and smart accessories, stood up straight, and was fastidious in her daily grooming. Rejecting the stout woman's foolhardy wish to "look inconspicuous," Smith believed "big girls" could always be "lovely to look at."[118] And she was. The dresses Smith wore on television flattered her figure, providing busy details close to her face; her makeup, hair, and jewelry were always elegant. In short, Smith met all of the criteria for personal beauty and outward attractiveness that Arlene Francis would later champion.

But the mutable context of daytime television forced a reevaluation of Smith's size. When Adrian Samish wrote Barry that NBC would soon have "a nice, fat hour to reprogram" after *The Kate Smith Hour* failed, the pun expressed a postwar remeasurement of Smith that ruled her dimensions too imposing for the small screen.[119]

"We Want Kate!"

Following her departure from daytime television in 1954, Kate Smith's special appearances on dozens of nighttime programs through the 1970s reinforced her link to a bygone era. During the 1950s, she regularly appeared on programs with strong ties to the past, like Ed Sullivan's *Toast of the Town*; she even starred in her own nostalgic evening special on 28 April 1957, in celebration of her 26th anniversary in broadcasting.[120]

After Collins's death in 1964, Smith's new manager, Ray Katz, advised her to take more risks. Mid-decade, Smith began appearing on the *Dean Martin Show*, where she was integrated into old-time musical comedy routines. During the late 1960s and early 1970s, Smith boosted ratings on several youth-oriented programs, such as *The Smothers Brothers Comedy Hour*, *Rowan and Martin's Laugh-In*, *Tony Orlando and Dawn*, and *The Sonny and Cher Show*. She fought to retain her dignity on these programs, refusing, for example, to play Oliver Hardy to Tommy Smothers's Stan Laurel, but as a woman in her sixties, she was cast for humor as the obsolete square.[121]

But Smith's public career—and her identification with the song that bound her immutably to patriotism—would find a new and quite remarkable venue late in her life. In 1969, the Philadelphia Flyers of the National Hockey League decided to play her song before home games rather than "The Star-Spangled Banner." Each time "God Bless America" was played, the Flyers won, and Smith became an unofficial talisman for the team. In 1973, Smith sang her song in person at the stadium for the first time, a performance that gained her a three-minute standing ovation. In 1974 and 1975, she sang again to open decisive games in the Stanley Cup playoffs, each time to cheering crowds chanting, "We want Kate! We want Kate!" When the Flyers won the Stanley Cup in 1974, Smith rode triumphantly on a fire engine in the victory parade.[122]

This transference from patriotism to team spirit confirms the signifying power of her person and her song. Distanced from an era when a careworn nation yearned for Smith's consoling figure, she and her song could nonetheless stir the zeal of unity and loyalty, now displaced onto sports. Moreover, she had aptly regained iconographic status in the home of the Liberty Bell and Independence Hall. A year after her death on 17 June 1986, the Philadelphia Flyers dedicated a commemorative bronze sculpture of Smith that would stand outside the hockey stadium, her arms forever outstretched as they were at the conclusion of her song.[123] In the homology of tropes, her revival in historic Philadelphia was entirely fitting.

As new possibilities for representing American femininity were put to the test on 1950s daytime television, the full-figured matron the nation had come to esteem during World War II slid into nostalgia. The failure of *The Kate Smith Hour* on NBC resulted from mistakes and miscalculations rival CBS meanwhile was doing its utmost to avoid. In contrast to Smith's aloofness from clients, CBS's cadre of personable male hosts from radio possessed a casual ease with women that gladly facilitated selling and played well on camera. In pared-down variety formats that kept costs under control, the decade's new breed of "charm boys" mixed audience participation, personalized commercials, and masculine allure to entertain women during the day.

4

The Charm Boys Woo the Audience
Garry Moore, Arthur Godfrey,
and Art Linkletter

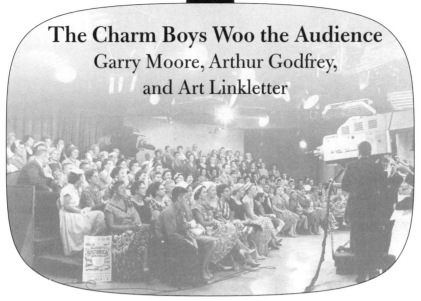

In 1950, as NBC showcased expensive female star power on *The Kate Smith Hour*, a succession of male celebrities began hosting more informal programs on CBS that cost less to produce and appealed to viewers more. *The Garry Moore Show*, vaudeo writ small, premiered in October 1950; *Arthur Godfrey Time* and *Art Linkletter's House Party*, prosperous CBS radio ventures since 1945, joined the daytime television lineup two years later.[1] All three programs are principal examples of a significant and far-reaching development in early daytime television: the rise of charismatic male stars who reigned over participatory formats aimed at women and whose assertive but toned-down masculinity secured a defining brand of male dominance in the daytime world.

Unlike the more brazenly patriarchal Dennis James on *Okay, Mother*, Garry Moore, Arthur Godfrey, and Art Linkletter were authoritative but judicious emcees whose well-tempered personae made them central agents in the advancement of participatory television and its entry into the daytime home. Relying as they did on audience interactions and a reputation for genuineness, each host laid claim to an unequaled rapport with women, and all three communicated a commanding but amiable deportment on air that eased homemakers into the virtual world of daytime television.

Time magazine called these pivotal hosts "the charm boys." While in 1954 the "unquestioned king" was Arthur Godfrey, *Time*'s list also included Garry Moore, Art Linkletter, Bob Crosby, Robert Q. Lewis, and Tommy Bartlett (the original host of *Hi Ladies*). In its characteristic style, *Time* said that from morning to sunset, television "turns loose an avalanche of masculine charm that would overwhelm any audience less hardy than U.S. housewives."[2] At its core was a modulated form of masculinity that not only incorporated boyishness, naughtiness, and humor but also included those traits traditionally associated with women—"sweetness," gentleness toward children and animals, deference to others, empathy, and attentive listening. Projecting these well-practiced qualities across the airwaves, Moore, Godfrey, and Linkletter disarmed their daytime fans and preserved male authority in a new feminine realm.

As embodiments of a masculinity deemed likable during the 1950s, these preeminent daytime stars enticed the homemaker into a new participatory world. By cultivating televisual practices that heightened a sense of intimacy, each host activated his charm to sell sponsors' products, and to woo the homemaker with an appealing but low-key sexuality.

Male Charm in a Participatory World

The charm quotient of Moore, Godfrey, and Linkletter did not rest exclusively on their personal magnetism. All three performers were able to work their magic by exploiting the new medium's potential for audience participation and inclusion, both in the studio and at home. As discussed in full in Chapter 1, early television's liveness and immediacy allowed participation shows to connect viewers and studio visitors in synchronous time, promising a friendly copresence. Like the participation shows discussed in later chapters that more formally structured the audience into the production (with greater ambiguity), the variety/talk formats hosted by Moore, Godfrey, and Linkletter instituted a place of amusement outside the home that was simultaneously made visible to the domestic viewer. On a daily basis, these three CBS stars orchestrated real-time intimacy in two social realms—the new public space of the television theater and the privatized workspace of the homemaker—and each host reveled in the pleasures that could be cultivated in both spaces.[3] The full force of their charm was expressed in their daily relations with women, and each program mobilized televisual and studio practices that enhanced the illusion of closeness.

In the studio, all three programs broke down the formal boundaries of the theatrical stage that characterized *The Kate Smith Hour*. Moore and Linkletter routinely breached the imaginary fourth wall of the proscenium arch when they bounded energetically into audience space, and Godfrey replaced the auditorium theater altogether with a simple raised platform surrounded by folding chairs.

To bolster contact with the home viewer, all three programs invented set designs and camera techniques that privileged close-up shots of the host. Because the discursive style of these performers imitated relaxed conversation, Moore, Godfrey, and Linkletter each perfected an expressive but natural rapport with the television camera. On air, Godfrey was "the master of the mildly distasteful grimace, the quizzical brow, the shrug of simulated incomprehension," as *Time* noted in 1950.[4] He had learned from his many years in broadcasting that radio was an intimate medium and that "television is more so because they can see you."[5] Moore had come to the same conclusion. Although he performed his daily program before a live audience in the cavernous Mansfield Theater in New York City,[6] he cherished his ability to captivate the home viewer via the camera. He maintained that he was able to talk "more honestly,

Art Linkletter considered the studio camera another member of the audience. He frequently directed his personable grin into the camera and communicated his responses to studio events through a range of facial expressions. Photo courtesy Linkletter Enterprises.

more intimately, and more intensely" in front of the TV camera than in his own home.[7] Linkletter, too, prided himself on his natural alliance with the camera. "I used the camera as another member of the audience," he explained in an interview with the author. "I would think of two or three people in their home, and if something happened ... [or] I wanted to look puzzled ... I'd look at the camera and I'd say [with my expression], 'How could I possibly have thought that a nice-looking young man like this would've been a head-hunter in the South Pacific?' Just an aside, just to my friends."[8] With a grin, a glance, or a wink at the camera, all three men took full advantage of early television's capacity for close-up contact in real time.

Maximizing these qualities of liveness, intimacy, and studio fun, the charm boys established for daytime viewers a spatial synthesis that fostered collegiality among women and attracted new fans to the daytime screen. Moore, Godfrey, and Linkletter skillfully translated to television programming strategies that had triumphed on radio and in the process infiltrated domesticity's private cloister with a seductive but softened mode of masculinity.

Construct No Barriers: *The Garry Moore Show* (1950–1958)

Garry Moore took a deep breath and plunged into what he called "Mr. William Paley's haunted fishbowl" in 1950.[9] Moore had just left a thriving five-year radio partnership with Jimmy Durante and had succeeded earlier in his own right as a daytime host on *Club Matinee*, broadcast from Chicago.[10] After Moore proved his aptitude as a TV natural in a guest appearance on Ed Wynn's network television program, CBS signed him to an exclusive five-year contract.[11]

The Garry Moore Show made its daytime debut in October 1950, broadcasting live on the CBS network every afternoon from 1:30 to 2:30, and it prospered on daytime television until June 1958, grabbing the attention of 8 million viewers each day.[12] Moore's career flourished, and he soon gained special prominence as the host of the primetime runaway hit *I've Got a Secret* (1952–1964).

At five feet six inches, Moore was a pixyish master of ceremonies, noted for his expressive face, crewcut, and bowtie, and he orchestrated a "kaleidoscope" of entertainment every weekday that journalist John Whitcomb of *Cosmopolitan* called in 1955 a "Moore-sized spectacular."[13] Moore's small ensemble cast and daily guests provided a mélange of vaudeville-style acts, interviews, and music. His regulars included an-

Garry Moore befriended a two-year-old lioness named Blondie and many other animals on **The Garry Moore Show**. *Photo courtesy Wisconsin Center for Film and Theater Research (WCFTR-22626).*

nouncer and sidekick Durwood Kirby, cast in part because his height (6'4") offered built-in visual comedy in sketches with Moore;[14] versatile singer and comedian Denise Lor, who often performed her songs dressed in unusual costumes, such as a kimono or Huck Finn overalls;[15] male vocalist Ken Carson, an accomplished horseman, who for dramatic effect at times rode across the Mansfield stage on a white horse; a small corps of musicians; and a basset hound named Morgan, whose drooping ears and implacable demeanor provided recurrent humor.[16]

Moore quickly learned that animals made for good television, and with the help of British zoologist Ivan Sanderson he tangled with a new species every week—including bats, anacondas, storks, boa constrictors, porcupines, zebras, crocodiles, baby elephants, skunks, monkeys, chimps, and a young lioness named Blondie. Llucky the Llama became a regular on the show (and even "married" Llinda Llama onstage), as did a capybara, whose Moore-ish hairdo guaranteed him repeat visits as the star's lookalike.[17]

Eccentric costumes were a central component of Moore's comic repertoire. Kirby in particular dressed up in a wide variety of outfits in keeping with his many characters, including Mayor Quagmire, a farmer named Mr. Littlefield, and "Jenny," a drag version of a "little old lady," whose friend was "Martha" (Moore, also in drag).[18] Intermixed with comedy sketches were occasional serious interviews (notably, Frank Lloyd Wright, Carl Sandberg, and Eleanor Roosevelt), or novelty visits from a hypnotist or the inventor of a 130-pound "gear machine" that did "absolutely nothing." Moore demonstrated many oddball inventions on air, including a revolving spaghetti fork and the Bantam Shredmaster, one of the first paper shredders. As a mentor to aspiring comedians, Moore featured a number of promising newcomers, among them Dick Van Dyke, Jonathan Winters, Don Adams, Don Knotts, George Gobel, and Carol Burnett.[19] Jazz and blues music completed the hour, welcoming a long line of guest musicians.

Although *New York Times* critic Val Adams labeled Moore a "perpetual juvenile" who was known to bounce on a trampoline, box a bear, or fly through the air on a trapeze,[20] when offstage, Moore was seriously reflective about his comedic style and spent long hours at the typewriter composing routines and "ad-libs."[21] Moore especially valued and fostered a kinship with his creative team of writers, two of whom were honored in 1957 for their scripted parody of Jack Webb's famous opening to *Dragnet*: "This is the flanagan. A teeming bortisneed of ten million snidlits. My job is to keep law and grifts. I'm a floop. The orken you are about to hear is plut . . . Only the girfs have been changed to protect the zahgen."[22]

From the start, Garry Moore valued the interactive mode and its potential to bring women together. Yet as one of television's earliest advocates and intermediaries, he also understood that his initial task was to promote daytime viewing itself. When Moore first previewed the audition kinescope of his show for CBS executives in April 1950, he placed a dust cloth on each chair in the viewing room to assure programmers he would provide the kind of entertainment women could watch as they worked.[23] Later, to encourage sustained viewing during station breaks, Moore flashed amusing messages on the screen, like "My! That fifteen minutes went quickly." Other slogans explicitly instructed women to keep watching, and all the messages—even an apparently contradictory one that declared, "You have fifteen seconds; read a book"—kept curious eyes fixed on the screen and familiarized spectators with daytime's new broadcasting flow.[24]

When *The Garry Moore Show* moved to a morning time slot in 1954, Moore and Kirby once again trained homemakers to take up a new viewing habit. Dressed in blazers and straw hats, they danced a soft-shoe together as they sang the praises of a.m. television (to the tune of "Carolina in the Morning"):

> Nothing could be greater
> Than this crummy old theater
> In the . . .
> Thanks to Mr. Paley
> We are coming to you daily
> In the . . .
> We're not broken-hearted
> It's the way that Godfrey started
> In the . . .
> Oh, how I've been wishin'
> I could be on television
> In the mor-or-or-ning.[25]

Appropriate to the exuberance of tunes like these, Moore advocated the participatory format as a source for daytime pleasure at home. He told Val Adams his function on *The Garry Moore Show* was to "maintain a mood of jollity and goodwill" for housewives, who turned to the medium as "a sop for loneliness" during the day.[26] While Moore rejected what he considered to be the gimmicky contest shows of the early 1950s and openly criticized the misery shows, he championed television's interconnection with women on his own terms. Preferring daytime broadcasting over primetime because he was freer to "rattle around" and get closer to viewers,[27] Moore celebrated what he called his "long love affair with the public,"[28] especially with the women who made up his daytime audience. According to *Time* magazine, Moore's "heart belong[ed] to his housewives."[29] "Be very kind to each other" became a familiar tagline at the close of his shows, and he often addressed the home viewer as "my dear."[30]

In his public statements, Moore explicitly cultivated his image as a man who admired women and who sought to connect with them in fun-filled interactions. "I reject the theory that housewives are stupid because they listen to daytime shows," he told *Time* magazine in 1953,[31] and he even advocated finding a new name for housewives, one with more dignity, glamour, and meaning. By the time Moore's 1953–1954 season began, well-formulated guidelines for his brand of success differentiated his show from other daytime formats: do not give away valuable merchandise, avoid humor at someone else's expense, never exploit human misfortune, and construct no barriers between the audience and the performers.[32]

In keeping with Moore's directive to construct no barriers, Moore and his producer Herb Sanford introduced a series of programming and staging practices that heightened the interactive possibilities of *The Garry Moore Show*. Many of these practices helped sustain Moore's vital bond with studio visitors, even within the mammoth Mansfield Theater—like Moore's casual audience warm-up before the show and a freewheeling "after show" for audience questions.[33] In contrast to the detachment between performer and audience projected on *The Kate Smith Hour*, Moore's approach embraced audience involvement.

Another Moore gimmick singled out studio visitors who would appear on camera during the broadcast. Before the show began, Kirby collected the names and hometowns of several audience members, under a vague pretext. During the broadcast, Moore asked these individuals to stand, pretending they were famous celebrities. As the camera caught their reactions, Moore might say, "There's Mrs. Everest, of Oak Bluff, Ohio . . . Mrs. Everest is the author of the famous magazine article which discusses the burning question: 'Should a girl who votes Republican be democratic on a sofa?' "[34]

Innovative camera positions also allowed Moore to ignore the traditional separation between the stage and the auditorium. Because two cameras were stationed at the back of the theater and a third movable camera was positioned on a side ramp, Moore was free to trek anywhere in the theater. To test the dictum that television productions required "movement," Moore jumped off the stage one day and improvised a sprint down the theater aisle, across a row of seated visitors, back to the rear of the theater, and up into the first row of the balcony, the camera on the ramp capturing his every move.

Moore's animal visitors occasionally departed the stage as well. Just moments after zoologist Ivan Sanderson reassured the audience that a six-foot-tall African marabou stork was unable to take flight from the small stage, the enormous bird lifted off and landed on the shoulders of a woman in the back of the house, and the pandemonium that followed was caught on camera.[35] In another episode, an East African monkey ignored the climbing structure provided to distract him and immediately scrambled onto the electronic equipment high above the stage. Unruffled and obviously tickled, Moore danced a mischievous jig.[36]

The Garry Moore Show's director Clarence Schimmel supplied exactly the ingenuity and workmanship Moore's freewheeling live program demanded, and he never lost sight of the audience. In one clever production number, Schimmel superimposed two camera shots to create the illusion that singers Lor and Carson were walking over the audience on a tightrope. As audience members glanced between the bare stage and the monitors, they broke into spontaneous applause, evidently appreciating a television trick that creatively integrated them into the performance.[37]

Home viewers were also urged to participate actively on *The Garry Moore Show*. From the beginning of his career in radio, Moore had relied upon home participation for his success. A radio fan had invented his stage name in 1940, winning $100 when she thought up an alternative to his cumbersome given name, Thomas Garrison Morfit.[38] On his television program one day in 1954, just "for laughs," Moore encouraged his viewers to each send a nickel to Mrs. Margaret Deibel, a housewife visiting the broadcast from Mount Pleasant, Michigan. The local post office was flooded with mail, and at week's end, she had collected $7,000[39] (when families' yearly median income was approximately $4,500).[40] In the spring of 1954, Moore sponsored a contest for the weekend ownership of Durwood Kirby, who would be "crated" and shipped via railroad to the woman who wrote the most persuasive letter. After thousands of letters were reviewed, Elly Morse of Chardon, Ohio, won Kirby as a weekend houseguest, and his arrival at her doorstep was widely publicized. Mrs. Morse's subsequent broadcast appearance on *The Garry Moore Show* in New York completed the interactive cycle.[41]

In another example, Moore found himself with time left to fill at the end of one program in 1955; he told viewers, "Here I am with a whole minute to kill. Something I've always wanted. I am going to make faces for you." Typifying his relaxed and personal style before the camera, he beamed a repertoire of improvised muggings over the airwaves for a full 60 seconds, richly displaying the close-up rapport with viewers that he and the other charm boys brought to television.[42]

Routed through interactions like these, Moore's puckish manner helped maneuver television into the homemaker's daytime schedule. As *The Garry Moore Show* began its 1953–1954 season, *Women's Home Companion* reported that Moore had somehow persuaded "millions of women to drop their work in the middle of a busy day, sit down in front of a TV set, and watch a variety show."[43] Moore's brand of masculine charm—which featured "feminine" qualities like his diminutive stature, his appearance in women's costumes, and his solicitous attitude toward housewives—prospered in the daytime sphere of women and paradoxically succeeded in validating masculine control.

Arthur Godfrey Time (1952–1959) and Godfrey the Great

Arthur Godfrey was a radio talent extraordinaire who ultimately transferred his magnetism and earning power to CBS's daytime television lineup. Yet in November 1948, Godfrey frankly expressed his anxieties about a move to television during a practice filming of his daytime radio broadcast. An opening long shot found Godfrey seated in his famous basement studio surrounded by orchestra, cast members, and studio visitors; when the camera cut to Godfrey in a medium shot, he began to joke ironically with his listeners. "Just think how wonderful it will be when we get this show on television," he teased. "You folks at home will be able, just with a flick of a switch, to be transported from your dull humdrum living room through miles of space through the miracle of electronics . . . to this dull hum-drum basement."[44]

Godfrey hoped he could replicate on television the same appeal that held together his virtual radio community, but he was apprehensive about how a picture of his face and body would affect the formula. "Then comes the big moment," he exclaimed later: "The camera swings to me—and your husband swings at the picture!" Godfrey feared that visibly inserting a male intruder into the home's daytime sanctity threatened to offend the man of the house. With these anxieties unresolved, Godfrey confided at the end of his monologue that he harbored doubts about televising *Arthur Godfrey Time*. "I don't know," he confessed. "Television may be the answer—or may not."[45]

Because Godfrey generated millions of dollars in revenue for CBS, his transition to television was carefully orchestrated. Fearful of jeopardizing the generous profits that sprang from his daytime moneymaker on radio but eager to capitalize on his unbeatable ratings, CBS transported Godfrey's properties to television in stages—beginning in primetime with *Talent Scouts* on Monday evenings in December 1948, followed by *Arthur Godfrey and His Friends* on Wednesday nights a month later.[46]

Any fears about Godfrey failing on television proved completely unfounded. Over the next four years, his stardom reached phenomenal proportions, with his two primetime television programs consistently placing in the Nielsen Top Ten. By the time *Arthur Godfrey Time* was launched as a 15-minute simulcast on daytime television in 1952, Godfrey's radio and television properties were projected to reach an estimated $11.5 million in CBS billings for the following year,[47] and Godfrey's total on-air time added up to nine and one-half hours per week. "People who like him can't get enough of him," said *Newsweek* in a cover story.[48] With Godfrey's career at its apex, the full radio version of *Arthur Godfrey Time* was soon broadcast Monday through Thursday from 10:00 to 11:30 a.m., and it thrived on daytime television in various times and lengths, including Fridays, until 1959.[49]

✦ ✦ ✦

Like Garry Moore, Godfrey served as a potent force in aligning daytime television with a sense of fun in a virtual community, for he had already mastered the studio/home conflation on radio. As a social scientist explained in 1954, during *Arthur Godfrey Time*, the housewife-viewer "entertains [Godfrey] in her home but at the same time, he invites her into his studio."[50] Godfrey's earlier fear of offending the man of the house came to naught as millions of his "goils" around the country[51] turned on the TV and eagerly welcomed him into their homes as an extra member of the family.[52] With a promise of relaxed, unpretentious entertainment, Godfrey advanced daytime television as a pleasurable new participatory activity for women, enjoyed simultaneously at home and in the studio.

The home audience participated every day through viewer and listener letters. *Collier's* reported that in 1953, letters selected from the 60,000 he received each month provided Godfrey with about half of his program material, most of it "cornball." Godfrey especially featured puns, the "bright sayings of children," and critical mail. Examples included groaners like "I have a model husband, but I wish he was a later model"; "I fell down today when I was ice skating. There was no one around to laugh, but the ice made some awful cracks" (from a nine-year-old girl); "My mother-in-law will fly you anyplace you want to go—on her broom"; and the simple declarative, "Godfrey, you stink!"[53]

Arthur Godfrey Time further reinforced the pleasures of participation by beaming across the nation daily images of women enjoying themselves in Godfrey's studio. On one episode, the camera devoted several minutes to panning across and through the audience while Godfrey sang a

*Arthur Godfrey, one of daytime television's most famous personalities, was
known for casually serenading his audience on the ukulele or guitar.
Private collection of Marsha Cassidy.*

comic ballad about Anne Boleyn of England. While Godfrey strummed
his trademark ukulele, the women whispered to each other, murmured,
and laughed. Entranced, they pointed at the camera and began to wave;
their hats tilted as they talked; they smoothed their dresses. "Ladies,
look at the camera," Godfrey told them. "When the lights are lookin' at
you, then you're on the air . . . See? That's right. That's you!" Godfrey
whistled to get their attention. "Sweetie, the camera's over there!" As

the camera continued to record sequined hats, dresses with fur collars, or lace-trimmed shirtwaists, Godfrey sang sardonically, "The ghost of Anne Boleyn walks . . . the bloody tower / With her head tucked underneath her arm."[54]

Unlike his counterparts, however, Godfrey eschewed elaborate audience involvement and shunned the bolder visual experiments that typified *The Garry Moore Show*. Although "King Arthur of the Airwaves" was noted for his unpredictable strolls around the studio on nighttime television, Godfrey favored a more stationary arrangement during the day, in part because a car accident had left him with chronic leg pain that hampered movement.[55] Moreover, because *Arthur Godfrey Time* for many years was a televised rendering of a live radio broadcast, Godfrey routinely remained seated on his raised platform throughout the show, typically wearing his headset and speaking into a table microphone marked "CBS."

Surrounding Godfrey's royal dais were "all the little Godfreys," arranged in folding chairs around the platform's perimeter. His musicians and singers changed over the years, as Godfrey gained a reputation for abruptly firing and replacing his staff, but his early troupe included announcer Tony Marvin; singers Janette Davis and the McGuire Sisters; guitarist Remo Palmier; orchestra leader and adviser Archie Bleyer; tenor Frank Parker; Hawaiian performer Haleloke; singers Marion Marlowe and LuAnn Simms; the Mariners, a racially integrated quartet; the Chordettes, female vocalists who sang a capella; and Godfrey's controversial protégé, Julius LaRosa.[56]

Camera shots alternated between long or medium shots of the orchestra or performers, close-ups of the sponsors' products (like Kellogg's variety packs), and a mix of medium shots and close-ups of Godfrey as he spoke to his guests. By 1956, the program had adopted the frequent use of the split screen. Simultaneous close-ups of Godfrey and one of his regulars added visual appeal to the star's conversations and kept Godfrey's face perpetually on screen.[57] Overall, however, Godfrey's daytime broadcasts conveyed a static look.

While the presence of a studio audience in high spirits was often verified in long shots, Godfrey minimized active exchanges with studio visitors except in the aggregate. By 1952, Godfrey had already begun to hold his fans at arm's length; because of his fame, he feared the average person could no longer relate to him in an authentic way. He told *Newsweek*, "It's no longer possible for Joe Blow to be himself with me. He becomes a phony when he's near me. He doesn't see me any more;

he sees a million bucks."[58] While Mrs. Joe Blow was sometimes shown to be savoring Godfrey's daytime festivities, she was treated more as an anonymous admirer, cheerful but passive as she experienced up close the magnetism of Godfrey the Great.[59]

Susan Murray has noted that Godfrey's persona was permanently tarnished after he callously dismissed Julius LaRosa on air in 1953, and his career waned thereafter.[60] Even so, Godfrey, whose "go-to-hell attitude" was integral to his appeal, remained a formidable competitor on CBS during the day.[61] In the 1956–1957 season, *Arthur Godfrey Time* still drew a winning 7.5 rating between 10:30 and 11:00 a.m.[62]

As the decade drew to a close, so did the program. In 1957 and 1958, Godfrey began pretaping some of his shows without a studio audience,[63] significantly reducing the participatory dimension. By then Godfrey's set had evolved into a denlike construction, furnished with bookcases, chairs, and simple sofas, and his only remaining audience was an admiring cast, who sat around the perimeter of "the den" and chatted attentively with their leader. The program ended in April 1959.

From the distance of 50 years, the appeal of Godfrey's uninhibited public persona—sarcastic, sentimental, abrasive, and disarming in turns—is enigmatic,[64] but Arthur Godfrey was a colossal figure in broadcast history, and his forceful personality attracted millions of women to the daytime TV habit. As his mail supervisor Doreen Partin said in 1953, "What's Godfrey got? Nobody seems to know—except the people."[65] Yet former Godfrey staffer Andy Rooney may have supplied a partial answer when he observed in 1959 that Godfrey did "not care much for the company of men" and was "more at ease with women."[66] This affinity for the company of women found singular expression during *Arthur Godfrey Time*, when, it has been argued, Godfrey appeared to achieve the status of a spousal stand-in during the day.[67] Godfrey's concern in 1948 that aggravated husbands would "take a swing" at his television image acknowledged his implied position as a friendly but potent male figure who kept the wife company at home after the husband left for work.[68] In this role as a spousal substitute, Godfrey perpetuated on television the hierarchy of gendered power.

Fun in the Studio: *Art Linkletter's House Party* (1952–1970)

Art Linkletter's House Party joined daytime television nine months after *Arthur Godfrey Time*, on 1 September 1952, but Linkletter abandoned the variety format altogether and chose instead to exploit his natural "likability" and ease with people to carry the concept of in-studio participation to new heights. Audience-driven segments were at the center of *House Party*, with two renowned standouts: Linkletter's daily incursions into audience space to quiz and rib studio visitors and his affectionate interviews with children, a feature that became his trademark and earned Linkletter the title the "Pied Piper of Television."

Early in his career, Linkletter recognized that his talent was interpersonal. After he graduated from San Diego State College with a teaching degree in English in 1934 and briefly taught junior high school, he decided to make a living in radio,[69] but he feared he lacked the kind of talent that would make him a star. "I didn't sing, play a musical instrument. I wasn't an actor and I wasn't a comic. There was no money in sports or news announcing then. So there was nothing for me to do."[70] The turning point came when Linkletter heard the CBS network show *Man on the Street*, produced from Texas. He remembered thinking, "I can do that!" and immediately went out and sold a man-on-the-street show locally. After stints in San Diego and Dallas, Linkletter moved in 1937 to San Francisco, where he exploited his "on-the-street" format to become the king of San Francisco radio, hosting up to 15 regular shows a week.[71]

Linkletter's competence in interviewing people evolved self-consciously. In contrast to the "entertainer," who is "automatically looking for *his* opportunity to be funny," Linkletter believes "[a] natural interviewer is really only interested in what the other person is saying . . . The best interviewers are the best listeners."[72] In Linkletter's view, success in broadcasting in the long haul required "somebody who really likes people and is interested and curious [about] people" and, most importantly, someone who is "likable." Without false modesty, Linkletter assessed the secret of his longevity in broadcasting. "I'm a very likable guy," he said, "and am not either overweening in my desire to be famous, or smarmy in my desire to please . . . just a guy you could consider to be a next-door neighbor that you like."[73]

In 1940, Linkletter and his lifelong colleague, producer John Guedel, teamed up to create the primetime radio hit *People Are Funny*,[74] followed by *House Party* during the day in 1945, proving that Linkletter was indeed likable. Linkletter's popularity followed him to television. In 1952, *People Are Funny* drew an estimated 15 million viewers each week,[75] and *House Party* was CBS's number one audience participation show in its inaugural year.[76]

Linkletter called his move to television "a very interesting transmigration,"[77] and he and Guedel deliberately waited to transfer both programs to TV until they had perfected visual techniques that supported Linkletter's ad-lib spirit. One of the most challenging hurdles was preventing cumbersome TV equipment from upstaging his studio interactions. To evoke "a real response from the audience," Linkletter said, people "have to listen and look and hear what you're saying."[78] Between 1950 and 1952, Linkletter and Guedel produced a weekly primetime program on ABC called *Life with Linkletter* that served as a laboratory for testing ways to keep microphones and cameras from blocking the audience's line of sight. Based on lessons learned from this trial program, *House Party*'s final setup made the cameras as unobtrusive as possible, freed up audience sight lines, and reduced distracting movement on stage.

To accommodate Linkletter's energetic movements within studio space, his longtime director, Michael Kane, perfected a three-camera arrangement that followed Linkletter everywhere and highlighted his quixotic reactions in close-up. *House Party* was the first daytime series produced in CBS's new "Television City" in Hollywood, and its stage design set the standard for audience participation shows, what one 1955 manual called an "ideal studio arrangement."[79] The cameras positioned in the rear of the studio adeptly recorded Linkletter's sojourn from stage to audience space and back again in medium shot and long shot.[80]

House Party's flexible camera techniques reminded viewers at home that daytime TV could function to unite audiences for lighthearted amusement. Each day, the program opened with a long shot that panned across a festive, mostly female studio gathering and found them chatting and laughing together, visibly enjoying the pleasures of a television party.[81] "Come on in," said the voice-over announcer, "It's *Art Linkletter's House Party*." In the next shot, the program's simple title card—a line drawing of a house, surrounded by flashing marquee lights—announced iconographically that the mission of *House Party* was to merge the brightly lit world of entertainment with domestic space.[82] Linkletter wrote in his autobiography, *Confessions of a Happy Man*, that he "tried to project an image of a happy man dedicated to fun and laughter,"[83] and his well-planned televisual methods on *House Party* beamed this image home.

Because *House Party* solved the transition to television in an exemplary way, Linkletter's charm with women and children in the studio did not disrupt his rapport with home viewers. "The television camera . . . is no longer a mere mechanical eye, with this little red warning light," he wrote in 1960. "To me it is a window looking into millions of homes, and

I like to feel that in each of them I am one of the family."[84] Without looking shifty-eyed, Linkletter was skilled at directing his varied reactions toward the camera, forging an intimacy with the home viewer through a wink or a merry widening of the eyes. For Linkletter, the *House Party* studio was "my living room," and through his interplay with the camera, he invited the home viewer to join the get-together. When Linkletter interviewed bachelor Phil Whitlow, who was asked to pair correctly three babies with their mothers on stage, the camera work cut rapidly between long shots, medium shots, and close-ups, but Linkletter managed to cast frequent meaningful glances at the appropriate camera throughout the stunt.[85]

Linkletter attributed part of the success of this interactive method to Kane, who not only capably followed Linkletter's jaunts through the studio but also recorded faithfully in close-up the subtleties of Linkletter's facial idiom. "[W]hen a child said something very unusual," Linkletter recalled, "the audience reacted but [Kane] cut to a close-up of me reacting. And I became a symbol of the audience surprise."[86] Linkletter and his production staff had mastered a transmission of looks that bonded the viewer to the festivities in the studio, a space Linkletter dedicated to daytime fun. "The world needs laughter," Linkletter declared, "and I intend to spread it around."[87]

✦ ✦ ✦

Linkletter's cheerful decorum served him well in his improvised exchanges with studio visitors. His athletic build—over six-feet tall, broad-shouldered, and muscular—granted him an authoritative stature in the audience, but his impish smile, his innocuous ribbing, and a concentration fixed on what guests had to say captivated and relaxed participants. Linkletter skillfully guided guests into camera range by exerting pressure on an elbow or by gallantly taking a woman's hand as she stood to converse. The respectful intimacy he expressed through body language played well on television and strengthened a mood of congeniality.

Linkletter's relaxed demeanor, combined with an intense focus on each guest, disarmed visitors to such an extent that the *Saturday Evening Post* in 1952 said Linkletter had "a sort of psychiatrist's effect on his audiences." The *Post* article surmised that Linkletter's "good-natured frankness" invited the people he interviewed to "come close to him and confide," even in public.[88] While guests on *House Party* were volunteers

*When Art Linkletter went out into the audience each day on **House Party**,
he put into action his belief that the best interviewers were the best listeners.
Photo courtesy Linkletter Enterprises.*

and never pre-rehearsed, they were all preselected before the show, often
by Linkletter himself, and seated near an aisle. "Picking people is very
important," Linkletter remembered, and he instinctively avoided "the
smart aleck, the pusher," the show-off. "[W]hat you want," he explained,
"is somebody who's nice . . . but extroverted."[89]

An example of shrewd preselection occurred one day when Linkletter
went out into the audience "to have a little fun by spelling." When Linkletter identified one of his contestants as a grammar school principal,
he turned to the camera with a look of glee. "If [only] we can spell him
down . . . ," Linkletter said hopefully. To everyone's delight, the principal misspelled "vacillate," and Linkletter triumphantly announced,
"[Y]ou have just gone back to the 5th grade!"[90]

Although Linkletter enjoyed interviewing men and women alike,[91]
his fame on *House Party* sprang in large part from his humorous exchanges with women and children. "I was, and still am, bewitched and
bewildered by the curious workings of the feminine mind," he wrote in
Confessions.[92] Day after day, women volunteers on *House Party* freely

confessed to Linkletter the embarrassing or intimate details of their lives. On one program, Linkletter inquired how wives had met their husbands. One woman confided that she was taking a shortcut through the park and encountered her husband for the first time as she climbed the gates and slid down a pole. Mrs. McWalters confessed that she met her husband when she double-dated with her "former best friend." Mrs. Don Hammond, more recently married, first set eyes on her husband as he was performing a handstand. "What a show-off!" responded Linkletter merrily. "Upside down he didn't look so good. Right side up you fell in love with him. That's reasonable."[93]

On another episode, Linkletter evoked from women "the silliest thing they ever did." Mrs. Camrit from Norway changed planes in New York City and boarded the wrong plane six hours later, ending up in South America (Linkletter: "Did you ever get back here? (PAUSE) Oh, yes, of course"). Gladys's maternity skirt almost slipped off; Elsie put her wedding dress on backwards (Linkletter: "You got married backwards!").[94] Visitors on another episode described for Linkletter "the most memorable events in their lives." Mrs. Janice delivered twins in an elevator; Mrs. Fishman drove from Indiana to California at age 73; Mrs. Stucey was revived from drowning; and Mrs. Aida Royas saw a sailor in his Skivvies (Linkletter: "This *is* a memorable moment!").[95] In his cheery affection for women, Linkletter effortlessly filled the role of interlocutor out in the audience.

Serving as an emblem for Linkletter's desire to uncover femininity's inner secrets was his ongoing fascination with women's handbags.[96] The idea to examine the contents of guests' purses had originated years earlier when Linkletter's radio producer, Helen Morgan, suggested the appearance of a woman's purse reflected her character and housekeeping abilities. From that moment on, volunteers had permitted Linkletter to peek into their purses and to expose even the most personal contents. Over time, Linkletter introduced game elements into the segment, sometimes planting a racetrack ticket, or offering a huge monetary prize to any woman who carried a rare object in her handbag, like an autographed picture of Clark Gable. Soon women began arriving on *House Party* "with their purses loaded"; one gray-haired lady held up an object so unusual that Linkletter didn't want to know what it was.[97] That it turned out to be a breast pump points to Linkletter's ambiguous position in the predominantly female domain of daytime television. On one occasion, a woman planted a rat-trap in her handbag,[98] a more explicit indictment of Linkletter's misplaced prying into feminine mysteries.

Linkletter solidified his rapport with women in a less intrusive way through his beguiling interactions with young children. His long-running "Schoolhouse" segment on *House Party* sealed his fame and gave rise to an entire media franchise.[99] The idea of improvising with children originated when Linkletter recorded an interview with his son Jack, age five, after his first day of school, and replayed it on the radio version of *House Party*. According to Linkletter, Jack refused to go back to school, explaining to his father, "I can't read. I can't write. And they won't let me talk." From then on, Linkletter interviewed four children a day, five days a week, for 26 years, some 27,000 children altogether,[100] retesting daily his old maxim, "Only children tell the truth."[101]

By the time the "Kids" segment reached television, Linkletter had finely honed his selection process and program routines. School teachers in the Los Angeles area selected participants, and the Board of Education required that children not be preinterviewed or rehearsed. To aim for the right group, Linkletter himself wrote a note to the teachers, requesting, "as a personal favor, would you please pick the four children you most like to have out of the class for a few blessed hours?"[102] Linkletter hired Mrs. Dorothy Gillespie, a certified public school teacher, to welcome and manage the young visitors each day.[103]

Before the program, Linkletter visited the children briefly in the dressing room. "[T]he only thing I did was to get down on the floor . . . and I let them see the kid in me," Linkletter remembered warmly. He then would prepare them for the inevitable laughter in the audience, explaining, "Now we're gonna go out there and it's a party. It's a fun game . . . And we'll be talking, and the people will be laughing because they're having such a good time and they like you and they like me." Linkletter believed this explanation blunted possible embarrassment and prevented audience laughter from scaring the children off. One of Linkletter's unbreakable rules, however, was that he himself would never laugh at the children, no matter how ridiculous an answer might appear to be. "If you . . . frighten a child by laughing at him, he pulls in like a tortoise inside of a shell."[104]

To achieve level eye contact with Linkletter, the children were seated in chairs on a raised platform. This fitting arrangement equalized the interview. "I wasn't talking down to them or I wasn't [talking] up to them," he said ardently, "I was speaking right to them close, face-to-face. And I was absolutely absorbed in what they had to say." When Linkletter asked one boy what he would do if he were a commercial airplane pilot whose engines had stopped, the boy explained he would parachute out. The

*The "Schoolhouse" segments on **House Party** earned Art Linkletter the title "the Pied Piper of Television." Photo courtesy Linkletter Enterprises.*

answer drew hearty laughter from the audience, but Linkletter sensed the child had more to say. After a pause, the boy explained, "I'm going for gas; I'll be coming back." Linkletter took pride in his ability to discern a child's meaning. "[B]y waiting and trusting my intuition that the kid was not being a smart aleck—he had something in mind that could be startling or interesting—that made it a marvelous interview."[105]

Because the format of *House Party* was unedited, even when the program moved from live broadcasting to tape to save production costs, the children's spontaneity supplied surprises at every turn. When Linkletter asked a young boy who wanted to be a lumberjack what lumberjacks yell when a tree comes down, the boy replied, "Help!"[106] One definition of a "wet blanket" was "the blanket baby lies on."[107] Over the years, Linkletter discovered that some questions were likely to solicit especially amusing replies. "Do you have any instructions from anyone today?" invariably uncovered family anxieties.[108] "My mother told me to be sure to keep my pants up" was one answer.[109] Sometimes the children made unintentionally suggestive remarks, but the network censors acquiesced. On one show, a boy told Linkletter he wanted to be an octopus so that he could hit all the bullies in his school with his "testicles"—a line that remained intact.[110]

Although Linkletter was never maudlin with the children he interviewed, his leading questions sometimes provoked affecting responses. In his essay, "Only Children Tell the Truth," he relates several poignant examples of children who revealed in an instant the hard reality of their own lives. In response to the question "What makes a happy home?" one boy replied, "A steady pay check." "Where do you sleep when company comes?" he asked another child, who replied, "Under the bed with all the dirt and dust."[111]

Remembering the warm familiarity he had nurtured with children, Linkletter said he especially valued a child's naturalness and recalled with affection how "funny and outrageous" some of them had been.[112] In 1956, Linkletter wrote, "People listen to kids, I think, with a kind of nostalgia. They remember their own childhood, when they could tell the truth with impunity."[113]

Time and again, the women and children on *House Party* responded guilelessly to Linkletter's unassuming manner. On the day before his 89th birthday, Linkletter recalled the comfortable alliance he had experienced with this daytime audience so many years earlier. "I just loved the camera and the microphone and everything," he said.[114] "It was *my* show," he explained. "*House Party* was *me* proving that people are innately funny ... I was proud of *House Party* from beginning to end."[115] Linkletter's interactions were not devoid of sentimentality and corniness (or commercial purpose); nevertheless, Linkletter exemplified a daytime host who opened his microphone to the unrehearsed voices of others and whose attentive listening skills mitigated a more suppressive male authority that characterized other programs (see Chapter 8). In this regard, Linkletter epitomized the physically imposing but discursively conciliatory male emcee of the 1950s, who granted women a measure of agency and, by transmitting deference, captured their allegiance.

Sales Appeal

In contrast to Kate Smith, who held fast to her role as "artist," the charm boys clinched their daytime success by applying their interactive charisma to salesmanship. Moore, Godfrey, and Linkletter each drew upon their distinctive public personae to endorse commercial products and to excel as on-air pitchmen, thereby guaranteeing the longevity of their stardom and the survival of daytime television itself.

Garry Moore was committed to providing a personal touch to his sponsors' messages, endorsing only those products he felt comfortable supporting, and "policing" all advertising copy to insure that product claims were not exaggerated.[116] *TV Guide* called this personable but low-key approach his ability "to sell softly."[117] Moore routinely integrated product pitches into skits or ad-libs, and then spoke affably to his viewers. In a 1953 program, Moore encouraged his viewers to "surprise Dad with a batch of . . . Ballard biscuits," while Kirby pantomimed a comic vision of the "hard-working husband" upstage. Moore ended the spot by promising the housewife at home in close-up, "No work for you, my dear." When a galago monkey escaped into the rafters later in the same program, Moore attempted to entice the animal down with a Ballard biscuit covered in jam and stuck on top of a pole. (This failed when the biscuit fell off the pole.) Moore promoted the biscuits one more time at the end of the show. "You can be the ever-ready hostess," Moore pledged with apparent sincerity, if "the boss comes home with hubby."[118]

By January 1958, when Moore decided to fold his still popular morning program, he cited his impatience with swelling commercial time as a deciding factor. In a farewell article published in *TV Guide*, Moore decried "the tremendous rise in the number of commercials on the show and products I must represent," which had grown from five or six accounts in the early years to some thirty different products at its peak. He had come to realize that "[u]nder present conditions the commercial aspect of the show now takes up more of my time than does the entertainment portion." Moore told readers, "That's simply not what I want to do with my life."[119] Selling softly by Moore's standards, while effective, ultimately threatened to overshadow his other talents altogether.

In contrast to Moore's softer approach to selling, Godfrey was famous for an irreverent mode of delivery that "razzed" and ridiculed advertising practices. Godfrey's mockery was carefully calculated. "I never made fun of the product," he said, "I kidded the shirt off the vice president of the company and the idiot agency that wrote . . . the most awful stuff . . . But I never did anything to belittle the product because I [wouldn't] represent a product if it isn't everything they say about it."[120] Susan Murray has concluded that while Godfrey's interventions "in the sponsor's address to consumers" temporarily disrupted and mediated the commercial aims of his program, his impertinent approach ultimately succeeded in selling the goods.[121] Godfrey's financial contributions to the profits of CBS during the 1950s were legendary, with estimates ranging as high as 12 percent of the network's overall revenues.[122]

On the 1948 radio show mentioned earlier, which was filmed for practice just before Thanksgiving, sponsor Nabisco Crackers presented Godfrey with a fully cooked turkey, decorated with parsley and lacy paper booties. With typical irreverence, Godfrey mocked the turkey, declared he hated parsley, and quickly concealed the greens between the turkey's legs. To the home listeners he said, "If you folks can guess where I shoved the parsley . . ."—a comment interrupted by hilarity in the studio. Later, when Godfrey read a comic ad line that flopped, he instructed the studio audience, "Laugh! Laugh! The client wrote that."[123]

Godfrey was proficient at interweaving product endorsement into the fabric of his programs, but he routinely did so with sarcasm or irascibility. On a 1953 episode sponsored by Pillsbury hot roll mixes—which opened with a graphic depicting Pillsbury pancakes floating in the sky like clouds—"rolls" became a discursive subtext. The announcer introduced the star as "Arthur, the hot roll kid, Godfrey," just as Godfrey introduced the McGuire Sisters as "three of the hottest rolls you've ever met." Soon, however, Godfrey became ostensibly irritated with Pillsbury. As he nibbled on a pizza made from the roll mix, he tried to read aloud the pizza recipe printed on the back of the box, only to discover with exasperation that it had been replaced by "easy kolachky." "What the heck is easy kolachky?" he complained to his entourage.[124]

In another example, after Marvin delivered a commercial for the rug cleaner Glamorene to open the show, Godfrey denounced television's commercial excesses altogether. "I can remember . . . when on radio and even on TV, they used to give you a little entertainment first, before they whapped you with the commercial . . . but no more," he protested.[125] Godfrey's outspoken annoyance with television's commercial structures seemingly aligned him with the viewer, yet evidence proves that in the end these complaints paradoxically served to strengthen his persuasive efficacy. Sponsors and top CBS executives tolerated Godfrey's brashness and no-nonsense attitude because he sold "the stuff."[126]

Art Linkletter was a businessman as well as a television celebrity—a star who made more money in business investments over the years than in show business[127]—and he, too, could sell the stuff. From the start, he rejected the advice of Jack Benny and other early stars of radio to avoid product endorsements. Benny and others "wouldn't even think of doing commercials," said Linkletter. "They were artists."

Eager to enrich his broadcast properties, Linkletter willingly volunteered to deliver commercial messages coast-to-coast. As time went by, Linkletter developed a distinctive personal style that effectively sold products, and he gained confidence in resisting erroneous commands from the "advertising agency guy" in the control booth. He learned to defend his individual mode of salesmanship. "[I]f I thought I did it right," he explained, "I'd say, 'No, I don't do it that way. That's not my personality . . . I know what I do. And that's what you're buying—me . . .' And they said, 'Yes, sir.'"[128]

Typically on *House Party*, Linkletter's commercial pitches began when a skirted product table was rolled out center stage. Without gimmickry, Linkletter smiled his way through the advertising copy, extolling the virtues of Swift's premium bacon with a low-key sincerity or endorsing the long string of other products including Geritol and Sominex that by 1961 sustained his program.[129] He attributed his smooth and letter-perfect delivery to his father's insistence that he read passages from the Old Testament without error as a boy. "Anybody who can do the Old Testament without a mistake can do a commercial," he said.[130]

Linkletter perceived that pleasing the sponsors constituted one of his most important responsibilities, and he traveled widely to make personal contact with his clients. "I knew all my sponsors. I went to the retail sales meetings; I went to the factories. I knew the Pillsburys. I knew the president of General Electric." After General Electric committed four years of single sponsorship to *House Party*, Linkletter carefully nurtured his relationship with GE's president. When the president confided to Linkletter that at times he was embarrassed while golfing with other company presidents to be sponsoring a show like *House Party*, hosted by "this fellow . . . who goes looking in ladies' purses and talks to little children," Linkletter assured him, "You tell 'em that I'm selling housewives electric blankets and refrigerators and other appliances," and the president conceded, "You're right."[131]

In the early days of television, the personalized salesmanship of Moore, Godfrey, and Linkletter worked to strengthen the financial security of CBS and to propel the expansion of daytime enterprises. Moore's relaxed but well-prepared comedy, Godfrey's familiar impudence, and

Linkletter's cheerful diplomacy appeased the era's sponsors and persuaded homemakers to purchase the consumer products that sustained daytime broadcasting.[132]

Sex Appeal/Gender Appeal

As charismatic intruders in a feminized sphere, Moore, Godfrey, and Linkletter role-played patriarch, husband, confidant, jokester, rascal, psychiatrist, and salesman all in one, but each also personified an understated seducer, whose masculine presence added a discrete sensuality to a viewer's day. Women's magazines of the era were eager to discover the "why's" of this masculine allure, and the "naturalness" of each host and his identification as a regular guy or a trusted friend were only part of the answer.[133]

Women loved Garry Moore, according to *Women's Home Companion*, because his boyish antics and undersized physique appealed to "everybody's maternal instinct."[134] Yet Moore added sexual innuendo to his performances too, as his question about Republicans behaving democratically on a sofa suggests.

Since Moore favored cross-dressing as a comic device, the vignettes in which he wore women's clothing permitted him to add erotic content in an innocuous way. In the sketch "Corsets from 1770 to Today," three young women scantily clad in old-fashioned underwear laced Moore into a frilly undergirdle. Although Moore was fully clothed in a suit, he took obvious pleasure in bodily contact with the models. This cross-gender stunt may have softened Moore's masculinity, but it also allowed for covert sexual playfulness.[135]

The recurring skit in which Moore and Kirby dressed as Martha and Jenny, two "little old ladies," also operated to introduce a paradoxical eroticism as a subtext. Wearing wigs, flowing skirts, and bustles, the broadly drawn characters often turned their attention to romance. As Herb Sanford noted, "They were man chasers."[136]

Kirby (in falsetto): Well, I was down to [the] General Store yesterday—and do you know what [Old Jed Hoskins] did?
Moore (also in falsetto): What?
Kirby: Pinched me.
Moore: No!
Kirby: Yes!
Moore: Where?

Kirby: Right between the cracker barrel and the rutabagas.

Moore: What did you do?

Kirby: I turned around real fast, looked him right in the eye, and I said, "Jed Hoskins, you do that three more times and I'll scream."[137]

Certainly Moore's small stature and his familiar appearance in women's clothing helped feminize his daytime persona, yet the exaggerated costuming in the Martha/Jenny sketches ultimately called attention to the fact that Moore and Kirby were both men, and these "men-as-women" freely intimated that women took pleasure in sex.

For *McCall's* writer Isabella Taves, the sex appeal of Arthur Godfrey also derived from his boyish demeanor—"a combination of small-boy naughtiness and genuine sweetness."[138] Known as the "Huckleberry Finn" of television, Godfrey often addressed women viewers in endearing terms. Yet Godfrey was equally notorious for frankly speaking his mind, and his "uninhibited mouth" frequently led to accusations of "blue language" or "innuendo"; by 1951, he had gained a reputation for having "an extremely earthy sense of humor."[139] One famous story detailed his handling of an ad for women's lingerie when he first started broadcasting on local radio in Washington, DC. After reading vivid copy about "filmy, clingy, alluring silk underpanties in devastating pink and black," he concluded breathlessly, "Whew! Is my face red!"[140] The anecdote evolved into a Godfrey legend not only because of its consequent sales success but also for its characteristic sensuality.

When Godfrey moved to television, some viewers began to discover salacious comments hidden in a gesture or expression, especially when Godfrey's broadcasts entered new markets for the first time. In 1951, journalist Jack O'Brian reported that Godfrey's "lifted eyebrows, smiles, his facial punctuation of any line, however innocuous, were lending a double, triple, and . . . quadruple meaning" to his remarks.[141] While Godfrey heartily denied offensive intentions, declaring he had grown afraid to say even the word "Chesterfield" on air "because of that first syllable,"[142] Godfrey's suggestive wordings and intonations were often transparent. Musician Remo Palmier recalled that Godfrey "was always making these double-meaning jokes on the air." On one occasion, according to Palmier, Godfrey claimed one use for Lysol Spray was to "spray your pet's area"; speaking quietly into the microphone, Godfrey whispered seductively, "Did you ever spray your pet's area?" In an improvised plug for Johnson's Glass Wax, Godfrey purred, "You rrrub-it-on . . . and you-rrrub-it-off."[143]

While Art Linkletter's innuendos were never as sensational, Linkletter understood that he, too, "skirted the edge." He explained, "I think because I'm who I am ... being a Baptist minister's kid and a family man, I can say naughty things. That aren't dirty. And [the audience] thinks it's cute."[144] When Linkletter displayed a harpoon made of whale-bone on one program, he remarked that older women would know that whale-bone was used in corset stays. "It held you in!" he teased, lifting his eyebrows rakishly for the camera. Other references were more blatant. Linkletter remembered one episode of *House Party* when he asked studio guests to describe the unusual circumstances under which they met the person they finally married. One woman met her husband when she was a stripper, wearing two tassels filled with sparkler material on her breasts. As she danced, spinning the lighted sparklers "like two spinwheels," one tassel flew off into the audience and landed in a man's lap. According to Linkletter, she told him, "By the time we put out the fire, he was in love with me."[145] *Coronet* magazine explained, "Linkletter's skillful use of the double-entendre is no accident. He plans it that way."[146]

Linkletter's healthy physique and his widely publicized accomplishments as an athlete continually affirmed his virility onscreen. Knowing winks and active eyebrows balanced out his tender ways with children and his well-honed listening skills, those qualities that veered toward the feminine. Some fans responded overtly to Linkletter's sexualized presence in their homes. Linkletter reported that about 3–4 percent of his mail was made up of "insane letters from women in love with me. Big red lipstick kisses ... Suggestions of what we'd do if I was there, what they were doing while I was 'there.'"[147] Like the other charm boys, Linkletter entered the domestic scene not only as a comedian, father figure, and confidant but also as a distant yet present paramour.

In a format that was at once both remote and intimate, Moore, Godfrey, and Linkletter enticed the daytime viewer into a new participatory mode of amusement by delivering a seemingly authentic self to homemakers. By means of innovative staging and a personal rapport with the camera, each man constructed his own brand of televisual charisma and sold consumer products in the process.

As interlopers in a subaltern sphere allotted almost entirely to women, each star also used television to perfect a figure of masculinity that viewers felt comfortable welcoming into the home's spatial field during the day. Moore, Godfrey, and Linkletter tempered their masculinity (and their sexuality) with humor, deference, and congeniality. In so doing, they constructed a gendered address to women that legitimated male privilege on daytime television. On the one hand, the charm boys sought to honor the daytime sovereignty of women, to establish intimacy with them, and to grant them agency; on the other, their striking presence in both the studio and in the home advanced daytime hosting as a male prerogative and reaffirmed the "natural" rightness of the decade's patriarchal order. This "loosening up" of masculinity, in Lynne Segal's terms,[148] still left male dominance intact and preserved the well-established hierarchies of gender relations.

Alongside these shows of amiability and humor—these "house parties"—another set of programs galvanized interactive participation to starkly different ends. Television's adaptation of radio's misery shows diverted 1950s housewives by dwelling upon the misfortunes and melancholy in the lives of many women and offered homemakers a more paradoxical pleasure.

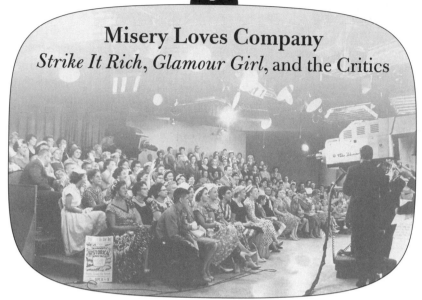

Misery Loves Company
Strike It Rich, *Glamour Girl*, and the Critics

In contrast to shows like *Garry Moore*, *Arthur Godfrey Time*, and *Art Linkletter's House Party*, which offered women lighthearted amusements, another category of popular daytime programs stressed the pathos of women's lives. Derisively called misery or sob shows, these variants of the audience participation genre required women to trade the public exposure of their life's problems for the chance to win prizes.[1] Women's confessions provided the nucleus for a number of successful television game shows during the 1950s, and victorious contestants acquired cash, consumer goods, and beauty treatments in reward.[2] By featuring the female subject in distress, two of the decade's earliest and most controversial examples of these confessional game shows, *Strike It Rich* (CBS) and *Glamour Girl* (NBC), exposed on camera the era's economic and social perils. By raising this ideological alarm, both programs predictably generated intense critical scrutiny in public and industry discourse. The case of *Strike It Rich* gave rise to a succession of ethical and legal disputes that ultimately implicated all "giveaway shows"; *Glamour Girl* provoked vigorous corporate debate too, as NBC's innermost circle confronted the show's questionable standards of propriety.

Strike It Rich was the first to come under fire. In November 1951, *New York Times* television critic Jack Gould denounced an episode he believed exploited the misery of a single mother who was considering giving up her child for adoption;[3] a little over a year later, criticism against *Glamour Girl* led to a pointed memo from David Sarnoff, then chairman of the board at RCA and NBC's interim president, that precipitated a wave of corporate deliberations. Heightened condemnation of all misery shows, *Strike It Rich* chief among them, reached a peak in early 1954, as the United States Supreme Court prepared to rule on the legality of all giveaway shows, deciding whether or not the FCC had overstepped its rule-making powers by regulating these shows as "lotteries."[4]

During this period, television's misery shows were consistently charged with advancing bad taste and contributing to the debasement of America's morals for network greed. "The crises that occur in the lives of individuals must not become grist for the morbid mill of TV," Gould proclaimed.[5] Critics like Gould framed their crusade against the misery shows within the decade's ongoing concerns over the quality of daytime television, warning against a replication of radio's denigrated feminine sphere (which included sob shows) and advocating "finer" programming for women that would uplift them (see Chapter 1).

On another level, however, this preoccupation with the "depravity" of the misery shows covered over a tacit desire to remove from view any image of Americans that belied postwar optimism. The very premise of *Strike It Rich* mandated the visible involvement of those who were socially marginalized—the sick, the poor, the unfortunate, and the disabled. Similarly, *Glamour Girl* paraded before the cameras society's ugly ducklings, whose discontent was visible in body and face. By giving voice to the "abject," *Strike It Rich*, *Glamour Girl*, and the other misery shows of the 1950s prefigured the "narrative irritation, complication, catch" that Gloria Jean Masciarotte observed in early *Oprah*. The revulsion with which the misery show was greeted by the era's television critics and social moralists suggests that these programs rendered the repressed visible, thus revealing the "contradictions of the social field."[6]

On both programs, female subjects in social distress were obligated to recount their personal intimacies in the presence of interlocutors, in keeping with what Mimi White calls television's "confessional discourse,"[7] and winning confessions earned therapeutic rehabilitation. *Strike It Rich* attempted to ameliorate the social inadequacies of its participants by lifting them closer to middle-class standards, awarding cash to the needy, donating a much-needed television set or washing machine, or returning "ailing" or "maimed" participants to "normalcy." Personal beautification revived contestants on *Glamour Girl*, a process that not only reinforced a new set of norms that had come to dictate feminine attractiveness and sexuality in postwar America but also promised contestants inner rehabilitation and happiness. In each case, contestants on the social margins exposed the failings of postwar America, offending the nation's social critics but offering women viewers the bittersweet pleasure of recognition and empathy.

Strike It Rich: Beyond Giveaways

From the beginning, *Strike It Rich* was conceived as a noble enterprise, committed to helping people realize the American dream. The show was produced by Walt Framer, an idealistic and openly patriotic son of a Russian immigrant, who developed the radio version in 1947 in part as an expression of gratitude for his own family's rise from poverty.[8] According to Framer, William Paley at CBS was receptive to the show's premise because both their fathers had faced difficult financial times together in the cigar business in Pittsburgh.[9]

From 1947 to 1950, *Strike It Rich* aired on the CBS radio network Sunday evenings, switching to NBC radio in 1950, where it continued as a morning program until 1957.[10] In an unusual contractual arrangement, the daytime television version debuted on CBS-TV on 7 May 1951, at 11:30 a.m., the network's first morning entry into national programming, while the radio edition remained an NBC property.[11]

As the radio show evolved, Framer discovered that the public favored contestants whose reasons for competing stirred up feelings of sympathy. By the time *Strike It Rich* arrived on CBS television, it was lauded for its do-good "welfare agency" mentality and known as a "quiz show with a heart."[12] Framer explained to *Newsweek* in 1953, "In anything I do, I want more than just giveaways."[13]

Each day, the program's on-camera announcer, Ralph Paul, introduced a succession of needy contestants (a mix of men and women) who were seated onstage in a set designed to replicate a comfortable living room. There the preselected participants confessed their troubles to host Warren Hull. After the interview, contestants proceeded to the quiz area, where Hull asked a series of incrementally more difficult factual questions that rose in cash value. In the "Heartline" segment that ended each episode, sympathetic viewers were able to donate additional cash or goods by calling a special hotline.

The hard luck segments in an episode that aired 28 November 1956 demonstrate the range and nature of the contestants' difficulties. The opening segment that day featured a married couple who had to carry water into their basement to wash clothes and were hoping to win enough money to buy a washing machine; during the "Helping Hand" segment, TV actor Paul Ford (of *The Phil Silvers Show*) played the game on behalf of Edna Austram, whose letter from Baton Rouge, Louisiana, explained that she and her invalid husband needed cash to build living quarters behind their store; near the end of the program, the camera panned the studio audience to surprise Michigan native P. G. Glazier, the father of 26 children, who had been compelled to work in Mexico as an itinerant farmer in order to support his family and who was chosen to compete for winnings the next day.[14]

In this typical episode, *Strike It Rich* operated to bring the needy and the disabled closer to the comforts of middle-class life. Each show opened with a shot of a treasure chest, from which arose a carton of Colgate-Palmolive's Fab detergent, as Ralph Paul spoke in voice-over: "It's the original show with a heart, *Strike It Rich* . . . where every day, Monday through Friday, people tell their own true stories and where, with our cash, you build your own fortune."[15] Throughout its run, *Strike It Rich* gathered on its television stage a diverse social collection of men and women marked as middle-class aspirants.

Central to the program's purposeful mission was the character of host Warren Hull, referred to on air as "Colgate's ambassador of good will."[16] Raised as a Quaker, Hull reportedly considered *Strike It Rich* a genuine public-service program. Framer remembered that when he first approached Hull to host the show after Todd Russell left in 1948, Hull accepted eagerly, pleased with the "help-your-neighbor idea" and even willing to work for scale. A Hollywood actor in B movies during the 1930s and an experienced radio announcer, Hull developed his interview skills on *Vox Pop* in 1941 and *Spin to Win* several years later.[17] His demeanor on *Strike It Rich* was congenial compassion, mixed with a slight awkwardness, and audiences found him to be charismatic and tender, with a hint of sex appeal. Radio historian Jim Cox, who attended one of Hull's public appearances during the series's peak popularity, recalled Hull's entry into a room: "The aura and magnetism that surrounded him . . . was nothing short of stunning. As he pushed through the crowd, his dapper, clean-cut features, flashing eyes and broad grin became overpowering."[18]

Part of Hull's compassionate image was his on-air tearfulness. According to *Radio TV Mirror*, the sad stories of some contestants so overwhelmed Hull that Framer prearranged for Ralph Paul to continue the interviews when Hull was overcome by emotion. Once, as Hull talked

*Raised a Quaker, Warren Hull, the host of **Strike It Rich**, was known to pray for his guests on the air and shed tears over their misfortunes. Photo courtesy Wisconsin Center for Film and Theater Research (WCFTR-10796).*

with a young boy suffering from leukemia, both of whose parents were also ill, Hull's eyes brimmed over, and Framer wondered "what words he could possibly find." "Suddenly," Framer told *Radio TV Mirror*, "Warren put up his hand and said quietly, 'Let's all bow our heads and pray for this boy.'"[19]

Hull's kindheartedness toward even the most wretched contestants was evident when Charles London, a destitute farmer from Riverdale, Georgia, competed for cash on 18 November 1953 in order to pay for transportation home. Elderly, gaunt, and missing several teeth, London walked haltingly to the quiz area on the arm of the announcer. When Hull asked London, "True or false? Colts, Garands, and Brownings are all different kinds of firearms," London kept repeating "Colts" as his answer, but Hull accepted the response as correct. To Hull's obvious chagrin, London was unable to identify correctly the tune "I'm Sitting on Top of the World" (although Hull repeatedly hummed the title melody for him). Finally, London risked all of his winnings on one last question. Hull asked London to fill in the blank in the famous saying, "Honesty is the best _____," but, despite audience attempts to help him and earnest coaching from Hull, London lost everything. Almost immediately the Heartline phone began to ring, and Hull literally leaped across the stage to answer it. To everyone's relief, especially Hull's, London was awarded $125. Grinning broadly, Hull held London's arm, patted him, and shook his hand good-bye.[20]

Although contestants on *Strike It Rich* were encouraged to tell their own true stories, Hull's interviews unmistakably guided and reworked people's narratives to evoke sympathy and concern for even the most miserable participant. Like other hosts of confessional game shows, Hull adopted a discursive style that blocked a contestant's full expressivity, but he did so to maximize empathy.[21]

In an episode that aired in the summer of 1952, Hull skillfully constructed the predicament of Mrs. Loretta Danny to sympathetic ends. Ordering her plight through paraphrasing, prompting, and asides, Hull kindheartedly presented the story of a heroic war widow. Mrs. Danny was an African American mother of two boys, seven-year-old Christopher and three-year-old Vaughn, both of whom were seated beside her.

> *Hull* (as the camera holds Mrs. Danny's face in close-up): Mommy, you wrote us that you're having quite a time.
> *Danny*: Yes, I am.
> *Hull*: That's why you came over here to *Strike It Rich.*
> *Danny*: Yes, that's right.
> *Hull*: So you tell me about it.
> *Danny*: Well, I would like to strike it rich because I want to finish my course at Franklin School of Science and Arts.
> *Hull*: You're studying to be . . .
> *Danny*: . . . I'm studying to be a medical technician.
> *Hull*: You're having a difficult time of it?
> *Danny*: Yes, I am having a very difficult time. I have to pay someone to take care of the children while I'm at school [. . .] Of course, there's food and clothing, books, supplies, laboratory fees. And I'm supposed to graduate in September.
> *Hull*: But you don't know how you're gonna get to September.
> *Danny*: No, I don't.

In this exchange, while Hull initially encouraged Mrs. Danny to "tell me about it" in her own words, he ingeniously began to build a narrative that aroused increasing solicitude for Danny's situation. As the interview continued and Mrs. Danny passed him a letter written by the president of her school, Hull's narrative crescendoed.

> *Hull* (reading from the letter): He says that you're a widow of a war veteran.
> *Danny*: Yes, I am [...] And I have had really a financial struggle.
> *Hull* (reading): He says that you have a fine disposition.
> *Danny* (laughing): Thank you.
> *Hull* (as we see a close-up of the letter): He says you have an excellent scholastic record.
> *Danny*: I try to. I try to be a good student and a good mother [...] It's rather hard; I try to be both of them at the same time.
> *Hull*: I'll say [...] that's two jobs ... (now reading directly from the letter) "She is thoroughly trustworthy and has the respect and admiration of all her instructors." Now that's pretty ... Huh?
> *Danny* (as the camera isolates Danny and her older boy): That's wonderful for him to say that.[22]

At a juncture in American history when the civil rights movement was in its formative stages, Hull's careful construction of Danny's image seemed crafted to position her as a "worthy" outsider who was seeking access to middle-class "normalcy." In retrospect, it appears that Hull's story functioned during its era to reassure a largely white audience that this remarkable African American war widow and single mother deserved full equality.[23] Hull enthusiastically sanctioned Danny as intelligent, well-spoken, hardworking, and "trustworthy"; moreover, her two young boys were also featured as polite, well dressed, intelligent, and sympathetic. In a touching family portrait, both Christopher and Vaughn nestled beside their mother during the quiz, and the camera frequently framed each of them in close-up. Just before Hull posed Mrs. Danny's final quiz question—on what city was the first A-bomb dropped?—Hull instructed Vaughn to cross his fingers.

Tension mounted in the studio as the camera framed Mrs. Danny and Christopher nervously consulting in whispers. When Mrs. Danny correctly answered "Hiroshima" and joyfully embraced Christopher, the audience applauded fervently. In this segment, under Warren Hull's guidance, *Strike It Rich* (and the supportive women in the studio) enthusiastically celebrated Mrs. Danny's inclusion in the social fabric of mainstream America.

By giving voice to the disenfranchised and sanctioning their images on television, *Strike It Rich* charted the "contradictions of the social field": Mrs. Danny's economic dilemma, P. G. Glazier's itinerant labor in Mexico, the struggle of a young woman to rescue her little sister from an orphanage, and even Mr. London's disorientation and unattractive teeth—all projected an unsettling spectacle of the desperate.

Like other misery shows, *Strike It Rich* featured a steady stream of disabled contestants, too, and the television camera often exposed the visual "irritation" of an "abnormal" body. During one episode, television director Kenneth Whelan remembered that he was instructed, against his own standards of good taste, to use a tight close-up on a male contestant who was lame.[24] Rosemarie Garland-Thomson has called one method of performance art used by the disabled "stare and tell," a technique of resistance that forces the audience to look closely at a disabled body while listening to the performer's personal story.[25] In the same manner, *Strike It Rich* offered the studio audience and home viewers an unfettered stare at the disabled body, even as Hull encouraged a contestant to describe her troubles.[26]

Representing disabled contestants on live television was fraught with risks, as unplanned embarrassment and even suppressed ridicule lurked just beneath the surface. At times, *Strike It Rich* and Hull himself struggled to govern these slippages. Under the gaze of the camera, Mr. London became almost laughable as well as pathetic, except for Hull's intervention. When a woman requesting a new hearing aid appeared on a nighttime episode, Hull was obliged to shout at her until Framer instructed Paul to halt the interview and break for an unplanned commercial. The very deficiency Mrs. Taylor had come to alleviate gave rise to a scene of mortification. Only Warren Hull's earnest kindheartedness prevented a collapse into farce. Hull resisted terminating the interview and reassured a befuddled Mrs. Taylor, "I'll see you after the show."[27]

Another technique that softened the presentation of a disabled figure was the use of viewer letters in the "Helping Hand" segment. On a daytime episode in 1952, Harry Steeger, publisher of *Argosy* magazine, played the game on behalf of Mr. George T. Hagler, from Charlotte, North Carolina, who remained paralyzed on his left side from an accident and had "lain prone" for eight years. Stapled to the letter was a tiny photograph of Hagler confined to his bed, and the camera captured this image in a fleeting glance. Through letters like this one, *Strike It Rich* embraced the impaired body but avoided the visual turmoil a lingering camera might interject.[28]

It was precisely the program's focus on America's excluded and forgotten that raised the critics' rancor. When the weekly evening edition of *Strike It Rich* reached the airwaves in July 1951, two months after the show's daytime debut, the program's inglorious stories of poverty, disability, and despair began to attract vehement public censure. On 9 November, Jack Gould inaugurated a campaign against *Strike It Rich* that continued for years. In Gould's opening offensive, he condemned a particularly appalling segment that featured a young single mother who was abandoned by her husband when she became pregnant. The frightened woman explained to Hull that she would have to give up her baby for adoption within thirty days unless she received financial help. Gould denounced the morbid buildup of suspense during the quiz segment, when the distraught mother was forced to answer trivial quiz questions to earn enough to keep her child. As she played, she kept repeating, "I just have to make it. I'm just hoping God's with me." When she ultimately won $500 in cash and a Heartline donation of $40 a month until she married again, the sentimental Hull reportedly wiped a tear from his eye. For Gould, however, *Strike It Rich* was "warped beyond belief." He particularly bashed the incongruous gaiety of the commercial message that immediately followed the segment, when a glamorous movie star in a negligee endorsed an underarm deodorant. "Here is a show," Gould wrote, "that callously exploits human anxiety to sell the products of a soap manufacturer and does it with a saccharine solicitude that hits the jackpot in bad taste."[29]

Gould's disdain for *Strike It Rich* helped frame the debate about the moral improprieties of all misery shows, no matter when they aired. Publicly upbraiding the Colgate-Palmolive-Peet Company, CBS, and Hull himself, Gould indicted both Framer's daytime and nighttime ventures when he asked, "What on earth do those connected with 'Strike It Rich' think they are doing?" And when Gould condemned the program as "a blatant capitalization of raw human emotions,"[30] he articulated the decade's central complaint against all sob shows.

Ironically, Gould's columns may well have increased viewership for *Strike It Rich*, daytime and primetime. Framer claimed that "every time Gould wrote a scathing column on *Strike It Rich* the ratings went up,"[31] and indeed, after Gould's first column appeared in 1951, ratings on the daytime edition climbed from October's 9.2 to 12.5 in November.[32] By early 1954, the daytime version was reaching 4 million homes, while the nighttime version attracted almost twice that number.[33] Defying Gould, Framer confidently defended his approach, telling *Newsweek* magazine that public response had guided his concentration on needy contestants.

*Despite public criticism, host Warren Hull and producer Walt Framer continued to support the idealistic aims of **Strike It Rich**. Photo courtesy Wisconsin Center for Film and Theater Research (WCFTR-10795).*

"We let someone on now with a trivial reason and we can't get away with it," Framer said. "They simply flood us with complaints."[34]

The mounting furor against the misery shows escalated early in 1954, with *Strike It Rich* the leading target. During an evening segment in January, George C. Poper, an ex-convict from Texas, who had recently been indicted on charges of theft and embezzlement, appeared as a sympathetic contestant on *Strike It Rich* and won $165.[35] The story was covered widely in the national press when the convict was eventually apprehended in upstate New York. Even though Framer cooperated fully with police, the show's screening process was roundly criticized, and *Strike It Rich* came under even more intense scrutiny.

Because needy contestants from around the country traveled to New York to compete for the chance to appear on *Strike It Rich*, New York City's Travelers Aid Society, as well as the city's welfare commissioner, Henry McCarthy, complained that *Strike It Rich* caused needy families to become stranded in Manhattan, burdening city resources. Travelers Aid reported receiving as many as five appeals a day from would-be contestants.[36]

Commissioner McCarthy was outspoken about the problem. In a number of printed interviews, he protested the show's power to attract "indigent fortune-seekers" to the city, many of whom were forced to apply for public relief when they failed to qualify as *Strike It Rich* participants. McCarthy claimed that 55 families were added to the welfare rolls during the first nine months of 1953 after striking out on their *Strike It Rich* auditions.[37] The experience of the destitute Jaskulski family from Port Deposit, Maryland, was one such highly publicized cautionary tale. The father, who spoke "poor English," had spent his most recent relief check to travel to Manhattan with his pregnant wife and nine children to seek help from *Strike It Rich*.[38] In what Framer later said was a preplanned tactic,[39] Travelers Aid intercepted the Jaskulski family at the bus station, and the New York City Welfare Agency immediately sent them back to Maryland. McCarthy told the *New York Times* that his department had provided for such indigents for over two years, but "we're not going to do it any more."[40]

McCarthy also assailed *Strike It Rich* in the city magistrate's court, charging the show with soliciting charity funds without a license by allowing contestants to receive donations from members of the audience during the Heartline segment. In response to this charge, *Strike It Rich* was obliged to open its books to public audit.[41] In December 1954, a New York magistrate ruled *Strike It Rich* was guilty of violating a city code—but only to the extent that it solicited contributions without a license from its studio audience. According to Magistrate Samuel H. Ohringer, local authorities could exercise no legal control over the conduct of the program as it was broadcast over the national airwaves, a jurisdiction assigned to federal bodies; he declined to fine defendants Walt Framer and Warren Hull, let alone send them to prison for three months. After the ruling was handed down, both sides declared victory. McCarthy hoped the judgment would mean "the end of this kind of abuse of public confidence," while Framer said he was gratified "the court found . . . the Welfare Commissioner cannot interfere with the format of our program."[42]

Meanwhile, a state-level legislative committee investigating the show's finances had determined that *Strike It Rich* had not mishandled its charitable donations (some $42,000 over three years), finding that 98 percent of the money collected reached the show's needy contestants.[43] To mollify the state committee, however, Framer agreed to prescreen each applicant and urged viewers not to travel to New York unless invited.[44]

Despite these concessions, the legal battle moved to the federal front. In 1949, the FCC had ruled that all giveaway programs violated the lottery section of the U.S. criminal code. The commission devised a set of rules whose violation would result in a revocation or denial of broadcast licenses, whereupon New York and Illinois courts issued restraining orders against the new FCC policy, ruling it interfered with constitutional guarantees of free speech and due process of law. The case reached the U.S. Supreme Court in February 1954, where all three networks, CBS, ABC, and NBC, rallied to argue against the FCC's position.[45]

Two months later, the Supreme Court ruled unanimously against the FCC, finding that the giveaway shows were not lotteries because the element of a "consideration" was missing. "The participation of a home audience by merely listening," said the Court, "does not constitute the necessary consideration." More importantly, the Supreme Court chided the FCC for its overzealous attempts to abolish the giveaway shows, concluding that the commission had "exceeded its rule-making power." While the Court did hint at the societal dilemma at the core of the FCC's actions, the justices concluded that "[r]egardless of the doubts held by the commission and others as to the social value of the programs here under consideration, such administrative expansion does not provide the remedy."[46]

While court proceedings failed to rein in the misery programs legally, momentum against the shows' excesses continued to build, particularly among influential religious publications. An editorial in the February 1954 issue of the *Christian Century* addressed the moral dimensions of the Supreme Court case. "The exploitation of [contestants'] misery makes a mockery of the ethical standards of treatment of persons needing assistance developed over many years by responsible social workers. When the scramble for profit reaches this level of depravity, it is time the churches speak up," the editorial exhorted.[47] *America*, a conservative Catholic publication, attacked *Strike It Rich* on the same grounds, quipping that Colgate-Palmolive "would soon be called upon to use some of its detergents to get rid of the noxious odor emanating from . . . *Strike It Rich.*" Asserting that a "civilized society—let alone anything like a Christian culture"—has other ways to care for the needy than to foster "morbid exhibitionism," the commentary urged the industry to "rule out such programs" in the public interest and common good.[48] A month later in the same publication, the Reverend Alfred J. Barrett, S.J., a professor of theology at Fordham University, argued that the existence of misery shows like *Strike It Rich* and *Glamour Girl* called for a ninth beatitude: "Blessed are ye who suffer—coast-to-coast." For Barrett, the misery shows violated the ideal of charity espoused in the Gospel of Matthew: "Therefore, when thou givest alms, do not sound a trumpet before thee, as the hypocrites do."[49]

Father Barrett censured *Strike It Rich* for another 'even more serious' reason: in his view, the misery programs served as "communistic propaganda."[50] According to Barrett, the "coast-to-coast indoctrination in how dismal life can be in these United States" poisoned minds against democracy, implying that America's government agencies failed adequately to help those in need. Commissioner McCarthy had reached much the same conclusion. He told Jack Gould: "Programs like these are a national disgrace . . . They create the impression that destitute people in the United States have no place to go." McCarthy, who was contemplating a bid for mayor of New York City, reasoned that every time the program's guests "expose their souls in public, we are playing into the hands of the Communists."[51] Even *TV Guide* agreed, objecting strenuously to "stupid publicity material" from *Strike It Rich* that served "Red propagandists" and calling the program "a desperate travesty on the very nature of charity."[52]

Gould fired another far-reaching salvo against *Strike It Rich* and all misery shows in February 1954. In a pique of moral outrage, he berated the genre's alignment with "nauseating spectacle" and "unspeakable bathos" and insisted that all misery shows be taken off the air. Gould called the creators of these misery shows "morbid hucksters" who debased the country by "exploiting the raw and private emotions of the unfortunate" and "catering to the craven curiosity of the mob." He exhorted those in the industry he held to be the trustees of the airwaves—William Paley, David Sarnoff, and Joseph McConnell (president of Colgate-Palmolive)—to abolish the programs at once. "These degrading and cheap exploitations of unhappiness and want have been a blot on TV for years," he wrote. "The sooner they go the better."[53]

It took almost a year before the trustees of the airwaves heeded Gould's advice. Colgate-Palmolive announced the cancellation of the nighttime version of *Strike It Rich* effective 19 January 1955.[54] The daytime edition of *Strike It Rich*, however, survived the country's righteous anger and remained on the air until 1958.[55]

Glamour's Gateway

On 6 July 1953, just six months before the denunciation of *Strike It Rich* reached its peak and even as legal action against giveaways was mounting, NBC introduced a daytime sob show of its own. Replaying the Cinderella story Monday through Friday at 10:30 a.m., *Glamour Girl* featured four women contestants competing for a glamorous makeover. Although *Glamour Girl* survived for only six months, what makes the program historically notable is the behind-the-scenes correspondence generated at the network when the show was publicly censured in the *New York Times*. NBC's highest-ranking executives, including the legendary founder of RCA and NBC, David Sarnoff himself, exchanged a series of memoranda that debated the ethics of the misery show. These papers, which have gone largely undiscovered for more than a half century, offer an inside look at the industry's private concerns and rationalizations about the difference between a "good heart act" and an indefensible exploitation of human misery.

On *Glamour Girl*, contestants explained in interviews with host Harry Babbitt or executive producer Jack McCoy (who took over hosting duties in October) their intimate reasons for wishing to be transformed; winners were selected by applause from the live audience. After receiving a key that unlocked the "gateway to glamour," the victor enjoyed 24 hours of beautification and pampering, returning to the studio the next day to display her new look to the world. Exploiting Hollywood's reputation as the globe's "glamour capital," the program was recorded in NBC's Burbank Studio #3 on 35 mm film for later network distribution from New York.[56] Although winners on *Glamour Girl* were reconstituted by means of consumer products and professional beauty advice—dramatically transformed by fashionable new clothes, a stylish hairdo, expertly applied cosmetics, and a complete line of beauty accessories—the program explicitly attached a psychodynamic value to each woman's beautification.

In her discussion of the "before-and-after" imagery favored by the cosmetics industry throughout the twentieth century, Kathy Peiss has linked the public remaking of a woman's outward appearance to her psychological restoration.[57] She explains that in modernity, beauty culturists promoted "the mutual transformation of external appearance and inner well-being," and the mass-market cosmetics industry promised that, with makeup, "a woman could not only change her looks but remake herself and her life chances."[58] In this approach, the body served as a reflection of the soul. According to Peiss, after new therapeutic language began to pervade advertising of the 1930s, the makeover became "a means of individual self-development."[59]

As a therapeutic visual spectacle linked to consumption, the public makeover was ideally suited to early television. While radio could supply beauty advice to women verbally, television permitted the close-up display of results. During the 1950s, the television makeover thus represented an intricate ideological crossroads, where the demands of daytime commercial television, financially dependent upon consumer-driven industries like cosmetics and fashion, intersected with long-standing traditions of feminine beautification and its therapeutic value. Evoking the decade's principle of psychodynamic refiguration, *Glamour Girl* selected a "lady" from the studio audience and glamorized her "into an exciting, thrilling, brand-spankin' new personality," according to Jack McCoy.[60] On *Glamour Girl*, television and the beauty industries were joined together in the mutual promotion of a woman's never-ending pursuit of therapeutic revival.

Personal restoration was further mediated on *Glamour Girl* through the imaginary of Hollywood. Not only did the show's opening sequence remind viewers the program was filmed in Hollywood—the "glamour capital of the world"—but each transformation was managed by Mary Webb Davis, consultant to the stars and the "finest glamour expert in America."[61] Whereas another 1950s program, the primetime celebrity show *This Is Your Life*, claimed to expose the authentic self within the glamorous star, as Mary Desjardins has explained,[62] *Glamour Girl* proposed the opposite—to bring to the surface the authentic glamour of the ordinary woman in a moment of televised celebrity. As Jack McCoy lucidly explained on air, beneath any repressed or damaged self lay a genuinely stunning creature. "I think almost every lady is basically very glamorous," said McCoy. "[It just takes] outside touching around" to bring out the glamour from within.[63]

Hollywood's central position in this fantasy of glamorous possibilities sprang not merely from the film industry's enduring status as the arbiter of chic modernity but also from the growing presence of Hollywood stars on television in purposeful cross-promotions.[64] The producers of *Glamour Girl* even considered adding the appearance of a Hollywood star (or "starlet") who would "tell how she made herself into a glamorous star from a plain jane" or help introduce guests.[65]

In the lexicon of *Glamour Girl*, the mark of social misfortune, inadequacy, or abuse was the unattractive body, presented for close inspection by the television camera. The damaged woman, after confessing the reasons for her displacement in the social world, won renewal in the trappings of Hollywood-driven glamour. And, like a modern-day Cinderella, every woman trapped by housework drudgery and isolated at the hearth was qualified to become a princess. A month into the show, *Glamour Girl*'s executive producer in New York, Adrian Samish, instructed the Los Angeles team to begin flying in contestants from around the country, to "give [the] audience the assurance they too can appear no matter where they live."[66] In an appeal for entries in October, Jack McCoy said to home viewers, "I know every one of you, no matter who you are, want[s] to be right here and see yourself transformed into a beautiful, beautiful glamorous lady."[67]

The story of each day's winner stigmatized her as a misfit within the gender structures of American life; at the same time, her plain, unsightly, or unconventional body supplied a reason for her marginal position within the social world. Jane Bennett, the ultimate winner on 1 October 1953, was an unmarried woman from Nashville, Tennessee, who told McCoy that she had been unable to "trap" a husband because "glamour [is] floatin' one way and me floatin' the other." McCoy immediately recognized Bennett's precarious position within 1950s patriarchy: "[You] represent lots of single girls in America who are a miss and want to be a missus."

On the following day, Elizabeth Launer of Hawthorne, California, won out over her competitors when she confessed, "I'm big. I want to prove you can be big AND glamorous." Elizabeth divulged that she had tried and failed to "reduce" and hoped to please her disapproving husband by demonstrating that big can be beautiful. Here, Elizabeth's substandard figure demarcated an erotic shortcoming that threatened to destabilize her marriage.

The next day, Joyce Torres's story exposed a much more volatile and disturbing marriage, on the brink of collapse. Torres, now pregnant with her second child, had been married three years, with a two-year-old daughter. She haltingly told McCoy that her husband thought she was not very glamorous and had threatened to leave a number of times because she didn't take care of herself. McCoy probed further. "Now, let me understand this properly," he continued, "Mr. Torres has criticized openly your appearance? . . . Have you talked this over with anyone?" Joyce conceded she had discussed the problem with a social worker, whose therapeutic advice turned out to be in accord with the ethos of *Glamour Girl*: the social worker advised Joyce to improve her appearance. After gently assuring Torres that her husband loved her and that she was a good wife and mother, McCoy asked enthusiastically, "Do you think glamour could help cohese [*sic*] this Torres home? Put it right back together the way you'd like it?" When she agreed, he added, "I hope it will do the trick . . . It won't hurt any . . . [Men need] a little help every so often." Despite McCoy's reassurances, Torres was reintroduced to the audience before the final vote as the contestant who wanted to be glamorized as a "last resort to keep her husband from leaving home."

As attentive interlocutors to each woman's therapeutic confession, the studio audience, almost exclusively composed of women, listened, evaluated, and then meted out deliverance, electing Miss Jane Bennett and the full-figured Elizabeth Launer by clear margins, while sustaining such wholehearted clapping for Joyce Torres that the applause meter pegged past 100 on her victory day. Women in the studio knew full well the jeopardy each winner faced under the rules of patriarchy.

Of course, for every winner there were three losers, and in just one week, audiences heard a total of 20 distressing tales. Like the players on *Strike It Rich*, woeful contestants on *Glamour Girl* sobbed out their stories day after day: a hardworking farm wife in her late 40s who never had a honeymoon; a polio victim who wanted to thank her husband for his life-saving support; a foster mother to 21 children who longed to attend her youngest daughter's wedding; a young woman whose face was disfigured in a fire; a wife who worked to put her husband through college while nursing a three-year-old daughter with leukemia; a mother of four abandoned by her husband; a mother whose husband was incapacitated by a chronic illness; a woman named Mabel McKinzie, age 43, who was widowed at age 17 and worked all her life to raise her children alone. Collectively, these stories reiterated a melancholic discontent, a secret longing for a life less prosaic. McKinzie summed up the bleakness of their lives when she said, simply, "The years have been long and the work hard."[68]

The accumulated narratives of these dispirited women, representing all possible gradations of misery from deep tragedy to the oppressive drabness of everyday routines, conveyed the lurking potential for despair in women's lives. Verifying the cheerlessness and daily drudgery that so often defined 1950s femininity, the television camera scrutinized in close-up how misery became discernible in a woman's appearance—in her face, her voice, the cut of her hair, her sloping posture, or the unattractive shape of her body. It was the repetition of these troubling images, coupled with the shallowness of a makeover solution, that ultimately aroused public criticism against *Glamour Girl* and set off NBC's internal dialogue about television misery.

Despite the stream of vituperation already visited upon *Strike It Rich* and other misery shows, *Glamour Girl* opened to strong reviews in July 1953. On 31 July, Adrian Samish bragged about the "great reviews" his program had received from all over the country and called for NBC to purchase print ads that stressed the press acclaim.[69] Ads for *Glamour Girl* were scheduled to run 25 August in the *New York Times*, the *New York Herald Tribune*, and the *Wall Street Journal*.[70] Among the plaudits collected, Ted Green at *Radio Daily–Television Daily* called the program a "sensational new hit" that "will be on the network for a long, long time"; Sid Shalit praised NBC vice president Charles Barry for creating "a sure-fire winner" that might, he joked, eventually provide Barry with enough votes from grateful housewives to propel him into the U.S. presidency. Harriet Van Horne of the *New York World-Telegram* was equally enthusiastic but more pragmatic, attributing the show's popularity to her conviction that "perfection of face and form is the dream of every woman still young enough to have a dream—i.e., under 80." And Hal Humphrey, the radio-TV editor for the *Mirror* in Los Angeles, gushed that the new daytime show "makes the author of 'Cinderella' look like a bum."[71]

NBC's sales department capitalized upon these reviews, preparing a hefty brochure geared to attract prospective clients. In a 19-page presentation, the pamphlet specifically targeted the country's burgeoning cosmetics and fashion industries, whose business was glamour: "[H]ere is the program especially produced for you . . . loaded with the proven elements of TV success"—feminine appeal, human interest, personal identification, and day-to-day suspense and continuity. With amazing "before-and-after" pictures of contestant Delores Napolitano, the brochure highlighted the drama created at the moment each day when the refurbished woman appeared before the cameras for the first time, accompanied by fanfare, music, and applause. "The effect is exciting and moving," the promotion read. "The audience can see that the girl is changed not only in appearance but also in her outlook on life. We see her poised, secure and smiling. This creation of a new personality has great human interest appeal."[72]

Glamour Girl Delores Napolitano, whose winning wish was to be glamourized for the G.I. husband she was going to visit in Germany. Before and after, with emcee Harry Babbitt -- who describes her beauty transformation and glamorous prize wardrobe.

An NBC sales brochure for **Glamour Girl** *featured the transformation of winner Delores Napolitano, who told host Harry Babbitt she wanted to be beautified before she visited her GI husband in Germany, but the show was roundly criticized for exploiting contestants whose reasons for competing were more pitiful. Courtesy Wisconsin Historical Society (WHi-26573).*

By the time critic Val Adams got around to reviewing *Glamour Girl* for the *New York Times* on 21 August, the show was already steaming toward success. Yet his two-column review precipitated an instant flurry of memo writing at NBC headquarters that continued over a three-week period and helped precipitate the show's ultimate demise.

The headline of Adams's review called *Glamour Girl* a "new twist in exploiting human misery," under which banner he composed a spirited excoriation. NBC's morning schedule "has deteriorated to an unbearably low level," he began; there is no excuse for a show "that exploits human misery and intentionally victimizes the innocent people who appear." He harshly criticized the program's narrative premise, expressing outrage that before NBC agreed to make a woman glamorous, she was "encouraged to tell pitiful and tragic things about her personal life." He derisively summarized the sob stories he had heard the day before. One woman "choked up and almost burst into tears" because her husband left her alone to support four children. "I can't get a job looking like this," she told Harry Babbitt. Another woman, whose husband had been ill for five years with an incurable disease, was mortified when she overheard a waitress describe her as a "Texas corn-fed gal." Adams exclaimed, "It is impossible to understand why NBC would choose to present such a cheap, vulgar program." While he conceded that a "glamour show for the ladies could really be fun," he ridiculed the approach NBC had chosen—"to play it offensively for tears instead of laughs." He concluded, "The whole shoddy business is a sin against the viewing public."[73]

This contemptuous essay caught the eye of David Sarnoff, who was serving as the interim president of NBC that August and, according to *Broadcasting/Telecasting*, was "acutely in command at the network."[74] Sarnoff's brief but stinging memo to John K. Herbert, his next-in-command at NBC, underscores the perceived danger of such sharp criticism to network interests. His terse (albeit polite) demand for an active response from Herbert and programming director Charles Barry set in motion a coast-to-coast discussion of propriety versus profits. The memo, in which Sarnoff mistakenly attributes the column to Jack Gould, reads in its entirety:

> This morning's criticism by Jack Gould in the New York Times of "Glamour Girl" is a pretty severe indictment. Is he justified in his criticism and, if so, what are we going to do about it?
>
> I should be glad to have the views of yourself or Barry, or both.
> D. S.[75]

The views of Sarnoff's subordinates began to take memo form immediately that Friday and continued to be typed and distributed around corporate offices and across the country for the next three weeks. Although the archival record is incomplete, the extant NBC memos offer an insight into the network's rationalizations about controversial but profitable formats, revealing that programmers sought to nuance the differences between a show with "a heart" and a misery show that merely featured the outpouring of "*acute* unhappiness."[76]

Over the course of the next few weeks, Adrian Samish, the NBC executive in New York who oversaw *Glamour Girl* and who was Herbert's subordinate, found himself at the center of the firestorm; his boss Charles Barry, NBC's director of programming, believed *Glamour Girl* needed "lots of work and careful planning" and instructed Samish to watch regularly "for review and criticism directed to McCoy."[77] In an attempt at damage control, Samish mailed several strong letters to producer Jack McCoy, "had numerous phone conversations" with him, telegrammed him at least once, and was prepared to fly to California for further meetings, if necessary.[78]

Samish's intense supervision of *Glamour Girl* began the same day Herbert received the Sarnoff memo. "You'll just have to watch it very carefully from now on, Jack," Samish warned McCoy, "as this kind of published criticism is not too good for your show, not good for NBC and not good for prospective clients."[79]

In this letter and subsequent correspondence, Samish labored to outline a rationale for McCoy that would allow NBC to retain *Glamour Girl* and still adhere to the high standards set by critics like Gould and Adams and professed by the network. Samish attempted to enunciate the subtle distinctions between "heart" and "misery" that for him seemed to elevate *Glamour Girl* above the other sob shows. Referring to the segments disparaged in the *Times* review, Samish accused McCoy of televising "the kind of story we agreed to stay away from, . . . the kind of thing we all agreed was wrong for the show." For Samish, the key difference between misery and heart was "inspiration." He told McCoy that the guest who recovered after suffering war trauma in a mental institution "was a *good* heart act for the show . . . This woman had fought her way back to sanity and gave a very strong message to other women . . . She was inspirational."[80] However, Samish ruled that the mere outpouring of severe unhappiness was "just plain bad taste" and did not belong on the show, particularly if misery was all the audience got out of a story.[81]

On Monday, Samish submitted a reasoned but candid summary of the situation to Barry. "I was just as disturbed as you were about the New York Times review of *Glamour Girl*," Samish began, but he bluntly reminded Barry that the misery shows generated sizable ratings and revenues within the daytime marketplace:

It is unfortunate that daytime television shows which appeal to housewives seem to require a measure of unhappiness in them to succeed. Strike It Rich, The Big Payoff, Welcome Travelers, and P&G's new show, On Your Account are going much further in this direction than does Glamour Girl and these shows are leading the pack in daytime TV ratings.[82]

Samish then recalled a meeting he and Barry had attended with Atherton Hobler, chairman of the board of the powerful advertising agency Benton and Bowles, producers of NBC's *On Your Account*. Samish remembered that Hobler advocated "what he calls the cancer treatment for successful daytime TV," meaning "a parade of the sick, the halt and the blind," a philosophy that had quickly yielded a 10.3 rating for *On Your Account*. Samish also stressed that NBC was "in a knockdown drag out fight with Arthur Godfrey for ratings" in the morning.[83] Reiterating the distinction between the exploitation of pure misery and the inspiration engendered by adversity overcome, Samish continued, "[W]e can't parade a succession of miserable, unhappy people before our cameras and feel we are contributing anything to the enjoyment and betterment of our viewers. What I am trying to get our Hollywood producers of Glamour Girl to realize is that there is a great difference between a guest who has an inspirational story coming out of hardship and a guest who simply gives a recital of her trials and tribulations." Samish told Barry he realized "full well that NBC has a greater obligation to its public than Mr. Hobler's desire to sell soap," but he suggested that the well-executed "emotional story" could be uplifting. "I believe a story of how a person is trying to use courage and faith to overcome their difficulties," he explained, "can be a help to viewers who are trying to gain the same moral strength for themselves and I further believe this kind of story is not distasteful to the average viewer and it has enough 'schmaltz' to get us a rating, too. The other daytime shows . . . do not make this distinction . . . [T]hey deal in plain misery."[84]

In a letter Samish sent to McCoy the same day he wrote Barry, he continued to accentuate the need for the right kind of heart act, "presented in the right way." Measured against the "inspiration" criterion, the "perfect heart act" in Samish's estimation was a story from a previous show of a young nurse who had fallen in love with a paralysis patient in an iron lung. Her wish was to be glamorous for her lover, who had only seen her in a nurse's uniform. Samish granted that the story "had sickness attached to it," but he praised its "great romantic twist," including "a theme of courage overcoming [a] great handicap," and culminating in possible marriage. He even told McCoy that in this instance, it would have been entirely appropriate to have "brought the guy to the show, iron lung and all, to see her transformation." He concluded, "No one could have criticized us for presenting this act and, if they did, I would have told them to go to hell."[85] For Samish, a TV executive held accountable for both decency and dollars, an inspirational story made misery defensible.

To Samish's chagrin, however, McCoy failed to grasp these fine distinctions. Two days later, Samish fired off a telegram to his wayward producer in Hollywood that began, "What would have been a great show today was spoiled by Mrs. Effie McCoy who had no good reason for wanting to be glamorous. Her act was a recital of her tough life and that's all. It was in questionable taste and the audience didn't like it any more than I did."[86]

No sooner had Samish chastised McCoy, when another more troubling memo arrived on Samish's desk, this one an NBC monitoring report completed by network executive Fred Shawn. In harsh terms, Shawn's report denounced *Glamour Girl* as "a maudlin parade of human miseries," "a very depressing, bad taste show," one that relied upon what Shawn derisively labeled "the Hearst newspaper treatment."[87] Mustering distinctions similar to Samish's, Shawn contrasted *Glamour Girl*'s depressing message with the "positive, inspirational theme" he praised as the foundation for NBC's *This Is Your Life*. Expressing mortification, Shawn outlined the stories of the four contestants competing on the day he watched. The first woman was forced to support her children alone after her husband deserted her; the second had suffered facial burns and severe disfigurement as a teenager; the third had delivered 16 children in 17 years; the fourth, pregnant with her third child, was also abandoned by a wayward husband. Shawn was especially disturbed when the burn victim's facial disfigurement "was accentuated by a revolting *close-up* shot," but he also objected to the program's underlying superficiality. "I can't help but wonder what emotional let-down these women must go through even if one of them is chosen to be glamorized for a moment," he worried. In an ominous warning, Shawn concluded, "If this day's show was typical of others in the series, it is not the kind of show that should continue on NBC."[88] On 2 September, Samish forwarded the report to McCoy, writing an exasperated cover letter: "I hope to God that, since my [last] letter to you regarding the show, you have gotten away from the museum of horrors and we will not get any more critiques like this one."[89]

Meanwhile, while Samish agonized over the fine points of acceptable misery and tried to keep McCoy in line from a distance of 3,000 miles, Barry composed a brief memo to Sarnoff on 27 August that was starkly pragmatic. Barry reassured Sarnoff that NBC had taken immediate action in response to his concerns and continued to remain vigilant. "Both Ade [Samish] and I are aware of the limitations of these over-done 'good heart' stories, and we are watching the show as closely as we can and exercising every bit of control which one can use from coast-to-coast." Then, using a calculated argument that disregarded Samish's philosophies, Barry conceded to Sarnoff that critics will harbor "strong likes and dislikes" regarding all of the misery shows, including *Glamour Girl*. He surmised, "You either like them or hate them, and it is more likely that the average critic will be inclined to slug rather than to praise shows of this type." To close, Barry appealed to Sarnoff as a hard-headed businessman. "We must give the audience a chance to vote as to the show's appeal," Barry reasoned, "and if we get the audience, that's what counts in this particular instance."[90]

A few days later, the controversy at the network over Adams's review apparently was beginning to wane. On 1 September, Herbert completed the exchange of memos when he wrote a final word to Sarnoff in answer to his original memo of 21 August: "Bud Barry's report to you represents my thoughts and completes our correspondence on this subject."[91]

At the bottom of Barry's one-page memo was a handwritten note that appears to have been written by Sarnoff himself to "F. F." In a scrawl signed "DS," the comment expressed Sarnoff's satisfaction with the adjustments he believed his vigilance had effected; for Sarnoff, Barry's correspondence verified "[t]he improvement that comes from top supervision."[92]

A few days later, columnist Sid Shalit published a brief commentary in the *New York Daily News* that read suspiciously like NBC doctrine. Shalit, who had already praised *Glamour Girl* when it first debuted, reaffirmed his view that the program highlighted the inspirational element Samish so valued. In fact, Shalit held up *Glamour Girl* as a positive model for the producers of "ill-conceived" giveaway shows, because *Glamour Girl* appealed to sympathy and good will, without sacrificing a contestant's dignity. "There's one thing we like best about *Glamour Girl*," Shalit concluded. "There isn't just one winner every day. Everybody in the studio and the audience wins; the prize—a warm feeling."[93]

As further evidence the crisis was over, on 3 September Samish telegrammed McCoy with praise. "Today's Glamour Girl show was top flight and just right," he wrote, "Please try to keep it on this track." Samish also suggested a way to appease critics who decried the neglect of contestants who lost. "When are we going to start giving each guest a watch after her interview[?]" Samish asked. "It's important so that we feel the losers are getting a worth while deal."[94]

Less than six weeks later, the audience got the chance to vote that Barry told Sarnoff was so essential. Two promotional announcements for a prize giveaway on *Glamour Girl* during the first few days in October drew more than 10,000 letters, a number so impressive that Barry circulated the good news to his superiors Herbert and Weaver with a handwritten exclamation scribbled in the margin: "Maybe it can happen!"[95] Two weeks later, Barry received even more good news: the show's Trendex rating had increased by 1.3, and its ARB rating was likewise showing a "good increase," even against *Arthur Godfrey Time*.[96] In Los Angeles, *Glamour Girl's* 3.2 ARB rating led all other NBC programs in the daytime lineup for 12–14 September, second only to *Art Linkletter's House Party* on CBS.[97]

Even more astonishing were the mail-in results for two consecutive promotions undertaken during the weeks of 5 October and 12 October. In the first week, *Glamour Girl* announced that its beauty experts would study letters and photographs from home viewers and offer suggestions for individual improvement over the air. When the program received 30,000 letters, the offer had to be withdrawn because "the glamour experts were up to their coiffures in letters and photographs," according to an NBC press release. The following week, *Glamour Girl* decided to select a single winner and reward her with "a trip to Hollywood, an appearance on the show, and a full glamour treatment."[98] The new contest drew 42,000 letters in one week; NBC calculated that between October 5 and October 16, approximately 1 in 10 viewers of *Glamour Girl* had entered the contest.[99]

Yet these hard numbers and the prospect of profit-taking could only temporarily quell NBC's anxieties about airing *Glamour Girl's* "museum of horrors." When columnist John Crosby criticized the show again in the *New York Herald Tribune* on 9 October, Sarnoff remained mum, but Barry reproached Samish again by asking, "[S]houldn't we be the 'Happy Glamourizers'[?]" John Herbert offered a prophetic final postscript to the August deliberations when he admitted to Barry about Crosby's review, "I think this guy is right."[100]

Within this uncertain climate at NBC, *Glamour Girl* could not survive for long. At a time of mounting public disapproval against all misery shows, NBC's efforts to sanitize the program through happier glamorization and moral lessons were too little, too late. Samish's well-articulated loophole of "inspiration" failed to salvage the show's respectability at a time when Weaver and his staff were planning to debut the more refined *Home* show in the same time slot. *Glamour Girl* aired its final episode on 8 January 1954.

Acts of Resistance

That the morning version of *Strike It Rich* remained on the air for three years after the nighttime show was deemed substandard underscores the second-tier status of daytime broadcasting during the 1950s. Fred Shawn enunciated a similar scorn for women's programming when he opened his critique of *Glamour Girl* with the telling words, "Maybe some women like this show."[101] This presumption of inferiority led the decade's predominantly male critics to frame debates about *Strike It Rich* and *Glamour Girl* within a context of moral inadequacy or "bad taste" and consequently to overlook the possibility that the programs offered viewers the hidden satisfaction of recognition and momentary defiance. For daily, on both *Strike It Rich* and *Glamour Girl*, emotionally charged words and pictures revealed the distress of women compromised by the economic and social structures of postwar America and, taken together, served to impeach the system.[102]

Susan Wendell, a feminist and disabilities scholar, notes that along with women, the disabled, the sick, and the old are ordinarily restricted to the private world, and those who enter the public world "with illness, pain, or a devalued body" encounter resistance.[103] *Strike It Rich* granted visibility every day to the sick, the disabled, and the destitute, freely exposing the devalued subject "to the pitiless stare of millions of curious strangers," in Gould's words.[104]

In this sense, the New York City welfare commissioner was right: *Strike It Rich* did create the impression that marginalized people in the United States had no place to go. Even the obvious insufficiency of the show's cash prizes, which could never eradicate contestants' suffering and poverty in the long run, articulated the impossibility of a complete resolution for people living on the social edges. In the poignant exchange of what Masciarotte calls "affective talk," the abject became daringly visible on *Strike It Rich*.[105]

Along the same lines, *Glamour Girl* emphasized the gender rigidities of postwar America by presenting to the nation an assemblage of women who were damaged and trapped by patriarchy. On a daily basis, the program linked misery to the bedraggled body and sanctioned public confessions that exposed the perils of gender inequities. Like women of an earlier era, contestants on *Glamour Girl* "staked a claim to public attention, demanded that others look," to quote Kathy Peiss.[106] As a remedy for body and soul, a Hollywood-style makeover served as a temporary but defiant gesture.

At the center of this insubordination on *Glamour Girl* was glamour expert Mary Webb Davis, whose team of beauty consultants transfigured each winner. A stylish woman herself, Davis spoke the language of supportive daring when she appeared on stage with the day's future glamour girl, kindly holding each woman's hand as she promised to use her expertise to bring out the "innate possibilities for a tremendous picture tomorrow."[107] To the full-figured Elizabeth Launer, Davis declared boldly, "There's no law that says all women should be slim . . . There can be BIG glamorous women, too. Glamazons . . . the Junoesque type."[108] To the pathetic expectant mother Joyce Torres, fearful of divorce, Davis pledged that the next day the world would see "one of the most glamorous mothers-to-be of all time . . . I promise this." Davis predicted that after the makeover, Mr. Torres "might feel like leaving, but for another reason . . . Every man [Joyce] meets will be so interested in her, he will get jealous."[109] The resistant tone of prescriptions like these accented the makeover on *Glamour Girl* as an act of opposition. Davis's philosophy of redemptive adornment liberated both the inner and outer self, a precept she called "psychology plus girdle."[110]

Viewed inside-out, *Glamour Girl* chronicled the dangers and disaffections of 1950s femininity and celebrated Davis's unruly remedies. Studio visitors and viewers alike were asked to gaze upon the bodies of distraught women, to listen every day to their stories of struggle and discontent, and to evaluate, adjudicate, and even ameliorate their lives of quiet desperation.

The impulse to rid daytime television of shows like *Strike It Rich* and *Glamour Girl* was powerfully ingrained in 1950s notions of vulgarity, morality, and "bad taste," and the predilections of trendsetters like Gould and Weaver brought to bear an extraordinary influence on programming choices. On 1 March 1954, NBC set out to correct the improprieties of *Glamour Girl* by debuting the *Home* show, an elite program of distinction for homemakers, a program in "good taste," above reproach, and primed to educate and uplift women during the day.

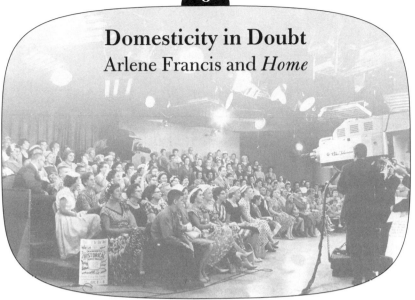

Domesticity in Doubt
Arlene Francis and *Home*

That Kate Smith and Arlene Francis were both born in 1907—Smith on 9 May and Francis on 20 October—is hard to reconcile with the contrasting images they projected on postwar television. By 1950, Smith already appeared matronly and old-fashioned, her discourse outmoded, while Francis, whose radio career in New York had closely paralleled Smith's during the 1930s and 1940s, emerged on daytime television in 1954 as a sophisticated "modern" woman and the energetic mother of a young child. If Smith's bulk and homespun personality never transcended wartime iconography, Francis's slim figure and Fifth Avenue charm offered television a mode of femininity updated for a new decade. Yet the persona of Arlene Francis turned out to be just as incongruous on daytime television as Kate Smith's, albeit for markedly different reasons. In her role as anchor of NBC's flagship homemaking program, *Home*, Francis was ideally situated to uphold emerging standards of suburban domesticity and consumerism at the base of postwar womanhood, but her urbanity and her reputation as a career woman destabilized the feminine mystique on a daily basis. Constrained by *Home*'s ambivalent mode of address and showcased on a modernist stage set that weakened homey naturalism, Francis came across on daytime television as a seasoned woman of the world trapped in an unstable new version of televised domesticity.[1]

*The urbane and witty Arlene Francis presided over a paradoxical world on **Home**.*
Photo courtesy Wisconsin Center for Film and Theater Research (WCFTR-3488).

With a more mature Francis as its "editor-in-chief," *Home* expressed an outlook toward feminine identity that reached back in time to the values of more progressive decades. Feminist historians who no longer dismiss the years 1945 to 1960 as the "dark ages" for women argue that elements of first-wave feminism survived into the 1950s and countered an unrelenting retreat to domesticity.[2] According to Susan Lynn, post-war women were free to pursue nondomestic activities "such as part-time work and civic and political activism" if they upheld their responsibilities as wives, mothers, and lovers.[3] In keeping with these transitional imbalances, Francis and *Home* regularly offered an ambiguous multivocality that cast doubts on a full withdrawal to homemaking.

The program was further unbalanced by its upper-middlebrow aspirations. Adding an urbane slant to the traditional homemaking formula confounded models for middlebrow suburban life that were validated elsewhere in the show, creating tensions that *Home* never fully resolved.[4]

Caught within the decade's historic shift in feminine representation, Arlene Francis and the urbane program she hosted served both to reproduce and to interrogate the decade's new standards for femininity. Not only was Francis the embodiment of an older woman who had grown up during a more optimistic time for women, whose sophistication transcended narrower models for the fantasy housewife, but two notable production elements on *Home* also challenged a rigid construction of the homemaker ideal. The first of these was *Home*'s segmented format, which intermixed 1950s homemaking advice with an array of features that were civic minded and politically aware. The second was *Home*'s elaborate circular stage, celebrated for its electronic gadgets and televisual wizardry. The imaginative use of this stage transmitted a modernist, self-reflexive aesthetic that stylistically exposed the false trappings of domestic fantasies. Through its contradictions, the *Home* show thus cast doubt on homebound femininity and projected the possibility for alternatives.

The T-H-T Triangle

While accounts of television's history have long acknowledged the significance of the durable *Today* and *Tonight* shows, *Home*'s early cancellation branded the program an inconsequential failure, and its historical importance has only recently been revised.[5] Yet between 1954 and 1957, *Home* was the middle note in NBC's "T-H-T" triad, the *Tonight-Home-Today* combination created by Sylvester "Pat" Weaver to expand nationally the method of segmented sponsorships adopted on *The Kate Smith Hour* and to extend network jurisdiction over a longer broadcast day. To these ends, NBC marketed *Today*, *Home*, and *Tonight* in an integrated sales package and even printed "T-H-T" stationery. While *Home* did not enjoy the longevity of *Today* and *Tonight*, it did succeed in strengthening NBC's national monopoly, displacing local productions late in the morning and securing an additional full hour of network control across the country. By 1956, *Home* reached 61 cities, drew a daily audience of

3 million viewers, had collected 40 sponsors, received 5,000 letters a week, and answered 500 phone calls a day.[6] In 1956, the T-H-T triangle was earning the NBC network $17 million annually.[7]

Home's debut was anticipated with hyperbolic publicity. A week before the show's unveiling, NBC ran a two-page ad in *Variety* that read, "March 1, 1954. Remember this date. In the future it will be known as the day that *Home* had its premiere."[8] This ad represented only one small part of the unprecedented $1 million Weaver spent to publicize *Home*'s introduction,[9] and reports of his extravagance and originality in launching the new show were widely circulated in the popular press. *Time* magazine heralded Weaver as NBC's "thinker-in-chief," declaring that his invention of *Today*, *Home*, and *Tonight* confirmed his reputation as a creative gambler.[10]

At the *New York Times*, however, critic Jack Gould made it clear that the construct for *Home* had already been amply tested in the nation's local markets, including New York City itself.[11] In his review of *Home*'s first week on the air, he wrote that the show "has not proved quite as startlingly novel as might have been expected . . . Most of the individual parts of the show have been seen on television before."[12]

Gould was right. As noted in Chapter 2, two-thirds of the country's prefreeze television stations were producing homemaking programs by 1952.[13] Even within limited budgets, over half the programs covered an array of homemaking topics and moved beyond a single kitchen set, adding backdrops that replicated living rooms, dining rooms, workshops, patios, and gardens.[14]

The homemaking genre that had grown so commonplace on local television emerged from a postwar trend to "professionalize" homemaking, as millions of women left wartime employment to become full-time wives and mothers. Elaine Tyler May has noted that as postwar women (even those who had attended college) "came to accept their domestic role as the center of their identity," they sought to turn homemaking and motherhood into vocations that were invested with "skills, prestige, and importance."[15] In response to this trend, the "science" of home economics began to blossom during this period, and home economists across the country avidly embraced television as a powerful new teaching tool. In 1952, two enterprising home economists advised their colleagues, "[I]t is timely to make use of the medium of television for furthering the education of many more homemakers than could be reached by ordinary public demonstrations."[16]

The shifting social economy after World War II further hastened the proliferation of the homemaking genre on television. Mary Beth Haralovich argues that a broad range of social institutions of the era, including the consumer product industry and television itself, promoted a social subjectivity for the middle-class homemaker that made her an essential component in a newly emerging economic structure.[17] "The economic importance of women's role as consumers [in the 1950s] cannot be overstated," agrees May, "for it kept American industry rolling and sustained jobs for the nation's male providers."[18] Local markets quickly discovered that daytime shows that targeted the homemaker as the family's primary consumer attracted enthusiastic sponsorship and led to lucrative profits, even if their matronly hostesses appeared unglamorous or their production values amateurish. In 1952, in Columbus, Ohio, for example, three homemaking programs that viewer surveys and home economists characterized as "dull," "untidy," and "unprofessional" were rated the best moneymaking formats of the season. "There is no difficulty in obtaining sponsors," station management asserted.[19]

Weaver believed that the proven success of the segmented homemaking model in local markets augured an economic bonanza for the network and offered sales advantages that could substantially enhance NBC's financial picture. Magazine-inspired segments on *Home* could be sold to a set of participating sponsors rather than to a single advertiser. Sponsors were offered purchase options that ranged from onetime participation to what *Variety* called a "full season's ride," following the *Today* show's selling strategy.[20] In the case of *Home*, NBC could market eight one-minute commercials per hour plus six 20-second product mentions.[21]

Weaver also reasoned that a network homemaking show would attract small-ticket advertisers who sold an array of women's products traditionally featured in magazines, and thus tap into a fresh source of revenue for the network.[22] Two weeks after the premiere of *Home*, Weaver commented in *Newsweek*, "It is inconceivable to me . . . that all that advertising money spent on women's products . . . has been allowed to escape [from network television]."[23] *Home*'s inaugural sponsors, which included Sunbeam appliances, Dow-Corning cookware, Wearever aluminum foil, Hallite utensils, American greeting cards, Broil-Quick, Lees carpets, Nacchi sewing machines, and Crosley television sets,[24] further bolstered Weaver's conviction that it was time for the networks to cash in on women's goods.

Finally, Weaver expected that a segmented magazine format like *Home*'s would allow the housewife to complete her work but drop in and out of attentive viewing as desired. As Spigel has noted, an NBC ad that appeared in *Good Housekeeping* in 1955 visually intermeshed the fragmented flow of housework with NBC's morning schedule of programs, represented in a succession of television screens around the page, including one for *Home*.[25] Sponsors could be assured that *Home*'s fragmented magazine format suited the daily activities of the busy homemaker.[26]

While the economic advantages of a network homemaking show were well grounded in theory and practice, cautionary NBC research and the experience of local programmers warned that televising the science of home economics on TV had its perils. Home economists around the nation had discovered that bland educational formats were short-lived. "The show must be entertaining," concluded expert Esther Lee Bride in *Practical Home Economics* in 1952.[27] Echoing this lesson, Ruddick C. Lawrence, director of promotion planning and development at NBC, said in a speech before a New York home economics group in 1952, "[A]s soon as you start to televise to women about home service exclusively you are no longer televising to them. They switch the dial." While lauding the educational value of home economics for the masses, Lawrence reminded his audience, "[Y]ou can't teach before you reach . . ."[28]

Lawrence also cited NBC research that overturned the notion that housewives used daytime television merely for instruction and education. According to Lawrence, Advertest Research had found that 58.3 percent of the women surveyed indicated they turned on their sets during the day "only to get entertainment," while another 19.9 percent used television viewing "to break up the monotony of their household duties." Lawrence cautioned, "It might be that the realities of domestic routine discourage the housewife from viewing this material on the screen."[29] In another survey, one housewife complained, "Why should I take time out to rest from housework, snap on TV for a few minutes' relaxation only to have some woman take 30 minutes to tell me how to clean a kitchen item that only takes me 10 minutes."[30] Some home economists and TV producers may have imagined housewives attentively absorbing professional homemaker tips as they dusted and mopped, but in 1953 NBC's Ted Mills urged that *Home* be designed not as a service show but as "an entertainment program with service elements in it."[31]

In the past, NBC's solution to offering homemaking advice had been to "sprinkle the home service segments in among programs basically designed to entertain," like the 10-minute homemaking segments on *The Kate Smith Hour*.[32] With *Home*, NBC's challenge was to endow a service show with enough entertainment value to keep large numbers of housewives watching. This predicament was a familiar one to Weaver in the early 1950s. By then he had adopted a philosophy of broadcasting that came to be known as "Operation Frontal Lobes," a view that promised to bring culture and education to the masses in a palatable form,[33] and he knew *Home* would have to put on a good show to succeed. For a man like Weaver, who built his reputation on extravagant spectacle, the problem was perplexing but not insurmountable. As a talent agent said of Weaver, "With Pat you can think big even about a cooking show."[34]

Under Weaver's guidance, *Home* overlaid the homemaking template with a lavish and unmistakable new look, an "NBC on Fifth Avenue Look" envisioned for the program by producer Richard Pinkham.[35] *Home*'s initial creative team, which included renowned Broadway director Leland Hayward of *South Pacific* fame,[36] designed a sumptuous, sophisticated, and electronically novel version of the typical low-budget fare found on TV stations across the country. Shamelessly assuming that upper-middlebrow urban culture (headquartered, like the NBC network, in Manhattan), represented American national culture at its best,[37] *Home*'s creative team, spending $50,000 per week, infused the program with Gothamesque style. *Home*'s roster of department "editors" directly linked *Home* to the intellectual, cultural, and entertainment elite. *New York Post* writer Dr. Rose Franzblau provided advice on family relations and child psychology; Dr. Leona Baumgartner, *Home*'s health expert, doubled as New York City's health commissioner; reporter Estelle Parsons, trained on the *Today* show, produced special projects; Vassar graduate Poppy Cannon, whose husband Walter White was president of the NAACP, headed *Home*'s food department; former actress and San Francisco TV personality Eve Hunter offered fashion and beauty advice; and Sydney Smith, daughter of Broadway star Loring Smith, handled home decorating.[38] Completing the team was junior editor Hugh Downs, Francis's assistant and a recent recruit from NBC's innovative programming in Chicago.

For an hour every Monday through Friday (11:00–noon in the East for two years, then 10:00–11:00 a.m.), the NBC network delivered live across its coaxial cables the empress of all homemaking shows.

Home's Mode of Address: From Gimbel's to the Senate

In her review of 489 nonfiction articles published in women's magazines between 1946 and 1958, Joanne Meyerowitz carefully documents the presence of "competing voices" during the postwar era[39] and argues that these various representations of womanhood "undermined and destabilized the domestic stereotype even as it was constructed."[40] She found that domestic ideals were counterweighted by "an ethos of individual achievement that celebrated nondomestic activity, individual strivings, public service, and public success." "All of the magazines sampled," she writes, "advocated both the domestic and nondomestic, sometimes in the same sentence."[41] For Meyerowitz, these discourses reflect "a diluted brand of early twentieth-century feminism" that had promoted "equality of opportunity" and "individual accomplishment" (237).

This same multivocality pervaded NBC's *Home* show, modeled as it was after the women's service magazines.[42] In 1953, NBC producer Ted Mills encouraged NBC to incorporate into *Home* the magazines' recognition that women were interested in issues beyond the home. He wrote in 1953 that the *Home* show should avoid relegating its audience exclusively to the "inner sancta of kitchen, bedroom and bath."[43] To this end, the founding design of the *Home* show duplicated the double enunciation of the women's publications. On the one hand, *Home* spoke to women as thoughtful citizens capable of achieving success in the public domain (within certain constraints). On the other, *Home* hailed its viewers as isolated domestic workers, eager to consume the nation's billowing list of consumer products. *Home*'s producers planned a daily rotation of segments that mixed domestic advice about cooking, gardening, fashion, home decorating, and beauty—all connected to retail products—with civic and cultural concerns, social issues, public affairs, and the arts. In oddly juxtaposed features, the program adopted a mixed mode of address that sometimes spoke to newly reconstructed consumerist homebodies, increasingly isolated in suburbia, and sometimes to women who sought satisfaction and influence outside the domestic arena.

As Spigel explains, *Home* implicitly integrated consumerism, housework, and TV entertainment, consistently addressing the viewer as "Mrs. Daytime Consumer," the composite housewife NBC research unearthed in its audience surveys.[44] According to Inger Stole, this seaming of program content to commercial message was a hallmark of the program. She cites a memo that Mills wrote to Weaver in 1953, which promised that *Home*'s "family of products" would be placed inside "as many service features as possible to make it difficult to tell where the commercial begins and the information leaves off."[45] A 1954 cooking segment serves as a characteristic example, when cooking editor Kit Kinney demonstrated how to prepare a meatloaf and proclaimed, "'H' is for 'Heinz' and for 'Home.'"[46]

This mode of address that equated consumerism and femininity was a defining feature of the *Home* text. A live remote broadcast from Gimbel Brothers Department Store in Philadelphia, orchestrated on location by Hugh Downs, stressed the central place of consumer products in *Home*'s depictions of femininity. Francis made this connection explicit in her introduction to the Gimbel's segment when she declared from the studio, "[A] woman's favorite pastime [is] shopping!" Over in Philadelphia, Downs reveled in the services and products meant to entice women to the store: a "you-ask-it box" (an intercom service that helped locate products); stylish baby layettes, Gimbel's "Talent Discovery Program" (which tested children's aptitude for musical instruments); free bridal and maternity services ("in that order," Downs said with a wink); Gimbel's International Food Fair; the "scientifically designed" Barcalounger; "summer-coated chocolates" that resisted melting in hot weather; a remote-controlled lawn mower; and even his-and-hers "busy pockets" aprons.[47]

Home's constant portrayal of womanhood in consumerist terms did not go unnoticed by the era's critics. After watching the show for a week, *New York Times* critic Jack Gould worried that *Home* "might become a 'television department store' just as easily as the women's magazine of video" it was purported to be.[48] A month later, in the *Saturday Review*, Robert Lewis Shayon damned *Home* for its preoccupation with things, rather than thoughts. "The Thing," he wrote, "is 'Home's' hearthgod . . . 'Home' appeared a heavenly department store, a valhalla of gadgets and gimmicks, a cloud of electronic dust returning to dust."[49]

Shayon was quick to indict the housewife herself rather than the industry (and the era) that was skillfully constructing a marketable version of her: "It frightens one again and again," wrote Shayon from the familiar stance of male superiority when speaking of women's culture, "that programs such as [*Home*] mirror the mind and the heart and the interests of the American wife and mother."[50] What *Home* mirrored was not the heart and interests of American women but a shifting representation of domestic femininity that postwar culture necessarily fostered. Shayon failed to notice that the 1950s economy required a hyped-up female consumer who was dedicated to buying the latest thing.

Yet *Home* was a television program that resisted an unqualified withdrawal to domesticity, and its mode of address sometimes shifted unpredictably to engage women who were well informed about the world and politically astute. In an interview with *Coronet* magazine in the fall of 1956, *Home*'s chief writer Fred Freed summarized this ambiguity of

*Nationwide remote broadcasts added prestige to the **Home** show. Photo courtesy Wisconsin Center for Film and Theater Research (WCFTR-10792).*

purpose: "Whenever we get a chance to stop treating the housewife like a dull dame with a dust mop . . . we give her something worthwhile."[51] At times, *Home*'s flow of interlocking segments circumvented narrow models of homemaking and consumerism. In keeping with Weaver's commitment to uplift, *Home* prided itself on features that *Home* producer Phyllis Adams Jenkins said "raised people's spirits and standards."[52]

Interspersed within its daily schedule, *Home* offered an array of segments that covered politics, culture, and social issues. In an interview with *Newsweek* magazine, Arlene Francis trumpeted the many examples of educational segments *Home* devoted to "child psychology, housing projects, comparative arts, teenagers' problems, and segregation."[53] Jenkins explained, "'Educate' sounds heavy, that was a sideline; [*Home*'s purpose was] stimulating emotions . . . opening doors visually and mentally."[54] Francis interviewed guests on the show who represented "the affirmation of life," in her opinion,[55] and these interviews served to edify viewers isolated at home, whose response letters, according to Freed, proved they were "intelligent, educated women, aware of the world and keenly interested in it."[56] Adopting a mode of address that imagined just such women, Arlene Francis interviewed Pearl S. Buck, Helen Keller, Frank Lloyd Wright, Joseph Welch, Cyril Ritchard, W. H. Auden, Archibald MacLeish, Thornton Wilder, Margaret Truman, Justice William O. Douglas, Norman Vincent Peale, Billy Graham, and John and Jacqueline Kennedy, among many others.[57]

Home also incorporated into its regular schedule remote broadcasts from around the country that focused on more than just shopping at Gimbel's. As part of its elaborative series called "Hometown U.S.A." viewers were transported to an A-bomb test in Yucca Flat, Nevada,[58] sight-seeing in Orange County, California, and even to Japan for the country's New Year's festivities.[59] In 1956, *Home* won the Ohio State Program of the Year award for its intimate portrait of an eight-year-old disabled boy named Dickie and his mother.[60]

Another regular feature on *Home*, a weekly segment that promoted the work of the General Federation of Women's Clubs, demonstrated *Home*'s grounding in the long tradition of volunteerism and community activism associated with women's causes from earlier decades, and acknowledged a viewer who was politically involved. One such GFWC segment aired on 12 November 1956,[61] when Francis promoted a Community Achievement Contest and the upcoming "State Teachers' Day." As the segment concluded, Francis was abruptly interrupted by her stage manager "Sam," who crossed into camera view to hand her a news bulletin, which she read immediately: "[Secretary-General] Dag Hammarskjöld said that Egypt has just accepted the United Nations police force" (to ease tensions in the Middle East). Looking straight into the camera, Francis ad-libbed, "Well, that's a pretty good bulletin to have. My, does that make everybody feel pretty good?" While assents were heard off-stage, Francis was also addressing the viewer at home, the "modern woman" Meyerowitz found in magazine discourse of the 1950s, who was encouraged to be politically informed and actively involved in public affairs, engaging especially in the altruistic work of women's clubs.[62] In 1956, the GFWC awarded *Home* a citation of excellence for its "promotion of individual responsibility."[63]

In typical *Home* ordering, however, the GFWC segment was wedged between a segment that highlighted "adult party clothes" and one that featured a fashion show, during which sewing expert Lucille Rivers told viewers, "Why not be feminine and exciting, too—in lace? . . . You'll feel like a doll and look as pretty." The slippage between these modes of address, clearly awkward as Francis moved from international news to sewing tips, characterized *Home*'s endorsement of multiple femininities in a transitional balancing act. If parts of *Home* evoked an activist model that harkened back to earlier attitudes, other segments reminded viewers they were vivacious, feminine dolls of the 1950s who spent their days sewing party clothes.

Francis's interview with Senator Margaret Chase Smith, an exemplary public figure of the era, expressed with clarity *Home*'s ambivalent representation of a woman's place in the public/private divide. Across the segment, repeated affirmations of Smith's femininity and domestic skills counterweighted her status as a woman of power and prestige in the nation's capital. Francis introduced the Maine Republican as "one of the most outstanding women in the world" and more famous "than any other woman in American politics," but she also avowed, "[T]his morning we are going to meet [Smith] not as a Senator but as a woman."[64]

In a dramatic and lengthy introduction, Francis recited a long list of Smith's academic degrees and awards, including the prestigious 1954 National Achievement Award for eminence in public affairs. On the same list, and regarded with the same awe, was the Charm Institute Award—an actual statuette Francis held up to the camera—which honored Smith as the "Most Charming Woman in Government." Francis observed that Smith's "combination of charm and brains" paid off in her reelection (1–4).

A recital of Smith's accomplishments in the Senate and film clips that showed Smith entering the Capitol Building and conversing with President Eisenhower and his wife, Mamie, confirmed Smith's place in the highest echelons of political power. "Yes, Margaret Chase Smith is one of our greatest Senators," Francis continued as the camera cut to her, "and as such her power and prestige are enormous. But she is more than that . . ." In the pause that followed, the camera framed the trademark corsage Smith wore on her dress in extreme close-up, femininity's emblem, then pulled back slowly and theatrically to reveal Smith in a "portrait" medium shot, as Francis concluded in voice-over, "She has invaded a man's world, but, having invaded it, remains very much a woman" (3–4).

This double theme of a woman's power in the public sphere, juxtaposed to her enduring ability to uphold traditional feminine values, teeter-tottered across the interview. Before any serious discussion of politics began, Francis focused her questioning on Smith's *homes*—her childhood home; her new home in Maine, where she entertained President Eisenhower at an outdoor barbecue; and her Maryland residence near the capital (6–9). Francis and Smith then discussed *recipes*, including Eisenhower's formula for cooking steaks on the barbecue and Smith's easy favorite, Lobster Newburg, made with Maine lobster and cream of celery soup (11).

When the interview finally turned to politics, Smith advised women busy raising families to become active in hospitals, school boards, club work, and civic affairs (15). The final lesson for viewers was delivered in domestic terms, however, as Francis recapped Smith's often repeated slogan that "we need less Government in the Home, and more Home in the Government" (8). At the end of the segment, Smith herself emphasized this interlink between a woman's purpose at home and her efficacy in the world of politics. "The structure of our Nation is only as strong as the structure of our individual homes," she affirmed. "We must protect and preserve our homes in order to protect and preserve our national security. Because life doesn't have much value without a home, we should do everything within our power to see that all of our people have a home. When that is accomplished, the insidious forces that seek to undermine our way of life will have been completely defeated" (17).

The incongruity of a noted female public official advocating a sociopolitical agenda that centered women's political activism at the hearth was rationalized in Francis's closing remarks. Francis explained that while women were capable of entering the political scene and bringing to it a set of feminine attributes like "gentle perseverance" and "freshness and idealism," the field was still very much closed to them. "[R]emember," Francis concluded, "as Margaret Chase Smith said, we can't *all* be in politics, and we must, for ourselves and the future, try to make happy homes" (18). As this example suggests, *Home*'s acknowledgment of a woman's potential agency in the public sphere was mediated by a reverse pull that sought to recast her in a more contemporary model of domestic confinement. This duality expressed the unresolved conflict between the ideals of an earlier time of activism, during which women struggled for political representation and the vote, and a revised set of norms for the 1950s that attempted to collapse women's political ambitions into the performance of domestic duties—a regressive version of "the personal is political."

The contradictions evident in *Home*'s mode of address, and in the image of Margaret Chase Smith as shaped by *Home*, were also embodied in Arlene Francis, whose persona mitigated a rigid equation between femininity and the homemaker/consumer, further allowing distanciation from postwar norms.

Of Pots and Puns

On 19 July 1954, Arlene Francis, looking regal in an off-the-shoulder ball gown and heavily jeweled necklace, appeared on the cover of *Newsweek* magazine. The story proclaimed her to be "as familiar a figure to TV viewers . . . as Willie Mays is to New York Giant fans" and "the queen" of television's new crop of "femcees."[65] Two weeks earlier her face had occupied the cover of *TV Guide*, and in May, just as *Home* debuted, *Look* magazine labeled her "TV's busiest woman."[66] A regular on the popular panel show *What's My Line?* (CBS) since 1950 and host of a U.S. Army talent program called *Soldiers' Parade* (ABC), Francis came to television from a highly successful radio career. During the 1930s, her deep-timbered voice was heard on more than 20 soap operas, and her gift for mimicry made her a versatile performer, landing her roles on *The March of Time*, *Cavalcade*, *Betty and Bob*, and *Forty-five Minutes from Hollywood* (in which she simulated the performances of famous movie stars, like Katharine Hepburn and Bette Davis). "I'd run from one studio to another in the same day, changing my accent en route," she remembered.[67] Francis spent the war years hosting a popular military dating program called *Blind Date*, which aired as a television program from 1949 to 1953 and started her on the road to fame in the new medium.

Francis was also closely associated with the New York theater scene as an actress and reviewer, which included a stint with Orson Welles's Mercury Theater troupe and starring roles in more than 20 plays.[68] In 1961, when director Billy Wilder recruited Francis to costar in the film *One, Two, Three*, Wilder considered Francis to be the third most famous woman in America, after Jackie Kennedy and Eleanor Roosevelt.[69]

During the years of her television fame, Francis and her husband

Martin Gabel, famed for his radio voice-overs and skills as a producer, mingled with the country's most cosmopolitan citizens, socializing with theater people, intellectuals, politicians, and society's elite. The public persona Francis brought to the *Home* show inevitably connected her to this fashionable social circle. Yet by all accounts, Francis excelled on television precisely because she did not come across as a snob. To audience and friends alike, she exuded "charm."

Lauded as the nation's founding femcee and preeminent "charm girl,"[70] Francis carried to the daytime screen a combination of brains and charisma she had praised in Margaret Chase Smith. Francis believed "that certain something" (called charm) stemmed from a woman's self-knowledge and a generous spirit toward others.[71] Being one's best and true self guaranteed the projection of authentic charm on television,[72] but for Francis, hosting the *Home* show brought into conflict her identity as a sophisticated career woman and the program's celebration of a more homebound female. The original producers of *Home*, Richard Pinkham and Jack Rayel, told *TV Guide* they had auditioned 200 women for the position of "editor-in-chief" before they thought of Francis. "We were looking for someone intelligent enough to handle an ad-lib show but simple and sweet," said Pinkham. "We figured our girl could be most anybody but a chic New York sophisticate." When they met with Francis for lunch, her charisma quickly changed their minds.[73]

One benefit to hiring Francis was her consummate professionalism as a TV saleswoman. Francis was eager to meet with clients and to endorse their products on the air, adopting a selling technique with a low-key "pitch" proven to win customers.[74] "The breathless, panting commercial in deep bass notes is no longer ringing up high sales," wrote one television adviser in 1954. ". . . [W]hen it's a subject that reaches deep into the heart of the home—women believe women."[75] Francis perfected this feminized style on *Home*. *Newsweek* reported that she spent more time rehearsing commercials than the script for the show itself.[76] Portraying herself as a woman who "dug" gadgets and who had to be honest with viewers about products she sold,[77] Francis said about her 40 sponsors, "I tried everything, did everything, ate everything and usually bought everything they offered . . . If I sold it, I was sold on it." In her autobiography, Francis recalls being presented with an award from the Sales Executive Club in 1956 for her skill in selling, joking that her earlier ambition to be "Actress of the Year" had evolved into being "Saleswoman of the Year."[78]

To make her seem more domestic, Francis's publicity universally emphasized her pursuit of two careers—"television and her home"[79]—and magazine photographs frequently captured her in the role of wife, mother, and hostess.[80] *TV Guide*'s 1954 cover story devoted one whole page to a picture of Francis in close-up with her seven-year-old son, Peter, a typical promotion shot.[81] Nonetheless, Francis's reputation as a polished New York actress and a determined career woman who earned $2000 per week on *Home* alone, divided her from the private world of her viewers. Francis was conscious of this enigma. "When they were first putting *Home* together," she said in an interview in 1956 with Alfred Bester, "they wanted the girl-next-door … I talked them out of it and persuaded them to let me do it my own way." In Bester's view, which typified the received wisdom about Francis at the time, Francis and a homemaking show didn't quite fit together. Bester wondered what such a "hip chick like Arlene" was doing on such a "square" show.[82]

While Arlene Francis was not exactly what Kathleen Rowe defines as an "unruly woman,"[83] Francis did violate 1950s feminine models in notable ways, as Pinkham and Rayel intuited. In the *Newsweek* cover story, she was called an "original contribution" to television's traditional patterns for female stars and more multidimensional than other "television girls."[84] In the public eye, she was a woman whose looks, age, verbal style, and wit transgressed feminine norms. Arlene Francis was "the quick queen of television," the ambiguous ruler of both "pots and puns."[85]

Francis worked hard to come across on *Home* as just one of the girls. "I'm a homebody," Francis went on to tell Bester. "Our show comes right into people's houses. They know me. They like me … and I like them."[86] To this end, she abandoned the formality of her look on *What's My Line?*, where she wore elegant evening gowns, to don on *Home* the 1950s uniform for stylish middle-class women, the shirtwaist dress, further imitating her audience, according to *Newsweek*, by "deciding not to wear a different dress every day."[87] Despite these attempts to project a homemaker image, Arlene Francis sold the promise of domestic fulfillment from a compromised position.

Francis's "true self" differentiated her from domestic femininity and gave her persona an unruly edge. Marginalized from standard ideals of beauty by age and imperfect features, her televised body belied the decade's growing preoccupation with the display of youthful gorgeousness on the airwaves. Photographs of Francis show her to be eminently attractive, but Francis's prettiness was viewed as somewhat unconventional. "Arlene, by Hollywood or Broadway standards, is no doll," judged

American Magazine, "her nose is long, her face isn't heart-shaped, and she's no youngster."[88]

During the course of her career, Francis avoided revealing her age. She writes in her autobiography that whenever she was asked, "Will you tell us how old you are?" she always replied, "Five feet five and a half inches. Next question?"[89] Francis was 47 years old and the mother of a young boy when *Home* premiered in 1954,[90] well outside the decade's statistical norms. The typical homemaker in 1954 married at the age of 20.3 years[91] and bore her first child 1.3 years later.[92] While Francis's age placed her in the era's life-cycle category of "older wives" or "matrons" (women over 45 with children over 15),[93] the young age of her son, Peter, excluded her, further affirming Francis's atypicality. Yet Francis's maturity also designated her as a woman who had come of age in an earlier, more encouraging time for women.[94] She was 13 years old when women won the right to vote, and the advancement of her personal life and career during the 1930s and 1940s benefited from the political achievements that had granted women greater access to education, equality in marriage, and employment.[95] Moreover, as a woman over 35, Francis stood in for the growing number of "older" women, some 13 million by 1956, who were reentering the workforce during the postwar decade.[96] In these diverse ways, Francis became the incarnation of a paradox: an intelligent, politically aware "matron" and career woman, as well as a homebody, a devoted wife, and a "young" mother.

In the popular imagination, her unconventional appearance and indeterminate age were coupled with an emphasis on her verbal talent and wit, qualities more directly associated with feminine rebellion.[97] "She is not beautiful . . . ," explained *Newsweek*, but "[p]re-eminently, she can talk. She can talk wisely, wittily, and continuously" although sometimes "too much."[98] As Rowe suggests, a woman's tendency toward excessive talk, and her inclination to make jokes and to laugh out loud herself are all qualities of the unruly woman.[99]

Her gift for unplanned humor, honed by her many years on *What's My Line?*, projected a measure of disruptive spectacle. Just a week before *Home* premiered, Lucille Ball appeared as the mystery celebrity on *What's My Line?*, where she spoke "Martian" (comic gibberish) in response to questions from the blindfolded panelists, in an attempt to conceal her identity.[100] In a crystallizing moment, Francis good-humoredly held an improvised conversation with Ball in Martian, quickly surmising the star's identity. For a few moments on primetime television, two women whose femininity consistently befuddled suburban standards and resisted domestic absolutes were speaking the same (unintelligible) language.

In 1956, *Coronet* magazine hinted at Francis's unruly tendencies when it reported that her too-sharp wit had almost cost her her career until she softened her wisecracks and became "kindlier."[101] By the time she starred on *Home*, any acerbic proclivities were well tamed and her quips mild and sedate. After rising to the surface in a diving bell off the coast of Louisiana, for example, she exclaimed, "Wow! Now I know what it feels like to be a champagne cork."[102] After a speedboat ride at 125 mph, she quipped, "Sure makes a girl yearn to cross the continent in a covered wagon."[103]

Another example of Francis's ability to ad-lib playfully occurred in a 1957 segment that previewed French hats.[104] In this presentation, Francis half seriously placed a large hat on her own head, then attempted to adorn mannequin heads as they spun past her on a rotating tabletop. The hats fell off; the hats drooped to one side; the hats she picked up were not the hats described in the script. "What's a matter, honey?" she said to a mute mannequin whose hat had slipped over its eyes, "She couldn't see where she was going?" As the heads continued to spin silently before her, she announced, "Traditional turban," but instantly realized the hat was NOT a turban and snatched it from the mannequin's head. "This girl doesn't seem to know what to put on this morning ... And it's because they're French hats and she's not used to them. Are you, darling?"

Francis's improvisational humor and her controlled delivery managed the daily uncertainties of live network television. Distinct from her competition on CBS, where traditional male personalities mediated daytime mishaps, Francis supplied a feminine control over pretape television that relied upon unfeminine skills.

Taken together, Francis's overall public presence set her apart from the feminine ideals of 1950s suburbia. Constant references to her career achievements, her social life in chic New York circles, her "whirlwind schedule,"[105] her intelligence, her distinctive appearance, and her verbal acuity separated her from the homebound world of the typical daytime viewer. In these ways, Francis's public image matched exactly the hundreds of portraits Meyerowitz discovered in popular magazines of the time—articles that featured individual wives and mothers who achieved public recognition through hard work. As Meyerowitz observes, "[T]he theme of nondomestic success was no hidden subtext" in these articles, which "tended to glorify [the] frenetic activity" required to balance home and career, a common theme in Francis's publicity.[106] Like the portraits in Meyerowitz's survey, the public Arlene Francis offered "a striking validation of nondomestic behavior."[107]

Francis's multifaceted identity reflected the transitional incongruities between pre- and postwar gender values. Francis had achieved public recognition through individual effort and fortitude; she was intelligent and politically astute; and she was old enough to have experienced continuity with progressive ideas from the past. At the same time, she was also the homemaker postwar suburbia expected her to be, a woman who loved gadgets and could decorate her own interiors.[108]

Francis's son, Peter Gabel, now a law professor and president emeritus of the New College of California in San Francisco, has contemplated in retrospect this issue of his mother's ambiguous femininity. Gabel believes his mother's performance style conveyed "spontaneous confidence in her own charm, goodness, and authenticity,"[109] a fitting way to describe Francis's innate self-assurance that she could retain her multilayered individuality on daytime television, even within the confines of *Home*'s paradoxical world.

The inevitable tensions between career demands and childrearing that women openly confronted in the feminist movement of the 1970s were concealed in public portraits of Francis during the 1950s. Reflecting on these years, her son remembered one way his mother attempted to resolve the dilemma of child care—she took young Peter with her to the *Home* set. "I did love going with her to *Home*. She loved it; everyone liked me; I was *with* her doing something fun."[110] Gabel's experience serves as a fitting final paradox, since Francis's double duty as public TV star and domesticated parent could only be achieved at a make-believe *Home*. Such a conflation mirrored the program's determination to reconcile the public and private sides of 1950s womanhood in the figure of Arlene Francis, contradictions notwithstanding.

Home's Televisual Style: Theater-in-the-Round

Arlene Francis performed her divided femininity on a television stage that further destabilized domestic certitudes. As *TV Guide* remarked, "*Home* is a misnomer. There never was another place like this."[111]

Costing over $200,000 to build—an unheard-of sum for the time—and measuring 60' 6" in diameter, *Home*'s innovative circular set was heralded as one of television's first attempts to "find designs and techniques especially appropriate to the [new visual] medium."[112] Countering the verisimilitude of the typical homemaking show, *Home* experimented with a modernist look and an innovative presentational style that called attention to the show's simulation.

The lavish studio was packed with electronic gadgets, stage turntables, platforms that moved up and down, and other well-publicized technological trickery that *Variety* declared to be in keeping with the "NBC-RCA electronic consciousness."[113] *Life* magazine ran a two-page spread when the show premiered that captured the essence of the mammoth set, providing an overhead shot of its round design divided into wedges that serviced the program's multiple departments, the cameras and crew stationed at the circle's center.[114] The gardening wedge or "growery" bordered the interior design arena; another platform simulated weather conditions like rain, snow, or sleet, unleashed at the touch of a button; a product testing area was outfitted with a mechanical hook that could turn over sofas or unroll and ripple rugs.[115] Another much-proclaimed innovation was the $30,000 remote-controlled "monkey" camera suspended from the studio's ceiling, whose telescopic arm could "extend to 29' in any direction, revolve . . . 360 degrees," and tilt 90 degrees up or down, permitting a "picture of any part of the set from any other part."[116] In Philip Hamburger's review of *Home*'s debut in the *New Yorker*, he praised the view from this camera that came to be *Home*'s signature transitional visual: " . . . [O]ne is privileged to see a full view of [the huge circular set] from above at various times. These panoramic views show us a number of cameras far below, and a good many figures scurrying about."[117]

Home's ingenious set design was created to attract housewives to a potentially dull service format. As Spigel has suggested, the show's circular stage, called by the network "a machine for selling," lavishly displayed "fragmented consumer fantasies" for the daytime viewer, teaching her how to buy products.[118] Yet the arena layout and the program's groundbreaking camera work introduced a self-reflexive televisual style, influenced by the Chicago school, which habitually dismantled fantastic illusions. Unlike the local homemaker programs that had aimed to simulate cozy living rooms or up-to-date kitchens to create intimacy with the viewer, *Home*'s set deliberately called attention to itself as artifice.

NBC executive Charles C. Barry, who sent producer Richard Pinkham his critiques of *Home* every day during its debut week, worried about "a kind of 'impressionism'" represented by the set: "I wonder if the intimacy and friendliness you want to establish between editors and viewer may not be made more difficult by this lack of natural surrounding. Think about this."[119] For Barry, the program's "impression-ist" set design contributed to a lack of hominess and to a fundamentally troubling "high polish" or "high gloss" that he feared would not appeal to "the average gal" in the mass audience.[120] In adopting a higher-brow aesthetic that esteemed modernist theatrical conventions, *Home* ines-capably transmitted a self-awareness that cast doubts on the very do-mestic and consumer fantasies the program was designed to promote.

In his daily critiques, Barry instinctively understood that *Home*'s tele-visual style and the set itself exposed a rift between suburban domestic naturalism that was commonplace on 1950s television and its signaled performance. He particularly disliked a segment, for example, during which a party game was demonstrated "out of the confines of a [stage] living room";[121] he also disapproved of a scene depicting the right way to get in and out of a car, featuring *Home*'s models and Hugh Downs seated in chairs. "I must say," he wrote Pinkham, "that the 'impression-ism' leaves me a little dubious. Frankly, I would have liked to have seen the girls piling out of a real automobile."[122]

In spite of Barry's admonitions, *Home*'s transparent theatricality be-came the program's defining form. From the very first week of the show, when *Home* devoted a segment to community theater in Greenwich Vil-lage (and urged viewers to start up their own companies),[123] portions of the program retained an "off-Broadway" style, often with a decidedly Brechtian flair. A brief tableau Francis and Downs performed in April that presented examples of women's bad manners (applying makeup at a restaurant table) became a familiar dramatic strategy.[124] Often on *Home*, short scenes using minimalist props and costumes replicated a modern-ist disdain for naturalism.

Phyllis Adams Jenkins believed that Francis's "background in the-ater" was one of her (many) strengths as *Home*'s editor-in-chief.[125] As a well-trained Broadway actress, Francis could perform these modernist sketches on a daily basis, one day portraying a rude luncheon compan-ion, the next day a ruthless auctioneer,[126] and, on special occasions, as-suming the role of a Wilderesque "stage manager" or even a participant-observer like Emily in *Our Town*, a character who moved freely from one level of diegesis to another. The ongoing, self-reflexive layers of these dramas routinely called attention to their own theatricality, as did the *Home* set itself.

An ambitious production during a remote from Philadelphia com-bined modest staging with fanciful televisual tricks to create electronic pageantry. As Francis prepared to retell the story of America's independence, she stood in the actual room of the Second Continental Congress, framed in a medium long shot between two "guards" wearing Revolutionary War uniforms.[127] "The year is 1775 . . . ," she began, as the camera pulled back to a long shot of the room and sounds of battle were heard in the background. A visual and sound montage then recounted the events leading to the writing of the U.S. Constitution in 1787, including inventive touches like a close-up of the guards listening to the "voice" of George Washington; a shot of leaves blowing on the ground as Francis narrated, "Let a year pass . . ."; and a slow pan across the room's empty chairs when Francis described the debates that ensued before the Constitution was completed. The montage ended with close-up shots of the cherished parchment, as strains of "My Country 'Tis of Thee" sneaked under Francis's narration. "From this single room, came the sunlight of liberty," she read dramatically, addressing the camera. "From this wonderful room came 33 presidents and 84 Congresses and the greatest nation on earth. (PAUSE). I'm glad we spent these moments in this room together." As Francis turned away from the camera to look once more at the room, the camera dramatically trucked back, moving ever so slowly past the entry doors to end in an artistic long shot, synchronous with the final notes: "Let freedom ring."

A more intricately layered performance occurred in the *Home* studio on 11 April 1957, when the program publicized a high-society fundraiser, the "April in Paris Ball," a benefit for charities in both France and America to commemorate the 200th birthday of the Marquis de Lafayette. The staging of this segment further disclosed how *Home* made obvious the theatricality of its interior plays. Early in the show Hugh Downs interviewed French film actor Jean Marais as himself, but the next time Marais appeared, he was costumed as Lafayette. Soon after, the camera found Francis, dressed in everyday attire, standing on a balcony above Downs and Marais, where she appeared to have entered an eighteenth-century soiree. As she promenaded past models costumed in elegant French gowns and descended to join Downs and "Lafayette," she declaimed the words President Franklin Roosevelt wrote to honor the French patriot. In a dramatic ending on ground level, "Lafayette" then orated the "Declaration of the Rights of Man." When time ran out, "Lafayette" continued to speak, but Francis silently waved to the camera, mouthed "Good-bye," and blew her audience a kiss. The scene then cut to *Home*'s standard overhead shot, revealing "Lafayette" still speaking, a stage manager waving his hands, and the studio cameras rolling heavily across the floor. *Home*'s stage set and televisual style first suggested and then nullified the fictive illusion of eighteenth-century France, while Francis once again represented a modernist presence who was free to enter and exit any drama at will.

Home's aesthetic of distanciation also uncovered the artificiality of advertising vignettes and served to dismantle televised illusions of domestic perfection, as advertising fantasies were shown to be mere fantasies. In a minidrama performed to sell DuPont bathrobes, for example, the semblance of a suburban bedtime scene was rapidly dispelled when the omniscient ceiling camera revealed the artifice of the bedroom set. A mobile camera tracked Francis off the bedroom wedge and across the studio's diameter to another quadrant, leaving commercial daydreams behind.[128]

An elaborate Cadillac commercial featured on Veterans Day 1956 demonstrates how *Home* displayed merchandise in the opulent visual style of the 1950s, but subsequently exposed its own trickery.[129] As the commercial began, the studio was cast in dramatic shadows, Francis declaring in voice-over, "The stage is set for an important glamorous debut." Chiaroscuro lighting, designed to show off the car's sculptured curves, gradually faded up as Francis announced, "And here for the first time on network television, the spectacularly beautiful 1957 Cadillac." After a long, loving shot of the automobile, a model dressed in a sculpted evening dress with sweeping skirt gracefully approached the car while Johnny Johnston provided piano music in the background. The woman slid into the front seat and sensuously touched the upholstery, as Francis cooed, "Mmmm . . . Yes . . ." Soon a fashion show began, the Cadillac now a motionless backdrop for the curvaceous flow of fabric over the female body—another gown, a "grand entrance coat," red velvet for the Southern belle, slinky black for the sophisticate. A stylish tableau ended the commercial, the models posed elegantly around the Cadillac. When the camera cross-faded to a more panoramic overhead shot, the well-wrought scene, which glorified the ultimate aspirations of the 1950s consumer, revealed itself to be yet another artful deception.

Day by day, the *Home* set, whose unique size and gadgetry could so often enact luxurious fantasies for consumption, conveyed at the same time the false front of its illusions. *Home*'s frequent use of the extreme long shot from overhead, or the moving camera that probed the studio and found the crew at work or revealed the cast rushing to other platforms, reminded viewers that the program merely simulated life at home.

By turning the dial a few clicks, homemakers could leave behind NBC's magnificent but vacant studio and join the visiting audiences assembled for programs like *Strike It Rich* or *The Garry Moore Show*. To counter this absence of in-studio audience participation, *Home* initiated a contest in which viewers explained why they wanted to travel to a designated country. On the Veterans Day program, the week's winners were Mr. and Mrs. Flexman, who hoped to be reunited with Mrs. Flexman's sister in Vienna, whom they had not seen in 18 years. As a surprise feature, *Home* screened a filmed greeting to the Flexmans from the Viennese sister and her children. Mrs. Flexman began weeping silently at her sister's image, while Francis offered comfort. Heightening the sentimentality, *Home*'s resident tenor, Johnny Johnston, stood beside the show's grand piano and crooned Mrs. Flexman's favorite song.

While this segment imitated the conventions of the misery show and centered everyday people on *Home*'s stage, the visual trickery of the conclusion nullified any sense of community experienced on more typical audience participation shows and verged on the comical. After the interview, Francis and Downs escorted the Flexmans to theatrical airplane seats, above which hovered a huge crown, representing the sponsor's aircraft. Soon the image of the seated Flexmans, topped by the crown, began to revolve faster and faster, until the swirl faded into a filmed picture of a spinning airplane propeller. Poof! The Flexmans were airborne and gone from the stage! Left behind, Francis exclaimed, "We wish you the happiest reunion and the most beautiful trip imaginable!"[130]

This act of sending studio visitors off into the ether epitomized *Home*'s impressionist aura of disconnection and detachment. The program's staging and production style repeatedly communicated theatricality, self-reflexion, and masquerade.

The Demise of T-H-T

By the time *Home* aired its final episode on 9 August 1957, the show had become an anachronism struggling to survive in a hotly contested marketplace. Even during its most profitable years, 1954 to 1956, *Home*'s Nielsen numbers had lagged behind the competition on CBS. *Strike It Rich*, which was scheduled against *Home*'s second half hour (11:30–noon), pulled an average 9.75 rating while *Home* delivered only a 3.0. In its final season (1956–1957), when NBC moved *Home* to an earlier time slot where the competition was less keen (10:00–11:00 a.m.), *Home* still failed to win its hour. On CBS, *The Garry Moore Show* averaged a 6.5 rating from 10:00 to 10:30 a.m. and *Arthur Godfrey Time* a 7.5 between 10:30 and 11:00, while *Home* slipped to a new low of 2.5.[131] *Vari-*

ety concluded that in the network's search for daytime dollars, "*Home* became an embarrassment in the overall daytime picture." While the rest of NBC's daytime schedule "kept hitting new rating and sponsor highs," the ultraexpensive *Home* was merely "holding steady . . . It had to go."[132]

Under Pat Weaver's direction, NBC had developed *The Kate Smith Hour, Home,* and (as the next chapter explains) *Matinee Theater* to establish its identification with prestige and opulence in the nation's daytime environment, but none of the programs survived for very long. By 1957, the television audience had shifted from a predominantly urban-centered demographic to a broader-based, more suburban profile, as Pamela Wilson notes, a quantum shift that "deeply affected the economic imperatives of the television industry," requiring networks to concentrate on programs with mass appeal and higher profit margins.[133] Weighted by pressures to beat CBS in the ratings, NBC ousted Weaver in 1956 and rejected his grandiose innovations.[134] Under the new leadership of David Sarnoff's son Robert and former ABC executive Robert Kintner, NBC began to register astonishing gains during the day when it acquired the controversial misery show *Queen for a Day.*[135] As Arlene Francis explained in her memoirs, *Home* became a "victim of the rating game."[136]

In 1960, Francis was able to joke, "I was born in Boston, raised in New York, and died in daytime television,"[137] but she was more contemplative and critical about her daytime experience in her later memoirs. She viewed *Home* as an intelligent, ambitious "educational" program that struggled to compete in a ratings-dominated business. "[S]ad to say," she wrote, "the networks have always demonstrated that it is not their job to educate the public. If that educational process happens along the way, that's gravy and groovy, but networks are primarily in business for the purpose of making money."[138]

Yet despite the generally gloomy assessment of the program's commercial success, *Home* did make its mark on television history. In the spring of 1953, a year before *Home*'s creation, NBC had found itself on the "affiliate 'hot-seat'" for failing to provide programs to fill the hours between 10:00 a.m. and 3:00 p.m.; stations complained bitterly that they were being forced to spend "a barrel of money" to program locally.[139] Although *Home* never did manage to dislodge CBS during the day, the program helped soothe affiliate dissatisfaction for several years, as the network sought to bolster its high-status presence in daytime programming.

In the longer view, *Home* also foreshadowed the possibility for multi-vocal femininity on daytime television.[140] *Home*'s segmented and inconstant mode of address, the appealing ambiguity of Arlene Francis herself, and the program's self-reflexive production style all served to reiterate the tension between narrow feminine representations that constrained women of the 1950s and representations that refuted these constraints. Built into *Home* was its own deconstruction.

During the 1970s, Francis was asked on air her opinion of the women's liberation movement. She replied, "I think we sometimes go too far." When scattered applause was heard from the audience, she added, "All of that applause came from men!"[141] The double direction of this exchange reaffirms the transitional conflicts Francis and *Home* came to represent during the 1950s. Every weekday for 893 episodes, *Home* performed 1950s femininity on a grand scale, and every day, the program exposed the perturbing instabilities in this gender shift. Arlene Francis and *Home* reminded viewers of a more progressive womanhood inherited from earlier decades and suggested that the revised femininity of the 1950s might only be a transitory phase. If Barbara Ryan is right that "the rebirth of feminism can be traced to the family-centered years of the 1950s,"[142] it is because the regressive forces of the decade's backlash were unable to suppress completely the momentum achieved during feminism's first wave.

The demise of *Home* coincided with the end of the Weaver era at NBC, as vacillating industry forces swept away the network's willingness to experiment on a lavish scale. In 1955, one year before Weaver was ousted as president, he authorized the third and final instance of NBC's remarkable daytime contributions, *Matinee Theater*, an even greater marvel of modernist staging and televisual design than *Home*. Like *The Kate Smith Hour* and *Home*, *Matinee Theater* strove to bring the extraordinary to daytime television and to secure NBC's reputation for elite quality.

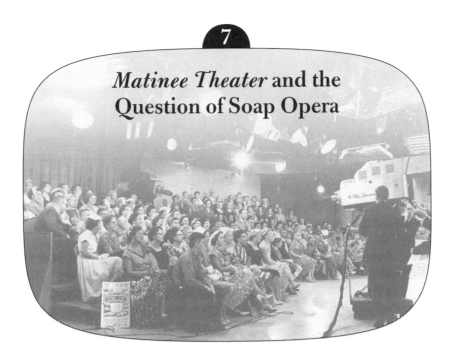

Matinee Theater and the Question of Soap Opera

A few weeks into the 1955–1956 television season, the peak year for live drama,[1] an advertisement appeared in *Look* magazine that promoted NBC's primetime theatrical productions in the language of serious art. Promotional assessments like "inspired performances," "skilled direction," and the "work of some of the most important writers of our time" cast an aura of selective taste around NBC's evening properties. Tagged onto the end of the ad was a promotion for NBC's brand-new daytime program *Matinee Theater*, which had debuted on 31 October. The copy read, "NBC MATINEE is a special treat for the lady of the house this season," a daily full-hour dramatic show in color and black-and-white "equal to the best of nighttime TV."[2] By grouping *Matinee Theater* with the network's most prestigious shows, the *Look* ad imbued the series with the highbrow reputation its producer Albert McCleery sought to secure. Even more than *Home*, *Matinee Theater* aimed to counter the stigma attached to daytime broadcasting's legacy of soap operas and misery shows and provide quality "adult" entertainment to homemakers. In a lengthy memorandum that articulated the show's founding ideas, Pat Weaver vowed to "upgrade dramatic entertainment in the daytime for women" by offering them matinee performances of theater at its best.[3]

The *Look* advertisement encapsulated the industry's self-awareness that live anthology drama in primetime was already supplying stature and sophistication to television in the minds of the era's cultural leaders. Influential television reviewers were exalting TV's new aesthetics, theorizing that live 60-minute plays exploited television's essentialist qualities of immediacy, intimacy, and naturalism to full advantage.[4] As discussed in Chapter 1, before postmodernist sensibilities recast aesthetic hierarchies, critics measured TV programming against a system of taste absolutes that proposed a wide gulf between the high and the low. Self-proclaimed "visionaries" like Weaver and McCleery—as well as prominent television columnists—aligned themselves with the values of highbrow taste and advocated the dissemination of cultivated entertainment to the growing mass of viewers who in their opinion required uplift. Weaver believed housewives could be persuaded to watch "something that they are not interested in if they have been sold on the idea that it is valuable or rewarding or inherently good," and he put his faith in women's desire to attain the elevated cultural status *Matinee Theater* presumed to offer them.[5]

Conversely, the era's defenders of "legitimate" culture deplored daytime programs that merely reproduced the "debasements" of daytime radio, especially the soap opera, and the team of Weaver and McCleery sought to recuperate broadcasting's dishonored feminine sphere by broadcasting another NBC program in good taste, like *Home*. The proclaimed mission of *Matinee Theater* was to offer housewives a daily dose of refined culture, and McCleery decreed that the merits of his dramas would reverse the perceived frailties of the soaps.

This issue was especially salient the year before *Matinee Theater* debuted, when serial drama's new vitality on television reanimated a public discussion of soap opera's defects. In 1954, Gilbert Seldes noted that TV soaps transferred from radio a set of negative presumptions about the genre's "middle-class-and-lower" followers,[6] and *Newsweek* observed that serials on the new medium continued to cater to this uncomplimentary fan stereotype—described in part as a dependent woman with "a dull imagination" and "routine ideas."[7] Even more alarming for many was the quick popularity of television's new arrivals. While only seven soap operas were on the air in February 1954, typically 15 minutes in length, they rated among daytime's most watched offerings. On CBS, *Search for Tomorrow* and *Guiding Light* ranked second and fourth in daytime popularity.[8] By December 1954, 18 soap operas were "rub-a-dub-dubbing" on television, in *Newsweek*'s words,[9] and the number of quarter hours of soap opera per week reached the decade's high point at 84 in 1955, the year *Matinee* premiered. Although this number fell back to 40 in 1956, a slowly rising number of television soap operas, most of them on CBS, began to coexist alongside the daily dramas of *Matinee Theater* as the 1950s drew to a close.[10]

Within this environment, Weaver and McCleery could not ignore "the question of the soap opera" in their planning for *Matinee Theater*. While committed to uplift, Weaver thought *Matinee* should try to capture some of soap opera's appeal, and he encouraged McCleery to consult with the best of the soap writers, even to the point of suggesting that McCleery commission Irna Phillips to write 10 shows a year.[11] That McCleery rejected Weaver's advice tactfully but decisively attests to his determination to position *Matinee* as prestige drama superior to soap opera in every way.[12] From the series's inception, radio and television's much maligned serial dramas served as a negatively charged default mode that *Matinee* resolutely sought to counter.

Inspired by anthology drama's golden reputation, McCleery and Weaver were well-matched television dreamers determined to endow their enterprise with a mystique of superiority they believed would trump soap opera. As this chapter explains, however, in retrospect *Matinee Theater* held an affinity with soap opera that was much more convoluted than its originators imagined. In an ironic twist of history, the very elements meant to differentiate *Matinee Theater* from soaps failed to sustain NBC's grand venture but ultimately found lasting expression in the lowly soap opera.

Spouting Theory

By 1955, Albert McCleery had earned a reputation at NBC as an innovative contributor to some of television's most esteemed theatrical productions. Positioned "between the muses and the masses," in Russell Lynes's vocabulary,[13] McCleery infused *Matinee* with just the right measure of intellectual and aesthetic loftiness.

McCleery's double training in community theater and early television prepared him well for the prodigious task of establishing an upper-middlebrow matinee series that would eclipse the appeals of soap opera. As a young man, McCleery had helped found a series of experimental theater troupes around the country. While he was quick to confess that he flunked out of Northwestern University's School of Speech and Theatre Arts, his time in Evanston, Illinois, did yield the first arena theater in the Midwest, the Georgian Little Theatre, founded in 1931.[14] McCleery explained that he was working "so hard on the theater project I didn't have time to listen to the professor spout theory."[15] In 1939, he moved to Broadway and coauthored *Curtains Going Up*, a best-selling book that documented the work of 300 community theater groups McCleery had personally visited across the country.[16] After a distinguished wartime career as a paratrooper, McCleery returned to civilian life as the director of drama at Fordham University, where he established the Department of Communication Arts and guided Fordham's University Theater to national prominence.[17]

In 1949, McCleery joined NBC-TV's programming department and was quickly promoted to senior executive producer/director. His entry into live television during its headiest days granted him creative autonomy and the freedom to integrate his ideas about community and arena theater into the staging of television drama. Despite his expressed impatience with "spouted theory," McCleery, like Pat Weaver, was able to articulate a lucid philosophy of TV aesthetics—and then test out these theories on the television stage. For McCleery, *Matinee* offered the unprecedented opportunity to establish a grassroots drama in reverse—a decentered "national theater" that was accessible, inexpensive, and egalitarian.[18]

In 1950, McCleery became one of the original forces behind NBC's revered *Cameo Theatre* (1950–1955), where he perfected a widely imitated camera technique that quickly became known as the "cameo shot." To save the cost of building sets, the cameo shot captured actors bathed in bright light in close-up or medium close-up, while the background was blurred or lost in deep shadow.

McCleery also directed 177 Sunday afternoon plays for NBC's *Hallmark Hall of Fame* (1951–1956), acclaimed at the time as another prestigious series.[19] It was during this experimental period at NBC that McCleery began collaborating with Weaver to devise a bold new anthology of daily dramas that would take five years to realize.[20]

During these early days, as critics in the press began to laud television's potential as an art form, McCleery discovered ways to adapt his dreams about a cutting-edge theater to the demands and possibilities of the new medium, a technology he said was "pregnant with excitement and ideas and imagination."[21] In this transformation, McCleery deliberately rejected the typical proscenium arch, using technology to imitate the effect of arena theater.[22] Instead of placing the audience in a circle around the drama, McCleery placed the television camera at the center of the dramatic ring, privy to the intimate action. "This was arena theatre turned wrong side out," he wrote, since "the camera (or spectators)

Albert McCleery, producer of NBC's **Matinee Theater**, *pioneered the "cameo shot" and brought his vision for a national theater of the air to daytime television. Photo courtesy Arts Library Special Collections, UCLA.*

were put in the center and the actors moved about them," combining the depth effect of staging with the fluidity of film.[23] McCleery's "suggested" settings further eliminated an overuse of the master shot, creating what Robert Lewis Shayon later criticized as the "'limbo' close-up" where characters floated in "no-worldliness."[24]

Simplified sets may have been an economic necessity for profitable television productions, but McCleery defended his "selective realism" on aesthetic grounds as well.[25] He lamented the fact that "TV has sold itself to the pseudo-realism of the movies ... It has gone set-happy."[26] Insisting that sets were unimportant and that a few imaginative props could indicate any setting, McCleery wasted no screen time shooting actors walking down halls or across rooms in filler long shots.[27] Instead, his well-planned cameo shots, in which human faces were sculpted by shades of dark and light, stripped away needless clutter to create an intimate canvas. *New York Herald Tribune* critic John Crosby raved, "McCleery demonstrates that a television screen can be as curt, concise and powerful as a line drawing by Toulouse-Lautrec."[28]

McCleery advocated other television techniques that fit the catechism for excellence preached by the country's most influential television critics. In the era's ongoing debate over the quality of filmed programs versus live drama,[29] McCleery remained adamant about live TV, believing it gave a show "more vitality and more of a feeling of heightened suspense" than filmed productions.[30] Because filmed programs on television were associated with formula stories and trite characters coming out of Hollywood during the mid-1950s,[31] McCleery upheld the strict aesthetic of liveness.[32] McCleery also furthered the artistic dogma that the writer of teleplays was the central auteur; as he said in 1956, "It is the writer who makes a powerful show, an entertaining show, a weak show or a flop."[33]

Acting style on television also demanded a new aesthetic standard, in McCleery's view, melding the performance requirements of the stage with techniques of the cinema. McCleery expected his actors to speak eloquently, as they might on stage,[34] but nurtured a naturalist speech style. "Human beings on television must look and speak like human beings, as their type and station in life requires," he theorized.[35] He further argued against the placement of a microphone six or seven feet above a wide shot because it resulted in a "dull flatness" and "a false aural perspective . . . where everyone seems to be speaking with the voice of God."[36]

To meet the demands of the camera close-up, McCleery coached actors to express their emotions with a "mobile face."[37] He reasoned that the small size of the home television screen often projected Lilliputians into American living rooms. "It is best to remember," he wrote, "that the average home screen is 12 inches wide . . . [S]how after show uses such wide shots that actors are often approximately 2¼ inches high."[38] Expert television acting, according to McCleery, reduced the broad gestures found on Broadway to facial expressions and subtler inflections of body language. McCleery told Philip Minoff of *Cue* magazine that he preferred movie to stage actors because "they know how to think with their faces."[39] He noted that while the audience cannot see a tear on the heroine's eyelash in Broadway plays, "on your living room television screen you can. Why not take advantage of it?"[40] In all these ways, McCleery upheld the era's dictum that television's best productions maximized "naturalistic performances, frequent close-ups," and dramas of "character."[41]

As NBC prepared to introduce *Matinee* in the fall of 1955, McCleery was primed to carry forward to daytime the new aesthetics of the teleplay and to produce a populist theater that satisfied Weaver's aspirations for what he called "a tremendous and exhilarating project that has more promise in it than anything we have ever done."[42] Working together as a creative team, Weaver and McCleery endowed *Matinee* with a grandiose vision, one that strove to adopt and then surpass the established aesthetics of 1950s TV drama.

Two memoranda served as a founding charter for *Matinee*—a lengthy treatise Weaver dictated to Jane Murray on 4 July 1955,[43] and McCleery's 17-page response, apparently written 12 September 1955.[44] These memos document the arduous deliberations that drove the design of the new series, the crux of which was Weaver's instruction that the show's "substantial diet from day to day" be "strong stories of interest to women[,] well written and well done." McCleery adopted this precept as "the *key* to our entire operation . . . our prime charge . . . and our most basic responsibility."[45]

The memos make clear that Weaver and McCleery shared an idealistic vision for *Matinee*, and McCleery addressed each of Weaver's wide-ranging suggestions with reverence and zeal, replying "point-for-point" to provide a progress report just weeks before the series debuted.[46] For McCleery, Weaver's propositions about script sources and a new talent pool were especially resonant. Weaver had encouraged McCleery to develop a "stock company" of actors[47] and to nurture a set of new stars and fresh writers, voicing a special enthusiasm for the re-creation of the big screen "Matinee Idol" so beloved by women before the war.[48] Enthusiastically committed to developing "*new* talent—and *new* Matinee Idols," McCleery replied that the cultivation of promising writers had already been "gratifyingly successful," and the series had contracted with several "new exciting male stars of tomorrow," including John Barrymore Jr., Lamont Johnson, and Peter Graves, and glamorous young leading women like Angie Dickinson and Vera Miles.[49]

Two other aspects of *Matinee*'s plan sought to raise the standards for daytime quality. The first was the decision to broadcast the series from Hollywood, not from New York. Hollywood's influence on programming excellence was still suspect in 1955, but McCleery welcomed his California location for its expansive facilities and creative environment. His drama factory incorporated a converted building at Vine and Selma in Hollywood that housed four rehearsal halls and eight offices. In Burbank, two of NBC's newest television studios alternated as McCleery's final rehearsal hall and broadcast center, each supported by 75 technicians.[50] For McCleery, the series's production site dislodged the pseudoroyalty of Broadway dramas and allowed *Matinee* to bring "American theater" to the grass roots. Of equal importance, Hollywood was brimming with exactly those aspiring performers, writers, and directors McCleery hoped to discover and nurture.[51]

NBC's second innovation was the mandate to broadcast the plays in color. Broadcasting in "tint" would place the show at the forefront of daytime technology, the network proclaimed. Weaver extolled color's "realism effect" and said he firmly believed that nothing was better looking than "big faces in color."[52] In Chicago, the NBC sales department invited dozens of prospective advertisers to view the first week's dramas on a new 21-inch RCA color receiver located in a conference room at the Merchandise Mart.[53] For RCA, which owned NBC, a side benefit of *Matinee Theater* was to broadcast a program that would permit dealers in every time zone to demonstrate the beauty of color during the day and encourage the purchase of color sets (only 0.02 percent of the country's approximately 31 million television households in 1955).[54] Critics noted that for the millions of women with black-and-white sets, the addition of color on *Matinee* was inconsequential. "Considering what fills most of the daytime hours," Harriet Van Horne wrote in the *New York Telegraph and Sun*, "most women would be happy to watch a good show done entirely in bottle green."[55] For prestige-conscious NBC, however, colorcasting was yet another promotable measure of the network's dedication to excellence.

NBC's prelaunch publicity succeeded in creating anticipatory enthusiasm for a quality show. In Chicago, *Sun-Times* critic Lucia Carter praised NBC's efforts to redeem daytime from the grip of soap opera. "Daytime broadcasting fare . . . all too often has been based on the arrogant assumption that the housewife is stupid," she began. "[T]he senseless soap epics . . . are an insult to the woman who turns on her TV set during the afternoon . . . Matinee [Theater] . . . will be of a different stripe."[56]

Under the grandeur of its charter, *Matinee* was slated to elevate daytime entertainment to new heights. "[S]pace, scope, sweep, mobility, bigness, stature, prestige—these are the qualities that we want," proclaimed Weaver.[57] And in the rhetoric of NBC, the accomplishment of these visionary goals would honor the taste and intelligence of the American homemaker by giving her an alternative to soap opera.

Not Soap Opera

NBC's audacious enterprise succeeded in calling nationwide attention to a daytime venture of unprecedented size. McCleery undertook the Herculean effort of producing five original color dramas per week, calling upon a literal cast of thousands. By any measure, *Matinee* was a gargantuan project, and McCleery, well trained by the U.S. Army to honor the chain of command, assumed the role of the operation's commander in chief.

Sold on a participating basis in the manner of *Home*, *Matinee* began its run with record-breaking advance sales, the total gross billings for the first 13-week cycle at more than $1 million.[58] By the end of the premiere week, sales had reached $5 million.[59] Early sponsors included Bab-O, Procter & Gamble, Alcoa, and Motorola.[60] Liggett & Myers cigarettes, Sylvania, and Johnson & Johnson signed on in December.[61]

With actor John Conte serving as host, *Matinee Theater* became a veritable drama factory in NBC's Burbank studios. Telecast live each weekday between 3:00 and 4:00 p.m. ET, the series employed a corps of some 275 workers, managed by three producers who reported directly to McCleery:[62] Ethel Frank, supervising story producer; Winston O'Keefe, talent producer; and Darrell Ross, the operations producer.[63]

The astonishing details of the enterprise filled the pages of the nation's newspapers and magazines and became a staple of NBC's own sales promotions. *Time* magazine reported that *Matinee Theater* mounted five concurrent rehearsals, worked on 50 scripts at once, retained access to 250 contributing authors and story doctors, employed 10 story editors in Hollywood, and maintained a permanent staff of nine in Manhattan.[64] In one season alone, an NBC press release exclaimed, series host John Conte was on camera 3,240 minutes (54 hours); enough makeup was used on the show to keep one woman "classically beautiful for 25 years"; 1,945 actors and actresses appeared in the series, requiring 5,030 costumes and 3,920 gallons of coffee.[65] The plays on *Matinee* were regarded as assembly-line productions, efficiently rolling onto live TV day after day, with McCleery cast as the "mastermind" and "field marshal."[66]

Through extraordinary effort, McCleery strove to realize an old dream: the establishment of "a National Theater in the truest sense of the word, a theater . . . brought within easy reach of everyone . . . and a theater that would be so sound that it would be truly permanent."[67] Yet the ambitious daily dramas of *Matinee Theater*, intended to re-create the best public theater of the past, ran side-by-side with soap opera, and

Matinee was inevitably measured against standards and biases that had censored the soaps for decades.

When *Matinee* broadcast its first play, "Beginning Now," on 31 October 1955, critics across the nation reflexively judged the series against soap opera norms.[68] John Crosby, critic for the *New York Herald Tribune*, devoutly hoped that *Matinee* heralded "the ultimate demise of soap opera," while at the *New York Times* Jack Gould raved that *Matinee* was making "a significant contribution to the evolution of a more mature TV," embracing the theory "that distaff viewers who enjoy intelligent dramas after dark do not suddenly become moronic clucks in the daylight."[69] *Variety* predicted that if the quality of the premiere continued, "the lordly and ladylike soap opera is in for big trouble."[70] For critic Donald Freeman of the *San Diego Union*, the arrival of *Matinee* on the daytime airwaves offered women a liberation from "drek": "women got the vote and they learned to smoke and wear slacks and now . . . they may be on the threshold of still another freedom—their deliverance from the soap opera. What's taken them so long, anyway?"[71]

Other reviewers across the country were more restrained in their praise, finding the play too much like its critical nemesis. The opening drama, adapted from a story by John P. Marquand and directed by McCleery himself, told the tale of a wealthy, irresponsible father whose automobile accident shocked his college-age son—and ultimately himself—into soul-searching reform. *Variety* said of the plot that it succeeded in striking "a midway level" between primetime and "detergent" dramas.[72] Roland Lindbloom of the *Newark News* appreciated the opening drama's "unusually good camera work" but adjudged "Beginning Now" to be "a year-long soap opera" crammed into 50 minutes.[73] Anthony LaCamera at the *Boston American* agreed, declaring that the teledrama "unmercifully threw [all the elements of soap opera] at us in one melodramatic lump."[74] At the end of the first week, *Broadcasting and Telecasting* appraised the new series as "tinseled soap opera" and "syrupy,"[75] while Larry Wolters at the *Chicago Tribune* wondered if McCleery was "writing down" for housewives.[76]

As time went on, the accusation of being "too sudsy" continued to haunt *Matinee*. Yet McCleery held fast to his initial precept that the series would serve as an enlightening beacon. "[W]omen have always been the cultural leaders of America" and would be treated as such by his productions, he had promised, and in March 1956, he reasserted that his plays introduced "sophistication to the ordinary person's life" and added to "the cultural tastes of people."[77] At the celebration of the series's

200th episode in August 1956, McCleery avowed, "[P]eople like honest, literate stuff at any time, not the soap-opera kind."[78]

For its first 200 episodes, *Matinee* collected a long list of national honors, including an Emmy for the "Best Contribution to Daytime Television,"[79] but McCleery soon learned that prestige alone could not sustain the high cost of quality. At the beginning of the second season, the series was only two-thirds sold and the network was assembling a "task selling force" to bring in more sponsors.[80]

While NBC vowed to uphold the series's mission of uplift, month after month of daily live productions created the need for balance and inevitable compromise. McCleery had discovered how to bring what he called a "catholicity of entertainment" to his schedule,[81] and the weekly lineup methodically mixed genres and moods.[82] "We are trying to please everyone," McCleery said in 1956.[83]

Even though only a small percentage of the dramas still survive on kinescope, a sampling of the extant films certifies the series's guiding principle to present an assortment of genres in a variety of tones: in "George Has a Birthday," Eddie Cantor starred in a farcical murder story; "Prosper's Old Mother" adapted a comic short story by Bret Harte set in the Old West; George Peppard, flown in for the occasion from New York, portrayed Jesse Stuart in "The Thread That Runs So True"; "Tall, Dark Stranger" imitated a moody film noir and starred Zsa Zsa Gabor and Hugh O'Brian as a sexually charged couple "irretrievably committed to murder and to each other"; "Give Me a Wand" and "The Bottom of the River" addressed issues of juvenile delinquency and teenage anguish; and a father learned to accept his "sensitive" and poetic 11-year-old son in "The Outing." Abbreviated renderings of Charlotte Brontë's "Jane Eyre" and Émile Zola's "Therese" also appeared on the schedule.[84] And in May 1958, *Matinee* presented William Shakespeare's "Much Ado about Nothing" in a two-part special.

These extant plays and the dozens of scripts on file in the Albert McCleery Papers at UCLA confirm the sweeping range of *Matinee*'s aspirations. As McCleery himself put it, from "the most realistic, experimental and artistic shows" to the play "with guts" about a social problem, from offbeat productions "with a gimmick twist" to Broadway adaptations and comedy, *Matinee Theater* did it all.[85]

These eclectic experiments could not rebuff daytime's legacy of feminized narratives set in the present, however, and *Matinee* tended to favor those formulas known to please the young married women at the heart of its audience.[86] Of the first 200 plays of the series, 35 were comedies,

*Nina Foch and Robert Horton starred in **Matinee Theater**'s production of "Much Ado about Nothing" in 1958, one of the program's "highbrow" presentations. Photo courtesy Wisconsin Center for Film and Theater Research (WCFTR-10772).*

20 were period pieces, 11 were classics, and 93 were "contemporary drama."[87] An NBC audience survey conducted in March 1956 discovered that even period adaptations of timeless romances were not well liked.[88] As proof, Chicago critic Lucia Carter found *Matinee*'s version of Emily Bronte's *Wuthering Heights* laughable. "There was something incongruous about [the actress] shouting 'Heathcliff!' all over somebody's

living room ... [T]he tragic events didn't quite ring true, and it was difficult to resist an impulse to giggle. In fact, it was impossible."[89]

By 1956, McCleery also championed the "upbeat ending." "If we can't solve a problem, we don't pose it," he told *Time*. "The afternoon is no time to wring people's hearts out ... If I were doing *Romeo and Juliet*, I would show their ghosts floating gently up to heaven, hand in hand."[90] McCleery attempted to leave viewers with a sense of elation. "We're not getting so arty that people want to drown themselves after having seen one of our productions."[91]

Yet even in its concessions and failures, *Matinee* hoped to distance itself from the perceived taint of daytime broadcasting. When Carter conceded "Wuthering Heights" was still "quite a step up from soap operas," she affirmed the series's reputation for unusual excellence in the daytime marketplace.[92] NBC tried to capitalize on this aura of superiority by continuing to play the prestige card in its marketing strategies. In October 1956, the network produced a sales kinescope called "Success Story" that promoted *Matinee*'s second season with this pitch. To prove the efficacy of the series's sales potential, excerpts from viewers' letters were featured prominently. One enthusiastic fan praised *Matinee* for complimenting the intelligence of its audience and promised that viewers like herself would "reciprocate and buy all [the] sponsors' products."[93]

The Matinee Habit

Because *Matinee Theater* was advertised as superior programming for housewives, NBC contended that each live presentation required a viewer's full attention. This approach originated in NBC's awareness that television was playing an increasingly conflicted role in a woman's workday, no longer merely replicating radio's service as a work companion. McCleery explicitly sought to cultivate *Matinee*'s leisure function, modeling his series on earlier entertainment forms that offered repose for women during the day. He told *TV-Radio Life* in 1955 that his purpose was to "recapture the matinee audience which was once the backbone of the theater and motion pictures."[94] As early as January 1956, NBC began promoting uninterrupted viewing of *Matinee* as a well-deserved break for the tired housewife, who was quite literally invited to take her shoes off and rest her feet. "[H]ere is a show of quality," the copy read, that the homemaker "can watch in solitary splendor."[95]

From the beginning, the critical reception of *Matinee* reinforced the series's pull toward pure entertainment, often expressing in a teasing way the program's power to disrupt a homemaker's scheduled responsibilities. In Chicago, where the show aired between 2:00 and 3:00 p.m., the *Sun-Times* rejoiced that modern science had devised "so many time-saving gadgets for the housewife" because *Matinee* might well "keep the missus out of the kitchen long enough each afternoon . . . to incite real havoc with the evening dinner menu."[96] Donald Freeman, writing in San Diego, worried that *Matinee* would "keep the breakfast dishes in the sink all day," since no woman interested in culture would "be able to wash a dish between noon and 1 p.m."[97] Taking a broader view, *Variety* understood that *Matinee* openly defied the hallowed precept that "daytime TV is tailored for the ears alone," arguing that the program's hour-long dramas required concentration and, possibly, "a whole repatterning of life."[98]

Matinee openly set out to encourage this repatterning. In March 1956, five months after the series premiere, NBC conducted a survey to assess the viewing habits of the *Matinee* audience. Summarizing the research, Bill Moseley reported in a memo to McCleery that home activities in the measured time zones significantly affected the matinee habit. Predictably, the largest sheer numbers of viewers were found in the East. The Central time zone drew the greatest percentage of viewers, while the Pacific zone was "by far the worst for us"; ratings for *Matinee* on the West Coast were markedly reduced by "handling children, eating lunch and viewing our competition."[99]

Other statistics from the survey suggested that, overall, *Matinee* was thriving in its function as a leisure activity for women of all income groups. Of the viewers surveyed, 100 percent were female; 67 percent were between the ages of 24 and 44; 90 percent viewed the entire hour, many three times a week, and "a surprising number" watched all five days.[100]

With this information in hand, NBC redoubled its efforts to promote dedicated viewing. In June 1956, NBC executive Thomas E. Coffin concluded that *Matinee*'s stiff competition on CBS, *The Big Payoff* and *The Bob Crosby Show*, required "less concentration and less devotion" than the NBC series. Coffin believed the major deterrent to watching *Matinee Theater* was the feeling of guilt an hour of uninterrupted entertainment aroused in homemakers. The antidote Coffin proposed was promotional material that depicted the *Matinee* viewer as "a hard-working woman who deserves an hour of relaxation and rest during the afternoon before she has to plunge into her evening chores. This hour of rest will make her a better wife and mother."[101]

Because the series aired live in four different time zones, homemakers were urged to plan their varied workloads around the broadcast. Host John Conte invited viewers to "join us for your daily hour of relaxation and entertainment on NBC"[102] and to "[p]lan your time accordingly and join us."[103] The promotional kinescope "Success Story" also highlighted testimonials from viewers across the country who arranged their workday to steal an hour of pleasure from the series. A viewer in Fort Worth, Texas, wrote, "It is the one daytime TV program that I absolutely must find time to watch every day." A fan in Dayton, Ohio, reported, "I especially like the time from 3:00 to 4:00 as it gives me a chance to relax before starting dinner," while a Michigan woman explained, "Most of my young married friends and I watch your Matinee while our babies are sleeping." McCleery asserted on the same kinescope that his series was "really becoming an American institution," reestablishing a film habit "practiced by millions of the nation's housewives" before the war. "Matinee is reviving that wonderfully relaxing time out," McCleery continued, "and doing it in the newest electronic fashion . . . Thousands of letter writers have told us about their new 'matinee habit.'"[104]

Sex in the Afternoon

In theory, *Matinee Theater*'s afternoon time slot sanctioned the production of mature drama for the thinking woman, and McCleery's boast that the program faced no bans in its treatment of "adult themes" imparted yet another air of urbanity to the series. "[W]e don't have any censorship of any kind," he proclaimed to *Variety*, "and as a result we can be and are the most sophisticated show on the air."[105] McCleery's story producer, Ethel Frank, who quickly established herself as a mentor for new Hollywood writing talent,[106] disseminated this message in her outreach workshops. "We'll read everything," she vowed. "Our only limitations are those of good taste. Writers of all kinds can service this show . . . [T]here are no taboos."[107]

McCleery maintained that because his afternoon audience was made up of adults, *Matinee* could ignore not only the "stringent censorship" of the early evening children's hours[108] but even the constraints of primetime. As proof, McCleery cited the instance when *Matinee* was allowed to broadcast the final lines of an Edith Wharton story between a wife and her husband's mistress ("I was married to him for 35 years"—"But I had his child"), while an evening version was forced to censor the ending.[109]

When sponsorship flagged at the beginning of the second season,

McCleery began plotting a strategy he thought would retain "the young married women between 21 and 29" already loyal to the program. Capitalizing on color television's capacity to convey "flesh tones," McCleery planned to focus on *Matinee*'s sex appeal. "Sex is important to us," he told *Variety*, "because our audience wants it . . . Sex is all a woman thinks about while she's sitting at home, and we can give it to her."[110] Robert Lewis Shayon lampooned this comment by McCleery a few months later in the *Saturday Review*, when he mockingly critiqued what seemed to be a rather tame schedule of forthcoming plays: "I felt certain," Shayon wrote, "that in the producer's hands these plays would yield their full harvest of sex and sophistication to my deceitful wife, who never does anything in the afternoon but lustfully watch 'Matinee Theatre.'"[111]

Shayon was right to scoff at McCleery's inflated claim that *Matinee* strove to seduce the housewife through desire alone, but McCleery did acknowledge the value of eros on television. He had told *Cue* magazine in 1951 that television owed "a debt of gratitude" to the curvaceous Dagmar, because "where you don't have sex, you don't have any profits."[112]

One way McCleery fostered *Matinee*'s mystique as a show with sex appeal was to promote host John Conte as an erotic new matinee idol—a twentieth-century "Lothario," according to the advertising copy.[113] A survey conducted in the summer of 1956 by Motivation Analysis, Inc., found that 82 percent of *Matinee* viewers responded positively to Conte. "John Conte is liked very much," the report said. "He is pictured as a friendly, poised, relaxed, smooth man, with a great deal of sex appeal in his voice, looks, even his clothes." In the words of one viewer, "[T]he emcee is Oh-oo, Ah-a-a, and Oomph . . . a honey."[114]

During the 1956–1957 season, NBC began exploiting Conte's appeal by giving him more to say during intermissions, casting him as the romantic lead in a number of daily dramas, assigning him interviews with actors at the end of performances, and generally promoting him as a major asset for the series. A sales promotion distributed in 1956 declared, "Conte has attracted millions of new feminine followers. They admire him as a winning host . . . persuasive salesman . . . appealing performer."[115] In 1957, *TV Radio Mirror* named him "Favorite TV Dramatic Actor" in daytime drama and acknowledged his role as a "*Matinee* idol," both as its host and recurrent star.[116]

In spite of McCleery's avowal that *Matinee Theater* was censorship-free, NBC's interoffice correspondence reveals that the Continuity Acceptance Department, which monitored network content, had its eye on the series from the start. The possibility of children viewing *Matinee*

*NBC promoted John Conte, the host of **Matinee Theater**, as a twentieth-century Lothario and afternoon idol. Photo courtesy Wisconsin Center for Film and Theater Research (WCFTR-10793).*

was not a trivial issue for NBC. Robert Wood, the continuity executive on the West Coast assigned to *Matinee*, advised his boss Stockton Helffrich in New York the day after the series premiered that *Matinee* would "get into the adult field" and noted that McCleery and the Continuity Acceptance staff would "have to be wary" about the possibility of children's presence in every time zone. Wood even promised Helffrich that on school holidays *Matinee* would schedule plays "aimed at full family viewing."[117]

Although Continuity Acceptance monitored a wide range of content issues,[118] NBC was especially skittish about overstepping the era's sexual norms. McCleery may have mandated that his plays appeal to the homebound viewer's assumed fixation on passion, but John Graves, editor of the department's Western Division, consistently strove to keep the preapproved scripts within the network's bounds of decorum, as stated in the network's codebook, *NBC Radio and Television Broadcast Standards*.[119] In reaction to the script for "Forsaking All Others," for example, Graves advised *Matinee* staff to add to the line "stay with me here," the phrase "at least a little longer," and to replace "nights of love" with "days of love."[120] In July 1956, in response to a viewer complaint, Wood chastised McCleery for permitting a moment of "open-mouthed kissing" on "The Lighted Window." In a memo copied to Helffrich, Wood wrote, "I feel it would be wise if you were to notify your directors that overly passionate love scenes could lead to a mass disapproval of such a well[-]integrated series, something neither you nor I would want."[121]

Because the NBC code book especially protected children, Continuity Acceptance repeatedly confronted the perplexing problem of young viewers. Although an audience survey in March 1956 indicated the typical viewer watched alone, without children present,[122] viewer grievances often revolved around potential harm to youngsters. Continuity's standard rejoinder reaffirmed that *Matinee* was not produced to entertain children, but Helffrich attended to these complaints with care. In 1956, Mrs. A. H. Kemp Jr. from Rochester, New York, wrote that she was outraged when three of her children and their friends, home for Easter vacation, became interested in a story that raised the issue of pregnancy outside of marriage. Helffrich defended "Singer in the Rain" as handling these issues "in the most healthy of contexts" and "in the most moral of settings," but he assured Mrs. Kemp that his long letter to her was meant to prove that "we do take our job seriously."[123]

Other examples also indicate that a play's strong moral center served as Continuity's best defense. When critic Gilbert Seldes complained in the *Saturday Review* that the sex scenes in "Eye of the Storm" were "highly immoral . . . as explicit physically as television dares to go,"[124] Continuity rejected Seldes's too strict Victorian code and praised the drama's "highly moral theme."[125]

Across *Matinee*'s years on the air, the mission of Continuity Acceptance was plainly effectuated—to guarantee that "moral standards" on the series "are and will continue to remain high."[126] While the adult content of its dramas was advertised as sophisticated theater that eclipsed the banality of soap opera, the series was in fact unable to escape the quotidian realities of domestic America and its middle-class mores. At the same time that McCleery publicly extolled the series's transcendent exploration of human, sexual, and familial relationships, cautious judgments behind the scenes held *Matinee* to daytime standards that were mainstream.

East Coast, West Coast, All around the Town

Over the course of its nearly three-year run, *Matinee Theater* was also forced to balance the aesthetic standards associated with New York's live anthology dramas, already in decline, with a late-decade shift toward the telefilm and the middlebrow taste associated with it.[127] *Matinee*'s West Coast production site placed the series at the epicenter of the growing cultural rift in the television industry between the high-brow values associated with New York and the more populist aesthetics linked to Hollywood, spurred on by an ever-more diverse and suburban TV audience.

A comparison of two plays produced on *Matinee* three years apart illustrates how these unstable issues of taste were explicitly addressed over time. "This One Is Different," produced early in the first season, and "Two-Picture Deal," which aired during the final months of the series (8 January 1958), capture the ongoing tensions that separated East Coast and West Coast taste values during the late 1950s and *Matinee*'s equivocal position within them. While New York City was shown to represent the cradle of elite culture in both plays, the 1955 teleplay validated the well-educated preferences of "Bohemian" urban life, while "Two-Picture Deal," more tolerant of Hollywood, depicted Manhattan's highbrow culture, and its inaccessible theater, as snobbish and effete.

"This One Is Different" follows a budding love affair between handsome Manhattan architect Tom Loring (played by John Conte) and Linda Gresham (Marcia Henderson), the daughter of a wealthy Wall Street broker. Tom, a Yale graduate, is a jaded bachelor rebounding from a "bad affair in Greenwich," and he speaks the voice of cynicism about America's new suburban world. Tom abhors the picture windows, dropped living rooms, and flagstone terraces he helped design on Long

Island and especially condemns suburban wives, who only think about sunlamps. "All these dolls have one thing in mind," Tom tells his roommate Bill, "a two-car garage with attached houses." Tom likewise disdains the "tribal ritual" of the Park Avenue set he expects to perform on his first date with Linda—a drink with Dad in the library, Linda's choice of a fashionable French restaurant, and a marriage engagement in three months. Contemptuous and superior, Tom equates marriage commitment with a middlebrow world and scornfully rejects both.

Linda, of course, turns out to be the one who is "different." In all matters cultural, her modernist predilections align with Tom's. Instead of suggesting a French restaurant, she prefers eating chicken paella at Tom's place, where she easily fits in with his friends and enjoys Chico Rivero's performance on the conga drums. Like Tom, she appreciates drinks, steaks, clam bars, art galleries, movies, and jazz ("I'm practically an addict"), and she impresses Tom with her understanding of the architecture of the United Nations building and her strong opinions about expressionist painting. After Linda fails to seduce Tom in front of his "functionalist" fireplace, she briefly dates an artist, but all ends well when Tom realizes he must overcome his fear of the "penitentiary" of marriage and finally proposes to Linda.

"This One Is Different" only occasionally ridicules Tom's self-importance. Linda tells him he's "really pretty smug," and Tom himself confesses that during his Yale years he was "very functional and pretty arrogant about it." Overall, however, the play affirms the superiority of Manhattan's highbrow taste culture, the very standards at the core of *Matinee*'s founding credo. Linda might express a soap opera platitude when she tells her girlfriend Casey that men are worth it—"They are, they are, they sure are"—but the play's trajectory casts doubt on "the penitentiary" of middle-class marriage and its dreary geography. After Tom and Linda marry, they plan to live in an "old broken down villa" in Italy, and then travel to Rome and Paris.[128]

By 1958, the emerging clash of power in the television industry between the taste culture of New York and that of Hollywood found full expression in "Two-Picture Deal."[129] In this play, the marriage of Josie (Mala Powers) and Frank Rawlings (Phillip Pine) is on the brink of collapse over career conflicts. Jo is a popular film star being pressured to sign a two-picture deal that would keep the couple in Hollywood, while Frank longs to return to New York City to pursue his career as a stage actor. Smarting from his reputation as "Mr. Jo Rawlings" and enraged by the Hollywood "weasels" who offered him a small film role only as a ploy to keep Jo in Los Angeles, Frank orders Jo to accompany him on the first plane back to New York.

Back in New York in act 2, the tyrannical husband and his obnoxious cronies become the play's central defenders of the city's theatrical scene, thus exposing Manhattan's once revered values as artificial and coldly intellectual. At a party with Frank's friends, Jo is ridiculed and demeaned for her ties with Hollywood. A renowned producer remarks derisively, "It's so nice to have a goddess among us." When Frank learns he will be cast in a plum part if Jo agrees to play the lead role of Sarena in García Lorca's fashionable new play, Jo confesses to Frank's mortification she has never heard of Lorca. Later, under pressure from Frank to land the part of Sarena, Jo reluctantly agrees to take acting lessons with Les, a haughty New York method actor who ruthlessly browbeats Jo in his workshop. "Flat! Flat! Uninteresting and untrue!" he screams about her performance. "There is no special treatment here! . . . You're raw material!" When Les grabs Jo's shoulders in exasperation shouting, "Don't play games!" Jo slaps his face and departs in a fury.

In the closing act, the couple has returned to Hollywood to attend the opening of Jo's new picture. Distraught over the turn of events in New York, Frank refuses to accompany Jo, telling her cruelly, "I don't escort the harem slaves anymore." Frank then presents Jo with an ultimatum—either she accompanies him to New York the next day or he takes the plane without her. After a tender moment of regret, when Jo admits she's not an actress but a "motion-picture personality," they realize each of them needs more "room," and Frank departs. Jo's final line of the play, "I have a kind of hope for both of us now," hints at the chance for marital reunion, but the split between the sterile mode of drama represented by the self-important Frank and the more populist dramatic form embodied in Jo and linked to Hollywood filmmaking remained irreconcilable.

These bookend plays reflect the ongoing tensions at the core of *Matinee Theater* itself, as esteemed live drama derived from a theatrical vitality centered in New York was set in dialectic with an increasingly more popular fare produced in Hollywood and making its way onto television. As William Boddy explains, ABC's move into telefilms after its mid-decade merger with United Paramount guided the television industry away from anthology drama and toward filmed productions originating on the West Coast.[130] The title of the song that opened "Two-Picture Deal" acknowledged this gradual migration in the industry from East to West, from live to recorded, from stage to film, from highbrow to middlebrow: "Hurray for Hollywood!"

Prestige till the End

Caught in the overriding industry movement away from live anthology drama[131] and toward more profit-conscious programming like soap opera, *Matinee* succumbed to economic pressures in June 1958. As early as January 1956, when Robert Sarnoff took charge at the network, sales prospects had become worrisome. NBC executive John B. Lanigan sent his colleagues word that the ratings on *Matinee* "are not such that the slide-rule type of buyer would be interested." Lanigan urged the team to "concentrate on our present advertisers and obtain renewals from them—it's the most important thing we have to do."[132]

Under Sarnoff's vigilance, NBC began to reassess the series's renewal for another season as it ended its first 26 weeks in March 1956. Even though two-thirds of sponsor slots had already been sold—adding new clients Fluffo, Tide, Maybelline, Ammident, and Saran Wrap[133]—consternation arose over the daytime competition on both ABC and CBS. ABC's afternoon replays of old films on *Afternoon Film Festival*, priced at 25 percent of *Matinee*'s advertising rate,[134] had already caused NBC some anxious moments with their L&M client. Lanigan reported that L&M "came very close to canceling."[135] While *Film Festival* was not a commercial success for ABC, Joe Culligan explained that "it acted as a 'spoiler' for Matinee," as its opening ratings equaled those of the NBC program.[136] In this increasingly competitive environment, Best Foods, an $800,000 order for *Matinee*, had slipped through NBC's grasp and signed with ABC. When Jerry Chester was asked to calculate the hard facts about NBC's investment in *Matinee* in March, he discovered production costs for the series to be $1,883,096, while net income stood at only $813,000, leaving an unrecovered program cost of over $1 million.[137]

Just as troubling was the news that in the ARB audience reports for April–May 1956, *Matinee Theater* lost to its CBS competitors *The Big Payoff* and *The Bob Crosby Show* in all but seven markets: New York, Philadelphia, Columbus, Omaha, Wheeling (WV)/Steubenville (OH), Rockford (IL), and Seattle/Tacoma.[138]

Financial contingencies and the merits of prestige were apparently persuasive enough to keep the program on the air another season. Chester reminded top executives that *Matinee* only cost about $175,000 more to produce over the first 26 weeks than NBC's previous entries in the same time period (*Ted Mack* and *It Pays to Be Married*), both of which were ratings and sales flops. He added that more than $400,000 of

Matinee's budget reverted to the network because it consisted of "NBC charges for the use of the Burbank color studio." Moreover, *Matinee* had yielded $433,000 in new revenue for NBC affiliates.[139]

Mitch Lipman, who worked in NBC-TV Sales Development, was quick to document that *Matinee*'s audience was almost five times greater than *Film Festival*'s, because ABC could not deliver a "meaningful nationwide audience," covering only 67 percent of U.S. television homes, compared to *Matinee*'s 89 percent reach. Lipman then listed 15 advantages *Matinee* held over *Film Festival*, emphasizing the program's prestige factor and even echoing the sentiments of McCleery that the series served in a way as "the country's first and only national theatre."[140]

Columnist Ben Gross, who caught wind of the possible cancellation, urged NBC to retain the series. After praising the overall brilliance of the productions, Gross argued that "a great network also has an obligation to those millions in its daytime audience who like good plays." If *Matinee Theater* were to disappear, he worried, "it would undoubtedly be succeeded by some typical afternoon item ... Heaven knows, there are plenty of these already!"[141]

In August 1956, a scheduling change placed *Matinee* between a popular lead-in variety show, hosted by Tennessee Ernie Ford, and NBC's newly acquired ratings phenomenon, *Queen for a Day*. Shored up by its new position, the ratings for *Matinee* jumped from 5.1 in November 1955 to 9.0 in August 1956, while CBS lost points between 3:00 and 4:00 p.m.[142] The temporary boost *Queen for a Day* afforded *Matinee* helped forestall the cancellation of the series that year, but the misery show's formula for profitability foretold *Matinee*'s future. Sales executive Joe Culligan lamented, "[A]long came Queen For A Day with its runaway rating success, and nobody would discuss Matinee."[143]

It came to pass that by November 1957, *Matinee*'s ratings had dropped back to a 7,[144] *Queen for a Day* was unstoppable, and the soap opera had begun to prove its ratings might on daytime television. While NBC celebrated an astonishing new profit growth in daytime programming overall, *Matinee* continued to lose $1 million per year.[145] The series's last live performance aired on 13 June 1958.

To the end, *Matinee* maintained its identification as a national theater of distinction, boldly defying the middlebrow standards linked to soap opera. McCleery purchased "Course for Collision," a controversial script written by Canadian playwright Arthur Hailey, as the final play of the series. In the story, set in 1968, the president of the United States thwarts a possible nuclear attack by the Soviet Union when he risks his own life aboard the presidential jet. According to the *New York Times*, CBS had rejected the script for *Studio One* because the U.S. Air Force found it objectionable and NBC officials feared the portrayal of the future president was in "poor taste."[146] Two days before its airdate, McCleery was quoted as saying the pressure from the California censors to kill the show was "tremendous," but "[f]ortunately, I was upheld."[147]

Even in *Matinee*'s final moments, McCleery tried to maintain his series's reputation for daring and uncensored drama. Yet Stockton Helffrich, who overruled the West Coast ban and allowed the play to air, suggested privately the controversy was nothing but a publicity stunt.[148]

Before the series finally concluded, another well-publicized development set the program apart. In an unprecedented grassroots movement, loyal fans began protesting the show's cancellation and stuffing money in envelopes addressed to John Conte. Within months, Ruth Conte had organized the "Foundation for the Preservation of *Matinee Theater*."[149] According to Mrs. Conte, who handled all of her husband's mail, viewers had begun asking, "Why can't *we* own the show? After all, it belongs to us." During the spring of 1958, she met with 105 viewer-homemakers in the Los Angeles area, from which grew a nationwide movement that activated 10,000 "chairmen" across the country.[150]

By November 1958, the foundation had collected $312,670.[151] Mrs. Conte's plan was to subsidize the series on any interested network until participating sponsors could be found. She believed that with "a mandate from millions of American citizens . . . [i]t is inconceivable that any network . . . could flagrantly disregard its responsibilities to the public."[152] In June, the foundation attempted to purchase commercial time on *Matinee* itself, in order to solicit support from viewers. Increasingly embarrassed by Mrs. Conte's enterprise, NBC rejected airing the foundation's announcement. "[*Matinee*'s] final broadcast will be June 27th," the proposed copy read in part. "However, through an unusual chain of events, it will now be possible for you, our viewers, to take an active part in returning *Matinee* to the air this fall without commercial sponsors and on a permanent and continuing basis."[153] To add to the uproar, Mrs. Dan Gerber of Gerber's Baby Food and Mrs. William Black of Chock full o' Nuts coffee promoted the foundation in a quarter-page ad in the *New York Times*. Both the Radio-TV Directors Guild and the National Association of Broadcast Employees and Technicians endorsed Ruth Conte's project. RTDG president Seymour Berns told the *Hollywood*

Reporter, "We deplore the reduction of good quality live dramatic programming which seems to be the forecast for the coming season."[154]

Despite this mobilization, the tide against live drama could not be turned. Ruth Conte mailed back every donation she could by March 1959 and donated the rest to charity. In her words, *Matinee* was now "dead and buried."[155]

The Fickle Bride

Even in its death throes, the series had clung to the grandeur of its promise, echoing the idealistic words Pat Weaver had delivered in a speech to NBC affiliates in 1955, just months after *Matinee* debuted. "[W]e [at NBC] have been against the know-nothings, the primitives," he declared, "because we do not believe that television should be run to give the people what they want. We believe that every NBC show should serve a purpose beyond diversion." According to Weaver's credo, knowledge from such programming would help society take "one more step forward toward sanity, maturity, and adulthood."[156]

After *Matinee*'s cancellation, McCleery clung fast to ideals like these. For 26 weeks, he produced *CBS Workshop* from New York City, another effort to foster new writers, directors, and actors through live drama; he then returned to Hollywood to try out a daytime soap opera of his own, *Paradise Bay*, which lasted just one season (September 1965 to July 1966).[157] By the end of 1966, McCleery had returned to the regional theater that he loved, temporarily saving the Pasadena Playhouse from bankruptcy and founding the Macloren Playhouse.[158]

In September 1960, McCleery reflected upon the interconnection that had evolved during the 1950s between television drama and what he called "the living theater."[159] By then, he discerned an inescapable chasm between "the public en masse" and a superior theater public, composed of "well-trained and knowledgeable sophisticates schooled to understand and appreciate" the aesthetics of the stage play. "For better or for worse, the American public is now wedded to television," he wrote disdainfully, but he concluded that the American theater was better off without such a fickle bride. "[T]elevision made our theater better," he said, "because it stole away the mediocre audience."

Although McCleery conceded that television could serve as a training ground for aspiring artists, he called TV "that black marauder of the arts" and concluded that it was only a matter of time before the mature artist, newly born, would return to the living theater "for future substance." Retreating to venerate again the intrinsic worth of what Bourdieu would call later "the pure aesthetic gaze," McCleery reaffirmed that "the artist produces not for the masses but for himself or for art or for other artists."[160]

As an advocate for the fixed taste hierarchies that pervaded 1950s cultural criticism, McCleery came to believe that the project of conveying highbrow programming to the masses via television was futile. Viewed in Bourdieu's terms, however, McCleery's mission was thwarted for other reasons. Television's universal reach inevitably devalued a refined cultural object as a class marker by making it easily accessible to the middle class, and cultural highbrows like McCleery could only reclaim their aesthetic purity by abandoning television altogether and reestablishing their elite authority in other media.[161]

Matinee was canceled by those whom Weaver might have considered "know-nothings" and "primitives," men like Robert Sarnoff and Robert Kintner, who had risen to network power at NBC during the late 1950s. *Queen for a Day*, later called the worst program on television by its own producer,[162] led NBC to record-breaking daytime profits as the decade closed. Soap opera, long declaimed as the blight of women's broadcasting, had already begun its slow but steady march to daytime prominence. In an inevitable reversal, two half-hour soap operas, *Today Is Ours* and *From These Roots*, replaced *Matinee* in the fall of 1958.[163]

In retrospect, it becomes ironic that *Matinee Theater* was not to be permanent, while soap opera—the "inferior," dramatic Other against which *Matinee* was forever measured—would soon achieve the stature of a national theater of the air and prosper on television as a stable dramatic form well into the twenty-first century, firmly establishing its own stock companies of writers, directors, performers, and matinee idols. The inexorable rise of the soap opera in the 1960s and 1970s appeared to turn the resplendent vision of Weaver and McCleery upside down. In NBC's high-minded attempt to position *Matinee Theater* as top-quality drama far superior to soap opera, the series paradoxically helped perfect the very elements that came to typify serial drama on television and to aid its acceptance. McCleery's close-up camera work in color; his insistence on more naturalistic acting styles; his commitment to sexual, familial, and adult themes; the advocacy of a new matinee viewing habit for women; and the vision of a populist theater within easy reach of everyone—all helped serial drama triumph on television.

Moreover, the era's strict divisions between high and low, which fostered a condescending attitude toward housewives and their supposedly dull imaginations, precluded any deeper understanding of soap opera's more subversive appeals, insights that feminists have since brought to light. In this regard, *Matinee Theater* may well have veered closer to soap opera than McCleery anticipated, but the program's sometimes pretentious mode of address weakened the more authentically populist tone that animated the subaltern sphere of soapland.[164]

As the decade passed the midpoint and *Matinee Theater* spun out its remarkable 660 hours of live daily drama,[165] the networks began to see a bright future for the television soap opera. Yet NBC, CBS, and ABC all achieved more immediate success in the latter part of the 1950s by exploiting another daytime favorite, the audience participation show, which featured on its stage the body and voice of the everyday woman.

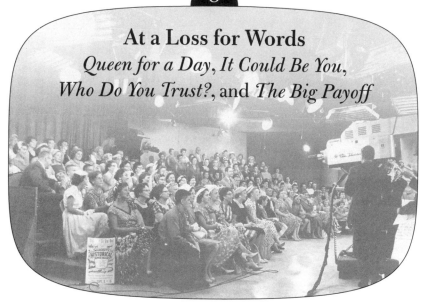

At a Loss for Words

Queen for a Day, It Could Be You, Who Do You Trust?, and The Big Payoff

During the second half of the 1950s, as *Matinee Theater* mounted its cameo dramas from an empty studio, everyday women continued to crowd the theaters of the audience participation shows, where female subjects spoke millions of words on camera. In the daytime world of television, the visibility and vitality of the speaking woman could not be denied, and her homebound sisters watched and listened faithfully.

While the steady procession of women on daytime television validated femininity's power to be seen and heard in a new public sphere, participation shows transmitted from their core a remarkably ambiguous feminine figure. Like the speaking subject in psychoanalysis and medicine described by Mary Ann Doane, the daytime contestant evinced "a very carefully constructed relation to enunciation." Doane explains that if a woman assumes the agency of speech, she must do so "within the well-regulated context of an institutionalized dialogue."[1] As this chapter will explain, the participation shows provided a range of well-regulated contexts that limited a women's full expressivity. Women's life stories, which served as the foundation for the most prominent daytime programs on NBC, CBS, and newcomer ABC, were entangled within pre-constituted frameworks, and more powerful agents retained authority over interpretation and meaning. Four of these programs—*Queen for a*

Day (1956–1964, NBC, then ABC), *It Could Be You* (1956–1961, NBC), *Who Do You Trust?* (1957–1963, ABC), and *The Big Payoff* (1951–1959, NBC, then CBS)—garnered impressive ratings as the decade drew to a close, and each program demonstrated the extent to which feminine speech was routinely prompted, interrupted, edited, summarized, and silenced.

At the same time that daytime television granted women the chance to speak publicly, the restrictions imposed on their speech and their moments of forced silence privileged a scrutiny of female bodies under the camera's watchful eye. In this speaking/appearing conundrum, television's visual track persisted in displaying women as feminine spectacle, eroticized or brimming over with emotion. On all three networks, game shows with a confessional element were mediated by genial but authoritative male intercessors. Jack Bailey, Bill Leyden, Johnny Carson, Randy Merriman, and Bob Paige resembled television's earlier "charm boys" in their generally cordial rapport with women, but they presided over formats that typically restricted a woman's free expression. Each of their programs in its own way paradoxically cast women as both talkative and silent, both agents of speech in a new public sphere and an object to be supervised and "overseen." The feminine subject on these shows was thus inextricably wedged between permission to speak and the obligation merely to appear. As the decade passed the midpoint, a convergence of historical factors sustained the preeminence of this ambiguous woman on daytime television.

Competitive Shifts, 1955 to 1960

At 4:00 p.m. on 3 January 1956, *Queen for a Day* debuted on the NBC network and signaled the company's new directive to compete transparently for profits and billings.[2] This new daytime strategy, conceived by Robert Sarnoff and Robert Kintner, succeeded beyond all expectations. Led by *Queen*'s remarkable popularity, NBC's daytime schedule quickly reversed its losses, and the network was finally able to challenge CBS's stronghold on daylight broadcasting.[3]

This mid-decade shift at NBC marked a more general move to ramp up competition during the day and to rely more perfunctorily upon tried-and-true formulas for success. NBC and CBS, now more evenly matched in ratings power, each exploited the reliable appeal of the confessional game show. In addition to *Queen for a Day*, NBC introduced another program in 1956 that centrally integrated studio visitors into the action, an original Ralph Edwards production called *It Could Be You*. Over at CBS, *The Big Payoff* was still in full swing, and Johnny Carson's *Who Do You Trust?* was only a year away on ABC.

Although arch rivals CBS and NBC continued to dominate the daytime marketplace, the decade's middle years served as a turning point for ABC, as the network finally gained a foothold in daytime scheduling. The late-afternoon children's classic, *The Mickey Mouse Club*, which debuted in 1955 (5:00–6:00 p.m.), established a forceful ABC presence before 6:00 p.m. that was exactly the visibility the network needed to build a solid daytime schedule.[4] In 1957, Oliver Treyz, the new president of ABC, began constructing a daytime lineup by capitalizing upon this youth appeal, running Dick Clark's *American Bandstand* from 3:00 to 3:30 and again from 4:00 to 5:00. In both time slots, it drew impressive ratings[5] and created an afternoon hammock for a program more specifically directed at housewives—a fresh daytime version of *Who Do You Trust?*, starring the irrepressible Johnny Carson.

Attempting to build on this late-afternoon bonanza, ABC announced it would offer a full daytime schedule beginning in the fall of 1958 that would target the homemaker audience.[6] Peter Levathes, director of media and television at the advertising agency Young & Rubicam, devised a selling scheme for this time period, called "Operation Daybreak," that permitted clients to buy spots at a rate based on the average audience from 11:00 a.m. to 5:00 p.m. and to rotate the airing of these spots across ABC's daytime schedule. Using this innovative method, Levathes assembled $18 million from seven clients in 1958, and ABC was at last able to offer its affiliates a daytime lineup from 11:00 a.m. to 3:00 p.m.[7]

Although these prodigious efforts reaped only modest results—four key programs were canceled within six months[8]—ABC nonetheless had made a leap into daytime competition that was a necessary move for the network's long-term survival. Leonard Goldenson, ABC's programming executive during the Treyz years, avowed later, "Pete Levathes helped save ABC by putting us into daytime."[9]

In the broader picture, the industry began to acknowledge the crucial importance of daytime programming to its bottom line. As many more viewers began to turn on their sets before 5:00 p.m., daytime productions became increasingly cost-effective. When the quiz scandals decimated the networks' most profitable primetime offerings after 1958, daytime schedules assumed an even greater commercial significance.[10] Such economic imperatives deepened daytime competition among the networks—which now included upstart ABC—and after 1955 helped propagate those reliable ratings-grabbers that focused their attention on ordinary women, with *Queen for a Day* the most notorious exemplar.

Queen for a Day: "You Promised You Weren't Gonna Cry"

Gilbert Seldes rightly observed in 1954 that real versions of soap opera miseries were already available to viewers on the daytime sob shows.[11] Not only did the misery shows imitate soap opera's melodramatic storylines—"the same widows and orphans; the same deaths and trials and tribulations"[12]—sob shows also reproduced the pressures between "speech and silence" melodrama exerted on the speaking woman.[13] As Sarah Kozloff reminds us in her work on women in film, melodramas are verbally overexplicit, but they nonetheless "hinge around *the not said, the words that cannot be spoken.*" Like stage melodrama from earlier centuries, these films rely upon the "melodramatic gesture" and scenarios of "tears and fainting."[14] Confessing subjects on the misery shows likewise reverted to somatic expression when their voices failed. Women on *Queen for a Day* were encouraged, indeed *required*, to tell their personal stories, yet their narratives were controlled, interrupted, and reworked so as to accent the emotion-charged gesture.[15] Even more completely than *Strike It Rich*, *Queen for a Day* expressed in the extreme television melodrama's passions and sobs. In frequent camera close-ups, women typically gestured their distress or wept openly.

Originating on the Mutual radio network in 1945, *Queen for a Day* began simulcasting on West Coast television in the late 1940s. As noted in Chapter 2, NBC initiated its attempt to acquire *Queen for Day* in May 1952, but legal battles with Mutual delayed procurement for four more years. In 1954, NBC's Charles Barry initiated a second effort to acquire the program, enticed by *Queen*'s 17.4 ARB rating in Los Angeles, which contrasted sharply with *The Kate Smith Hour*'s meager 1.0.[16] In this round, NBC decided to wait until the program could be contracted "with no strings attached,"[17] a miscalculation that stalled negotiations for another year.

As NBC scrambled again to strengthen its deteriorating late-afternoon lineup in January 1955, talks with Mutual reached a fevered pitch. In a telegram marked "Rush, Rush, Rush, Rush," Tom McAvity, writing from NBC's corporate offices in New York, instructed his West Coast team to solve any existing problems regarding the deal for *Queen* at once: "Time is very much of the essence . . . Still think *Queen for a Day* best bet. How can we solve this? What is the problem?"[18]

Host Jack Bailey opened each episode of **Queen for a Day** *with the same question: "Would you like to be queen for a day?"* **Queen for a Day** *Souvenir Program. Private collection of Marsha Cassidy.*

The push to acquire *Queen* reached even greater intensity in March, when the show achieved "sensational ratings" in several test markets. George F. McGarrett concluded that *Queen* showed all the "symptoms of being one of the greatest smash hits in daytime television." He wrote Sam Fuller, "I have alerted the west coast boys to stay on top of this whole situation and I will . . . try to obviate any possibility of letting this slip through our fingers when it becomes available."[19]

NBC did not close the deal in time for a fall debut, but within a year of the program's launch in January 1956, *Queen for a Day* had pulled NBC out of its daytime doldrums.[20] As NBC anticipated, the show became a smash hit. *Queen*'s performance increased NBC's average afternoon rating to 10.2, up 44 percent from pre-*Queen* programming. Delivering 4,222,000 homes for NBC every day, *Queen* attracted more viewers than 20 of ABC's primetime offerings.[21] In February 1957, NBC boldly claimed that the network's triumph had fostered "the most pronounced change in afternoon television program viewing habits in the medium's history." NBC attributed the additional 750,000 sets in use per average minute between 2:30 and 5:30 ET to its programming brilliance, anchored by *Queen for a Day*.[22] By April 1957, *Time* magazine reported that nearly 10 million viewers watched the afternoon program each day, securing an audience rating of almost 50.[23]

The show's high numbers rapidly sold the alternating and multiple sponsorships that had become the daytime norm; even in advance of its premiere, *Queen* acquired 15 committed sponsors, among them television's advertising giant, Procter & Gamble, which purchased 65 quarter hours.[24] Based on estimated weekly costs for one half hour of daily programming five days a week, *Queen for a Day* spent only $25,000 on production,[25] allowing a handsome profit margin. (*Matinee Theater*, by comparison, was budgeted at twice that figure.) By the fall of 1957, Carl Lindemann considered *Queen for a Day* "the financial backbone" of NBC's daytime structure.[26]

Like *Glamour Girl* and *Strike It Rich* before it, *Queen* was scorned for honing a formula that exploited human affliction to serve industry greed. Jack Gould wrote of *Queen*'s debut on the national scene, "What hath Sarnoff wrought?"[27] Each day four women selected from the studio audience (five when the show was lengthened to 45 minutes) narrated their troubles to host Jack Bailey on the stage of the Moulin Rouge in Hollywood. While *Strike It Rich* was criticized for forcing needy people to answer arbitrary quiz questions in order to win assistance, *Queen for a Day* was lambasted for escalating the sob factor. Because the studio audience served as both interlocutor and final judge—a queen was selected on the strength of audience applause—each contestant vied to tell the most tear-jerking story possible. As a result, *Queen* attracted a steady procession of distraught contestants in dire circumstances. Former queen June Kaufman, the mother of two chronically ill children, recalled the severity of her crisis in 1958, when she appeared as a single mother in need of a wheelchair. "I was *very* emotional," she remembered. Virginia Kellman, a model on the program, confessed she learned how to "tune out" the unhappiness she observed every day. "I couldn't hardly handle hearing some of the sadness," she said.[28]

One of the program's cameramen, Ed Payne, remembered that the women in the audience were "true fans," primed to commiserate with the plight of their comrades.[29] Day after day, an audience packed with 500–800 sympathetic listeners offered a measure of solace to troubled women. Millie Brown, the very first queen ever selected on radio (in 1945), whose wish was to visit her soldier husband in Italy, felt surprised and moved when the audience applauded her story. "I was so overwhelmed that [the audience] stood up for me. I'm not an actress or anything. But I had a standing ovation."[30]

Yet *Queen*'s narrative limitations guaranteed many more unfortunate losers than ecstatic winners. "Once the Queen was elected," the show's longtime producer Howard Blake admitted, "the losers were deliberately ignored," their disappointment and tears never shown on camera.[31] The abandonment of needy contestants after the vote alarmed *Queen*'s critics, but reviewers also decried the inhumanity of the program's pre-show screening process, during which many more anguished women were cast aside daily. In a rush before the program aired, Bailey and his producers preselected winning stories and sent dozens of disappointed women back to their seats in the audience.

In April 1957, Bailey told *Time* magazine that the interviews on *Queen* were authentic and spontaneous. "We don't have any more idea than the viewer at home of what people will say," he said,[32] and Blake echoed this claim: "No candidate for Queen was ever planted, prompted, or rehearsed."[33] Payne agreed that contestants were encouraged to "tell the truth in their own words," but he also explained that producers had devised a set of checks that ensured contestants would "come across on television" and "keep those ratings up."[34] While the selection of the queen was never "phony" or "fixed," the vetting process before airtime, coupled with Bailey's active interventions on air, manipulated the tenor of each story and restricted a woman's free expressivity.

As the screening process began, producers reviewed hundreds of "wish cards" from audience hopefuls, judging each request against television's entertainment principle. According to Blake, the reason for a contestant's wish "had to make a good story." Producers narrowed the field to 20 or 25 just before airtime and, with Bailey's help, selected the contestants who "would provide the best entertainment."[35] During this process, the show's producers "stir[red] the pot," according to Payne, encouraging women to "spice up" their stories.[36] The final selection process gathered frenetic momentum as airtime approached. Out of the original 20 women, 10 were rapidly eliminated; the final five were often chosen within three minutes of the live broadcast, raising the emotional stakes even more.[37]

Familiar with the core of each woman's story, the loquacious Bailey adopted a rapid-fire interview style during the broadcast that managed each narrative arc. Exploiting his Iowa cadence of speech and idiom to appear unpretentious, he nonetheless overpowered women in his verbal transactions, permitting them to speak only in brief interludes. Bailey's experience as a circus-carnival barker and department store salesman[38] had taught him how to sustain an incessant patter that was commanding. If Warren Hull's awkward kindheartedness directed his line of questioning, Bailey's interrogations were shaped by a glib folksiness that rapidly alternated between humor and tear-making gravity. In an episode that aired on ABC 19 October 1960, typical comic pleasantries began Bailey's interview with Carol Williams.

Bailey: Have you lived in the South?

Williams: Yes, I have.

Bailey: Well, I thought there was a little Southern dialect leakin' through. Whereabouts in the South?

Williams: Well, I've lived in Long Beach. Mostly in Bakersfield.

Bailey (laughing as audience laughs): That's way south. A real Southern girl! That's 40 miles south of here . . .

In the next breath, however, Bailey asked Williams for her wish, and she explained that her five-year-old son Rickie needed educational toys and a collie dog because he recently underwent surgery to remove a brain tumor. For a moment, the pathetic story unraveled in her own words.

Williams: Last Easter Sunday they found he had a brain tumor.

Bailey: Oh, for heaven's sake.

Williams: And they operated on him that Sunday.

Bailey: Yes.

Williams: They couldn't get the roots.

Bailey: Uh-huh.

Williams: And they still didn't after radiation treatment.

Bailey: Yes.

Williams: And it's slowed him down.

Bailey: Sure, it has.

Bailey's momentary shift to the role of earnest interlocutor abruptly reversed again, however, when he joked about the benefits of a boy dog over a girl dog (no worry about puppies) and then summarily ended Williams's interview.

Appropriating the familiarity of a small-town friend, Bailey extracted a contestant's story while never relinquishing rhetorical power. A visual sign of Bailey's supremacy over speech was his possession of the wand-like microphone he waved back and forth to permit alternating talk. As Williams recited her pitiable story, the camera stayed close-up on her face while the microphone was thrust in and out of frame.

In the presence of Jack Bailey, women were tossed between expressing their most intimate stories in their own words and succumbing to his quips and paraphrases. This swift verbal parrying was standard procedure on *Queen for a Day*.

Another sign of Bailey's control over narrative outpouring occurred just before the day's voting, when the camera panned the face of each contestant in close-up. At the very moment when the audience selected a winner, Bailey was allowed a final recapitulation. Kellman believed Bailey favored certain contestants and could subtly manipulate the voting outcome. By slanting a woman's presentation or gently editorializing, Bailey had his way of "swaying the audience."[39]

To mask this firm management of contestant narratives, Bailey frequently praised a woman's speaking abilities. At the conclusion of Mrs. Singer's interview, which was fraught with nervous pauses and prodding, he exclaimed, "You told it like a million bucks!" After she won, he repeated his praise, "You're the queen! You told it right!"[40] "Telling it right" on *Queen for a Day* meant submitting one's voice to immutable constraints. As Mary Ann Doane observed about film melodrama, *Queen for a Day* "simultaneously grant[ed] a woman access to narration and with[held] it from her."[41]

Buffeted between segments of full expressivity and silence, contestants on *Queen for a Day* spoke their own true stories in mere fragments; when their words failed or were abridged, their bodies recorded suppressed sentiment. As *Time* magazine joked, one contestant seemed destined for victory because she "had all the tearmarks of a winner."[42] During every phase of the program, the television camera focused close up on these ardent responses, doggedly tracking the kinetics of distress. An intensely nervous Mrs. Singer squeezed Bailey's hand so hard during her interview that he joked about it after she won: "You like to wither my hand squeezin' it!"[43]

During another even more poignant interview, contestant Angie Ward swung between speech and uncontrollable weeping as she recited her pitiful history. The camera followed the kinetics of muted desperation in close-up, while the garrulous Bailey sustained the verbal arc.

Bailey: [Is] your home here?
Ward: Ah. Well. No. (Nervous laugh.)
Bailey: Yes and no. Where do you live most of the time?
Ward: The last six months, I've just kinda drifted [. . .] My home . . .
    (She begins to cry and turns her head away from the camera.)
Bailey: Now, now, now. You promised you weren't gonna [. . .] cry.
    That's all right. You had a pretty bad thing happen. Do you want
    to tell why you've moved since six months ago?
Ward: Um . . . (She is so choked up she can't speak.)
Bailey: I'll tell them for you, if you don't mind. Your husband—her
    husband passed away about six months ago.[44]

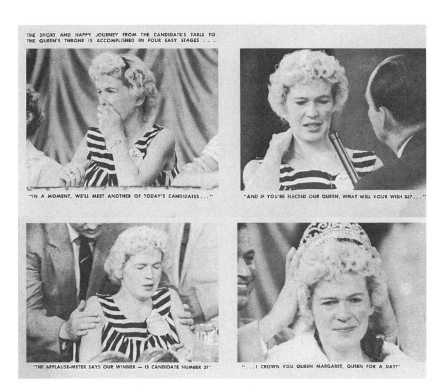

THE SHORT AND HAPPY JOURNEY FROM THE CANDIDATE'S TABLE TO THE QUEEN'S THRONE IS ACCOMPLISHED IN FOUR EASY STAGES . . .

"IN A MOMENT, WE'LL MEET ANOTHER OF TODAY'S CANDIDATES . . ."

"AND IF YOU'RE ELECTED OUR QUEEN, WHAT WILL YOUR WISH BE? . . ."

"THE APPLAUSE-METER SAYS OUR WINNER — IS CANDIDATE NUMBER 2!"

". . . I CROWN YOU QUEEN MARGARET, QUEEN FOR A DAY!"

Queen for a Day's *Souvenir Program spelled out the emotional steps to the queen's throne. Private collection of Marsha Cassidy.*

Like other guests on *Queen for a Day*, Mrs. Ward was caught in the paradox of melodrama, expressing herself in gestures of the heart, while Bailey provided the words. In this discursive split, Bailey reigned as King of the Word, talking nonstop. When Mrs. Singer was elected queen, she wept with joy, quavered as she was crowned, was unable to catch her breath as she reviewed her prizes, and finally sobbed with happiness when she won a coveted trip to Tennessee to see her disabled brother. All the while, Bailey prattled on about her winnings.

By means of these winnings, *Queen for a Day* explicitly tied the reconstitution of distressed women to material goods and beauty. Howard Blake clearly understood television's stake in the inseparable connection between the confessing subject and the marketable consumer products that were supposed to restore her. "A candidate had to want something we could plug," Blake remembered, "a stove, a carpet, a plane trip, an artificial leg, a detective agency, a year's supply of baby food."[45] For economic reasons, the panoply of gifts the queen received soon surpassed her initial wish. "[T]he more gifts we gave the Queen, the more money we made," Blake recalled, since advertisers paid for product mentions. "We *loaded* the Queens with gifts—at the rate of a million dollars a year."[46] When Mrs. Viva Birch became queen in an episode from 1960, the product presentations that ended the program lasted a total of 5 minutes and 30 seconds.[47] Day after day, troubled women were reborn as idealized middle-class homemakers, acquiring everything from dinette sets to washing machines to the improbably named "insinkerator."[48]

According to Kellman, added to the original premise of the program was the extra bonus of glamour.[49] In between the program's fragmented tales of misery were staged fashion shows, during which consultant Jeanne Cagney presented the therapeutic trappings of femininity intended to transform the anointed queen. Former queens remembered they were treated "like Miss America" and entered "a fairyland" that was "a big thrill." In the psychodynamic mode of *Glamour Girl*, the winners enjoyed a complete makeover: they were clothed in fancy gowns, covered in "thick makeup," and treated to a manicure and new hairstyle. They each experienced a "moment of celebrity" that enhanced their morale and lifted their spirits. One winner danced with Clark Gable; another met Bob Hope and Hedda Hopper at the Ice Capades; a third woman said she thought she had "died and gone to heaven" when she was introduced to movie stars. One queen remembered "the elation of it all." For these ordinary women with troubles, "[i]t was a big deal." As Kellman expressed it, "Jack Bailey made them stars."[50]

At the end of each show, the queen, now enfolded in an ermine-trimmed robe and crowned with a diamond tiara, sat in regal silence upon her dais, flanked by lovely young attendants. As Bailey and his announcer speedily pitched the virtues of the consumer goods destined to revive her, the excessive words of men rendered the queen speechless, reinscribing her into a mute tableau and the sanctioned reticence of 1950s femininity.

It Could Be You: "We Know All about You"

Earlier in the day on NBC, another popular game show featuring women's stories at its nucleus modulated the melodramatic tone of *Queen for a Day*. *It Could Be You*, produced by *This Is Your Life* innovator Ralph Edwards, accentuated a mood of fun, amusement, and humor in the telling of everyday tales. The unusual premise of *It Could Be You* was to surprise audience members in the studio and at home with funny and touching stories about themselves—and then to reward participants with gifts. As emcee Bill Leyden explained in one episode, "We don't ask" people in the audience to talk about themselves, "we tell *them*."[51] Posing as a good-natured surveillance show, *It Could Be You* gained information about participants from the show's "spies" and "investigators."[52] "Our spies tell us another child is due in August," Leyden revealed about one woman,[53] or "Lynn Hamilton, do we know things about you!"[54] With this premise at its foundation, Leyden and his prescripted monologues habitually superseded the speech of women, even though it was women's life adventures that fueled the production.

Originating from Hollywood, *It Could Be You* aired daily from 4 June 1956 to 19 December 1961,[55] featuring between six and ten pranks and anecdotes each day. According to Sue Chadwick, media consultant for Ralph Edwards Productions, a team of four writer-researchers, with the help of a script secretary, met regularly with Leyden, his producer Stefan Hatos, director Stuart Phelps, and announcer Wendell Niles to explore the personal stories of unsuspecting members of the studio and viewing audience. Aided by family relatives and employees at NBC affiliates, the writers developed a series of "acts" for each show and fully scripted each surprise. On air, Leyden read these scripts from well-concealed teleprompters attached at eye level to cameras, retelling participants' private tales of humor, embarrassment, or woe. Chadwick remembered, "After the first few shows, suggestions came from everywhere, from viewers, from station personnel, the grocery clerk, anywhere. Luncheons and just ordinary conversation produced many ideas."[56] At the close of one episode in 1956, Leyden thanked viewers for their help and praised the hard work of his research team, whose files were "loaded" with material. "Thanks, staff!" he concluded.[57]

Routinely springing into the studio audience with a microphone in hand, Leyden—labeled "the man who will amaze you with what he knows about you"—radiated a playful, teasing manner as he startled guests. "It's America's great surprise show!" announced Wendell Niles on 8 November 1956, and he pledged that Leyden, as the guardian of inside information, would "update you with what he knows about you."[58] On 11 September 1957, a typical day, Leyden entered the audience space and declared, "We're lookin' for someone who wants something . . . It's you, Penny . . . Penny Taylor, will you stand up, please?" Handing her 10 $10 bills, Leyden explained he would take one away for every question about herself she missed. "We checked into your background; we know all about you . . . You think we don't investigate!" (Penny could

*Bill Leyden, host of **It Could Be You**, surprised guests each day with anecdotes about themselves. Leyden's inside stories, compiled by a staff of researchers, unexpectedly thrust studio guests into the television spotlight. Photo courtesy Ralph Edwards Productions.*

not remember the name of her first cat and other details about her past, winning only $50.)[59] In the same jesting tone on another episode, Leyden reminded an amazed guest about the time she got out of the bathtub to get soap and her daughter teased her by saying her friend "Mr. Marlowe" was coming. Announcer Wendell Niles descended the audience steps wearing a barrel in case Mr. Marlowe ever showed up again.[60]

Paralleling the espionage in the studio, secrets were collected about members of the viewing audience as well. Each day two or three home viewers took part in the studio performance as Leyden announced they were receiving prizes at their homes—"right now." "Go to your door," Leyden told Mr. and Mrs. Charles Moody via camera, because "our spies" in Grand Rapids, Michigan, tell us it's your silver anniversary today.[61]

The constant repetition of the show's catchphrase—"It could be you!"—underscored the program's all-inclusiveness. "You," as an empty signifier, interpolated simultaneously the visitors in the studio and the viewers at home, fostering a relay of identifications. These unstable possibilities were immediately evident in the show's introductory sequence. As the camera panned an applauding studio audience, the voice of the announcer twice declared, "It could be . . . YOU!" Each time, a Zoomar camera lens and a roving spotlight isolated unsuspecting audience members in sudden close-up. The announcer's third intonation, "Or . . . it could be . . . YOU!" was pointedly redirected at the home viewer.[62] When Leyden appeared on stage, he reinforced this rotating referent by skillfully shifting his gaze from the camera to the studio audience and back again. In a double-directed look during one episode, Leyden simultaneously told the studio audience and home viewers, "Oh, what we don't know about you!" Without skipping a beat, Leyden then altered his address to speak directly through the camera to Mrs. Messer, a mother of 10, who lived on a farm near Cincinnati, where an Amana freezer was being delivered to "your door." With finesse, Leyden then broke eye contact with the camera, picked up his hand microphone, and bounded into the audience to joke with a startled participant in the audience—yet another "you."[63]

Leyden's reiteration of the "you" signifier also enforced his authority as the unquestioned "master" of surprises told in the second person. While Jack Bailey guided, paraphrased, and interpreted a woman's utterance, Leyden recited an already constructed script. Although Chadwick said Leyden was free to change and ad-lib the lines written for him,[64] the show's "you" narratives were all scripted and often dramatized. In every segment, Leyden structured a woman's story for her in the second person, and she was cast as the spectator, "narratee," and respondent to her own past.

The utter silence of women was most apparent during segments about home viewers, a common feature on *It Could Be You*. In these segments, participants appeared as mere photographs in a snapshot, if they appeared at all, and Leyden fully controlled the second-person story. Over a photograph of Miss Patti Kipper from Omaha, Nebraska, Leyden explained, "We have spies at KMTV in Omaha [who] tell us you're just about the top 4-H gal in the country . . . We know you're 16, you help mom and dad take care of your four younger brothers and sisters. We know about the fire that destroyed your home last year and also mom's sewing machine went with it . . . I know you're embarrassed about borrowing other people's sewing machines, so don't bother them any more. You're going to have a beauty." After Leyden plugged the sewing machine fully pictured on camera, he concluded, "We want you to be the 4-H national champ, Honey . . . Good luck, Patti, we're pulling for you."[65]

With in-studio guests as well, Leyden perpetuated this verbal authority, rattling off complicated anecdotes that permitted women only limited speech. In a telling example, Leyden said to Mrs. Mann from the stage, "Remember last week, you went to the movies to see the latest Mr. Magoo cartoon? You thought you were going to have a ball, didn't you?" It was soon apparent that Mrs. Mann had no access to a microphone and could not be heard, a mistake that in no way hindered Leyden's continuation. "You forgot your glasses!" he went on glibly, "We don't want you to have any trouble finding your glasses again, Mrs. Magoo, I mean Mrs. Mann, so here are some spares for you. A basketful of all sizes and shapes and styles."[66]

In many cases, the stories Leyden narrated were anchored to a dramatic set piece. Dozens of preplanned vignettes starred unsuspecting audience guests, but the heroines remained virtually silent during most of the performance, relegated to the role of astonished and passive spectators to a reenactment of their own lives.

One cleverly prefabricated act typified this quieting of studio guests. In this case, a "silent movie" recorded the life of amateur artist Marion Zimmerman, and affirmed *It Could Be You*'s sovereignty over women's speech. In a parody of a silent film, old photographs of Zimmerman were projected onto a screen and intercut with decorative titles. "AT FIRST SHE WAS A SIMPLE OUTDOOR GIRL," for example, was followed by a snapshot of Zimmerman in knee stockings. Throughout the movie, piano accompaniment embellished the photographs; the piano played "Charleston" when Zimmerman was shown dressed as a flapper. Out in the audience, Zimmerman and Leyden were seated next to each other, watching the film together. While Leyden lounged back and heckled the screen, the studio camera found Zimmerman covering her face with her program ticket, awkwardly throwing one arm across her waist, squinting, grimacing, or concealing her mouth with her hand—never certain, it seemed, whether to laugh or cry. Like other women on *It Could Be You*, Mrs. Zimmerman was consigned to the role of onlooker in her own life, and she responded with gestures of embarrassment.[67]

During other segments, *It Could Be You* added elements of tearful sentiment to its fun-filled surprises. Especially during the program's final "reunion climax," when an audience member was unexpectedly reunited with a long-lost loved one, women contestants were submitted to affecting revelations. During this "heart-warming" part of the program, three women selected from the studio audience tried to guess from aural clues the identity of the person in silhouette behind a screen. In each case, the contestants on stage reverted to unrehearsed body language when words failed. When Mrs. Ludwick was reunited with her mother, she was so flustered she was unable to speak her mother's name.[68] When Mamie Stevens began to suspect it was her beloved sister-in-law behind the screen, she tensely clasped and unclasped her hands, then impulsively grabbed the shoulder of the contestant next to her.[69] When Nancy Higley accidentally peeked and saw her mother behind the screen, her hands pressed upon her heart, then flew over to Leyden's chest.[70]

Another carefully composed scenario on *It Could Be You* veered toward the sentimentality of *Queen for a Day*. As Ann Kempel was summoned to the stage to the tune of "It's a Most Unusual Day," Leyden set the surprise in motion. "Someone here in our audience," he began (referring to Kempel), "got quite a surprise a few years ago when she hurriedly went over to someone's front door and opened it, like this." Leyden then flung open a stage door to reveal Wendell Niles, who was quickly shooed away.

Kempel was discernibly agitated by the time she arrived on stage, and she suspiciously eyed the now-closed door. "I'm nervous," she confessed to Leyden. Undaunted, Leyden determinedly recited her drama as scripted, explaining that Kempel's husband Bill, stationed in Alaska, hadn't seen their baby daughter yet. In a rapid narrative surge, Leyden then described the time Kempel mistakenly suspected that Bill (then her fiancé) was seeing another woman; to check out her suspicions, Kempel had boldly walked into the other woman's house, uninvited.

> *Leyden*: [Y]ou went right over to the house, didn't you? You walked
> right in (Leyden walks toward the stage door) and you threw open
> the door, just like this!

Behind the door is a man in uniform concealed by shadows. Surprise! It's her husband Bill! As Ann collapsed weeping into Bill's arms, the audience applauded fervently, and dramatic organ music swelled. But Leyden's story was not over yet. On cue, Bill's mother appeared from behind the curtain carrying the Kempels' sleeping infant; the baby was handed to her father for the first time, with organ music in complement, and tears of joy overflowed.[71] Yet within the whole of this emotion-charged minidrama, Ann spoke exactly 20 words, two of them "Oh!" in a muffled cry. Leyden's theatrical "you" narration rendered Ann speechless and restricted her expression of sentiment to the heartfelt gestures of melodrama.

On occasion, women singled out on *It Could Be You* did attempt to resist Leyden's authorial agency. Edna Beeman told Leyden, "I'm afraid of you . . . You know too much." Leyden draped his arm around her shoulders to reassure her, declaring, "NAH!" but, before Beeman could speak again, he immediately launched into a scripted monologue detailing the sad story of her widowhood.[72] Faye Coffey's truthfulness was tested in a wacky lie detector that looked like an electric chair and registered "TRUE" or "FALSE" to her answers. When Leyden asked her what she did with her son's baseball bat in the kitchen, she responded, "Do I have to tell?" "If you don't tell," replied Leyden, "the machine will." Coffey won a new stove when Leyden revealed she used the bat to prop closed her old oven door.[73]

Leyden's interchange with Mrs. Moropolis in 1960 demonstrated the show's ambiguous relationship to women's free expression.

> *Leyden*: Tell of the time your husband won $65 playing a [Las Vegas] slot machine and you insisted right at that moment he quit.
>
> *Moropolis*: So a gentleman came up and put in 50 cents and won the $200 jackpot. Then he said, "See, what did I tell you? I could have won $200." I said, "You should be satisfied with $65. What if you didn't get the $200 jackpot?" He said, "You should listen to me once and a while. You're always nagging, nagging, nagging."

At this point in her story, Moropolis began to laugh uncomfortably as she noticed that Leyden had turned slightly away from her, rolled his eyes, and crossed his arms in mock exasperation. He then exclaimed, "I bet he does listen to you!"[74]

Leyden's implication that Moropolis (and all women) talked too much and forced men to listen was offered as a truism even though it was he himself who spoke incessantly on *It Could Be You*. As Kozloff explains, "[W]hen women *do* talk, their speech is redefined as inconsequential, nonstop chatter."[75] Even though Leyden had instructed Moropolis to tell the story in her own way, he quickly intervened and teased her for her "feminine" wordiness.

Every day women who appeared on *It Could Be You* seemed eager to accept the compromised agency the program granted them, apparently relishing the chance to participate in a new form of leisure and to enjoy their high visibility in a far-reaching public sphere. Chadwick recalled that the show's researchers were "careful never to delve into anything unsavory or unduly embarrassing . . . We never had a guest balk."[76] "If we had," she said, "that would have shown inadequate research."[77] The women on *It Could Be You* comported themselves as good sports, accepting their role as Leyden's confederates. Because Leyden might suddenly thrust any one of them into the television spotlight, a mood of cheerful empathy among studio members prevailed. Leyden also conveyed a measure of courtesy and grace in his interactions with women. "Thank you so much," he kindly told Mrs. LeSeur and Mrs. Mann in one episode, "for letting us delve into your private lives for just a moment."[78]

While most women readily yielded to the strictures of the program, some participants managed to preserve a small measure of enunciative agency. ("I'm nervous." "You know too much." "Do I have to tell?") In one episode in 1960, studio guest Marie Vattel momentarily disrupted a well-planned setup. As she participated in a prescribed stunt onstage, she retained the role of a feminine subordinate, but her spontaneous playfulness and flirtation sent the program's fabricated scenario into disarray.

Vattel appeared in a segment of *It Could Be You* in which a surprise Hollywood star performed a stunt with an audience member. Ava Gabor, Lou Costello, Tennessee Ernie Ford, and Mickey Rooney were a few of the many secret stars who appeared in various segments.[79] On 26 March 1960, Vattel was conspicuously dressed in a maternity blouse as she joined Leyden onstage, serenaded by Hawaiian music. When Leyden handed her a hula skirt, she joked that it wouldn't fit, but she agreed to wear it anyway.

"You're on the beach," Leyden began, leading up to a tortuous pun ahead. "You're looking out over the water. A raft appears." At this moment, George Raft entered upstage behind Vattel, and Vattel was asked to guess what "raft showed up." Leyden finally turned her around to meet the famous actor, who asked if she would "dance for us."

"I'm not in any condition to do that," quipped Vattel, to the audience's amusement. Awkwardly abandoning the script, Leyden asked, "Where do you go from there? . . . It is *Mrs.* Vattel, isn't it?" Raft laughed heartily and declared, "I guess it's all right then," and Leyden warned him, "Daytime television . . . no remarks!" But Vattel mischievously diverted the conversation one more time. "How did I get up here with two such handsome men?" she teased. As Raft bowed gallantly, Leyden responded, "I'll quit there. The show's gone!"[80]

Vattel's good-natured resistance offered a brief respite from Leyden's customary dominance. In an unusual reversal, it was Leyden who was surprised, as Vattel's noticeable pregnancy forced him to discard the script. Improvising, Leyden resorted to sexual innuendo to affirm Vattel's traditional place in femininity ("It's *Mrs.* Vattel, isn't it?"), and Vattel herself relied upon the standard wiles of womanhood to speak out. Yet her flirtation as an expectant mother unnerved both Leyden and Raft, and she used this discomfort to comic advantage, intimating that a woman could be erotic and pregnant at the same time. For once, it was Leyden who was speechless.

Moments of resistance like these were notable, and pleasurable, because they were unexpected. On most days, Leyden politely but adeptly curbed the voice of the female subject.

Who Do You Trust? Your Wife?

In the fall of 1957, ABC acquired *Do You Trust Your Wife?*, previously a CBS evening program starring ventriloquist Edgar Bergen, as a new property for its daytime schedule. When the network was unable to reach an agreement with Bergen to host the program during the day, ABC turned to Johnny Carson, who obtained a release from his contract with CBS. The series premiered on 30 September 1957; a year later, it was renamed *Who Do You Trust?* and Ed McMahon was hired as Carson's announcer.[81]

The format of the daytime version required one partner of a couple to answer three quiz questions, worth $25, $50, and $75; after Carson described the topic of each question, the male partner, usually a husband, decided if he trusted himself or his wife to answer the question correctly. In the final round of the contest, the couple with the greatest winnings each day competed in a lightning round against the previous day's winners. In this segment as well, the man determined which partner would proceed to the soundproof "isolation booth" (two windowed areas on each side of the stage, set into what looked like a modest brick house) and try to win an extra $500. Another feature of the series, called the "Scrambled Name Game," incorporated home viewers. Each day, Carson randomly drew a viewer letter and telephoned the home contestant to determine if she could identify the celebrity name scrambled on a game board.

The daytime version of the program, produced by Don Fedderson, filtered the popular elements of the interview and quiz formats through the comic persona of Johnny Carson. While each episode was outlined and couples were interviewed in advance, according to a staff member at Johnny Carson Productions, the program "was basically open-ended" and "much of it was spontaneous."[82] In keeping with ABC's youth orientation, Carson perfected an onscreen persona whose jokes and antics aligned him with a likable but irreverent adolescent male. He retained an unaffected Midwestern civility toward women during interview segments, kindly complimenting a woman's hat or inquiring about the children, but the program was preferential to male contestants and unapologetically played up Carson's shenanigans.

The interstitial cartoon graphics on early episodes highlighted the male slant that was so bluntly stated in the program's original title. In one line drawing, a woman was shown driving the family car through the wall of the garage; in another, a husband was seated in an easy chair as his wife returned home from a shopping spree, overloaded with packages. In keeping with this iconography, for the first year of the program, the "you" in the title addressed an indulgent but exasperated husband who could never decide whether or not to trust his wife. Within this context, the foibles of the "little woman" were courteously, if condescendingly, indulged.[83]

Bolstering male camaraderie, Carson often joked knowingly with husbands to achieve a sexually charged laugh. John McClonnen was introduced as a "pitchman" who fast-talked customers into buying gadgets in department stores. After McClonnen confessed that he and his wife would like to have another child, Carson retorted, "Well, keep pitchin'!" and the audience, slowly catching on, began to applaud and roar with laughter.[84]

During another brief moment when Carson engaged in masculine teasing, Cindy, the program's model, wheeled in a display table topped with a large potato and a "potato stretcher," so that McClonnen could demonstrate his pitching skills. Picking up the potato, McClonnen said, "That's a real nice potato, isn't it, John?" As if on cue, Carson stood on tiptoe to get a better look at Cindy, and leered, "Yes, it certainly is!" then turned his roguish face to the studio audience for the laugh.[85] On a later episode, the female contestant was an attractive blond model, atypically a single career woman. "Things are picking up around here on the show," Carson told McMahon as he met Lola. When Lola explained she once modeled an aluminum bathing suit, Carson joked, "Two sauce pans and a roaster?"[86] In these instances and throughout the series, Carson sustained a posture of roguish innuendo that suited the program's tone of masculine fraternity.

Carson also delighted in the oddities of his guests' talents, and contestants were selected whose unusual occupations allowed for amusing conversation, usually with the husband: a butcher who was also a chiropractor, a weather insurer, a tea-taster,[87] and a fencing instructor.[88] Carson asked the chiropractor if he ever got mixed up and wrapped a patient in brown paper. In another exchange, Dr. Berkenfield, a surgeon, told Carson he "lost a patient" because he appeared on TV. Answering Carson's look of concern, Berkenfield explained that one of his older patients selected another surgeon because he didn't trust "show people." (The patness of this exchange suggests it was pre-rehearsed.)

During the quiz segments, too, masculine power (and Carson's impudence) reigned. Male contestants were granted the authority to decide which partner would answer each question. "First names of famous people" and "famous songs" were typically assigned to wives, while men tackled "U.S. history" and "world geography." Masculine expertise routinely ended each program, as male contestants squared off for the lightning round. Dr. Berkenfield retained his championship by naming in 10 seconds nine countries of Europe that were republics.[89]

With Carson in charge, *Do You Trust Your Wife?* added physical humor and farce to the quiz format, with Carson himself joining in on the slapstick. After McClonnen demonstrated the potato stretcher, for example, Carson attempted to use the gadget to peel a potato himself, pretending to stab his finger, crossing his eyes in a goofy look of pain, and finally turning the spiral-cut potato into a miniature accordion.[90] Later, Carson invited McClonnen to illustrate his sales technique by pitching Jello Instant Pudding, one of the show's sponsors. In a speedy monologue that surpassed even Leyden's pace, McClonnen delivered a torrent of words in just one minute. During the recitation, the camera pulled back to frame Carson paying close attention and reacting comically to McClonnen's every word. "Beautiful!" Carson exclaimed, applauding along with the audience after McClonnen's final rush of words. "John, I hate to follow you! A hard pitch to follow!" All the while, Mrs. McClonnen smiled and listened passively, only occasionally framed in a two-shot with her husband. As McClonnen strutted his verbosity, the little wife looked on in silent admiration.

A classic example of Carson's affinity for farce occurred earlier in the same program, when Mr. Niederkirshner, a fencing master, dueled with Carson onstage. During the interview portion, Mrs. Niederkirshner remained taciturn as Carson fooled around with her eccentric and exuberant husband.

When Carson asked Niederkirshner to explain the difference between a good fencer and a bad fencer, Carson preempted the answer by surmising, "I suppose the bad fencer is dead!" Here the energetic Niederkirshner began to kick and dodge, thrust and parry, as Carson cast the audience his now-famous look, at once befuddled and derisive. "Welcome to zoo parade, folks!"

Carson initiated the farcical duel when he asked Niederkirshner how duels start anyway, and Niederkirshner instantly exploded in pseudo-rage, claiming Carson had insulted his wife. After the men exchanged a few blows, Carson ran away and attacked Niederkirshner from behind, poking him in the buttocks. Later, Carson explained to a cheering audience, "I'm cowardly when I fight. That's the way to win. Never kick a man when he's down; he might get up."[91]

In moments like these, and on other occasions as well, Carson's slapstick served to destabilize the codes of patriarchy affirmed elsewhere, in this case making gallantry appear ridiculous and Carson an amusing weakling. On *Who Do You Trust?* Carson regularly projected a compromised masculinity that could revel in standard male banter but simultaneously convey a degree of playfulness about gendered behavior. In his own Jello Pudding commercial, Carson even assumed the role of housewife as he demonstrated how to make pineapple-strawberry parfait, with hapless results. The cellophane wrapper fell into the bowl, he added the pineapple too soon, and he flubbed his lines. "You simply add one 'crup,' uh, 'cup' [of pineapple]." Carson's spontaneous gender reversal ultimately redeemed the commercial, however, as he shifted seamlessly from competent homemaker to inept male in the kitchen. "If you have a crup in the house, add that," he improvised. "It doesn't make any difference." Laughing at himself, he concluded, "It looks great! . . . Not like *I* made it! Get some. For my sake! Next time you shop!"[92]

While Carson's comically ambiguous masculinity softened the blow, the format of *Who Do You Trust?*, with its celebration of male speech and a reliance upon visual clowning, succeeded in marginalizing women as subsidiary players. With Carson in command, women spoke less, laughed and listened more.

The Big Payoff: "Ladies Love Fashion"

If *Who Do You Trust?* attenuated women's speech to exult in masculine escapades, *The Big Payoff* limited a woman's personal expression to luxuriate in the tropes of feminine attractiveness. *The Big Payoff* allied women almost exclusively with what Kozloff has described as "bodies/beauty/silence."[93]

The Big Payoff serves as a fitting final case study here not only because the program spanned almost the entire decade of the 1950s (31 December 1951 to 16 October 1959) but also, and more significantly, because its format so fully exposed the enduring schism beneath TV's representations of the decade's female subject. More than the other three programs discussed in this chapter, *Payoff* celebrated the decorative woman, an archetype of beauty whose language was habitually constrained. At the center of this tension between speech and display was the striking figure of cohost Bess Myerson, Miss America 1945. In her role as coanchor, Myerson was granted the power to speak, but her status as a glamorous beauty queen simultaneously elevated her to preeminence as visual spectacle. Myerson thus embodied the very conflicts all women who appeared on 1950s television confronted.

Payoff was Walt Framer's second daytime project, and the program remained one of television's most successful properties across the 1950s. First airing weekdays on NBC from 3 to 3:30, the program moved to its permanent home on CBS in 1953 in the same time slot, where it thrived until the network terminated all big-money quiz shows after the scandals.[94] By 1955, at the end of the show's third season, the series had already given away 104 mink coats and trips to Europe, 62 automobiles, and $975,000 worth of merchandise.[95] In 1956, *Variety* called *Payoff* "one of the most fabulous money stories in daytime television"; in combination with *Strike It Rich*, Framer was netting $1 million per year, with Colgate investing $4 million in the dual sponsorship.[96]

The premise of the program required men to speak on behalf of women, first by submitting a letter explaining why "his" woman "deserve[d] a reward,"[97] and then on the air, when men pretold a woman's predica-

*Costars of **The Big Payoff**, Bess Myerson (1951–1959) and Bob Paige (1957–1959), divided hosting duties according to gender, with Paige conversing with men and Myerson describing fashion and beauty products to women. In December 1958, Myerson was about to "break a record" for women hosts on CBS by completing her seventh consecutive year on daytime television. Private collection of Marsha Cassidy.*

ment for her. In early versions, the female contestant did not even arrive on set until after her male partner had explained the couple's dilemma to host Randy Merriman. Contestant Frank Stillman told Merriman man-to-man, "I'm in the middle of a new business venture and it costs money to get married these days and I'd like to give [Dorothy] a mink coat and a trip to Paris."[98] On later shows, the woman contestant was sidelined on a raised platform at stage left, seated in the "Colgate Wishing Chair," while Bob Paige interviewed her partner. On an episode that aired early in 1958, Florence and Robert Conway were the contestants. Although Paige briefly included Mrs. Conway in deferential questioning, the two men commanded on-air voice and visual dominance as they were distanced to her right. Camera work heightened this masculine/feminine divide, the camera framing Mrs. Conway either singly or positioned off to the side in a three-shot but recording the men together in a medium two-shot as they conversed. Before long, the men's conversation evolved into an interchange about Mr. Conway's background, career, and experiences in New York City.[99]

During masculine exchanges like these, women's words and women's stories all but disappeared. As Paige talked with Sergeant Charles Buchanan on another episode, Buchanan recounted the details of his war career, his awards for good writing, and his outstanding honors in the Army Air Corps. In this typical focus on male achievement, the woman's story was trivialized or even forgotten. For the Buchanans, the sergeant's heroism appeared to be their only qualification for competing.[100]

If motives were offered on *Payoff*, no matter how trifling, they were offered by men, who often expressed a desire to repay a woman's many sacrifices. An airline pilot lamented, "We've been married 24 years and [my wife's] never had a home of her own"; a longshoreman explained, "My [work]clothes come first ... I go through an awful lot of them, handling acids, grease, tar, and cables." In the constituent terms of *Payoff*'s formula, men endeavored to compensate women for the insufficiencies in their lives by attaining for them all the luxuries of feminine embellishment.[101]

From its inception, *Payoff* revered material adornment. In the opening moments of an early episode, the announcer declared, "Yes, it's *The Big Payoff*, where each day, Monday through Friday, a man may earn for the lady of his choice, clothes from head to toe." Over harp music, the camera framed an array of products she might win, including shoes, hosiery, jewelry, lingerie, "stunning dresses," "chic hats by the world's greatest designers," and matched luggage. Culminating this list was "the big payoff itself," a trip to "gay Paree" and "the breathtaking gift of a woman's dream, a beautiful mink coat." As organ and harp music swelled to reprise the program's theme song, the camera framed the back of Bess Myerson as she modeled the coat and fanned out its pleating.[102] With an elegant twirl, Myerson then turned to face the studio audience,

Bess Myerson, crowned Miss America in 1945, became **The Big Payoff**'*s permanent beauty queen, adorned daily in a lavish mink coat. Private collection of Marsha Cassidy.*

and the program's overdetermined message was greeted with thunderous applause: on *Payoff*, women aspired to Miss America glamour and display, aided by their "handsome knight in shining armor."[103]

By 1958, the program had codified its purpose even more explicitly, calling itself "television's only daily parade of elegant fashions" and "the show with the fabulous prizes." By now Bess Myerson's routine costume was a ball gown, and she had matured into "America's lady in mink," flaring the coat each day at the top of an elegant staircase and then descending dramatically to join Bob Paige center stage.[104]

Before each quiz question, Myerson's task was to describe the lavish goods to be acquired—all accoutrements of 1950s femininity. Sometimes she displayed the fashionable products exclusively to the seated wife, who smiled and nodded in longing approval. At other times, fashion segments were more elaborately produced, the glamorous prizes presented sumptuously on the staircase or in front of a stage curtain. Some segments achieved a theatrical storyline of their own, narrated by Myerson and acted out by staff models. A model sang "Just You, Just Me" during an abridged love story, as Myerson narrated in voice-over the story of shy Judy's love for a ventriloquist (and the stunning clothes worn by Judy's rivals). In another example, three staff models played musical chairs with a male contestant as Myerson described the women's stylish outfits. Other fashion segments created an atmosphere rather than a story. One segment mixed "exotic music of the East" with images of Oriental sculptures and chiaroscuro lighting; models displayed their opulent clothes as they posed on the darkened staircase. In each case, the spectacle of feminine beauty was glorified.

During the quiz segments especially, women were nonessential, their speech suppressed. As questions were asked and answered, the camera captured the host and male contestant in two-shots, while the woman, sitting passively to the side, was only glimpsed in reaction close-ups. Women on *Payoff* admired male knowledge from afar and waited with eager anticipation to receive the bounty of femininity's masquerade. The array of feminine treasures promised Mrs. Conway in three successive payoffs typified this coveted opulence: a turquoise velvet dress, gold Monet jewelry, a flowered pillbox hat, a two-piece dress ensemble, a luxury handbag, a pure silk tissue taffeta dress with a harem skirt "designed for romance," a printed designer cap, a fitted carryall by Evans, My Sin perfume by Lanvin, Trapeze sports shoes, an orchid corsage, Fifi hosiery, a turban hat, a basic beige water-repellent coat, and a two-piece linen chemise.[105] Glamorous figuration subsumed all else on *Payoff* and consigned women to compulsory reticence.

Bess Myerson herself served as an ideal incarnation of the pressure between speech and spectacle daytime television imposed on 1950s women. As a rare female cohost, Myerson possessed the power of utterance usually reserved for men: She addressed the camera directly; she bantered with the host and even dared to correct him (the next show is "Monday," not "tomorrow"); she provided frames for contestants' stories during her brief introductions; and, in voice-over, she narrated fashion tableaux and product vignettes. On her successful primetime program, *I've Got a Secret* (1952–1964), hosted by Garry Moore, Myerson spoke on an equal plane with panelists noted for their verbal repartee (wits like Steve Allen, Jayne Meadows, Betsy Palmer, and Henry Morgan). During the day, however, in contrast to NBC's loquacious Arlene Francis, Myerson repressed her well-known capacity for self-expression.

During her reign as the country's first Jewish Miss America in 1945–1946, Myerson had gained a reputation for being outspoken. A graduate of Hunter College, Myerson was widely praised for her dignity, intelligence, and eloquence, but she had encountered bitter anti-Semitism as America's beauty queen. By the winter of 1945, she recognized that her Jewish heritage was creating real difficulties for the pageant and its sponsors. "They had wanted me," she recalled, "because I was a lady, educated, well spoken . . . However, some of the people I had begun to meet didn't want me because I was a Jewish lady." Shunned at "restricted" clubs, openly insulted by anti-Semites, and rejected for jobs because corporations declined association with her "Jewish name," Myerson began to feel "deeply frustrated." Although outwardly she remained "sweet and dignified and calm," she admitted, "[i]nwardly I felt a rage that has never left me. . . I was trapped in the disguise I myself had agreed to wear."[106]

To appease her anger and to cross over into "the serious world" she aspired to enter, she joined forces with the Anti-Defamation League of B'nai B'rith to speak out publicly against bigotry. Her frequent and highly publicized appearances, in person and on radio, drew harsh recrimination from the Miss America Pageant's director, Lenora Slaughter, who feared Myerson had fallen into the clutches of Jewish Communists from New York's Garment District.[107] Ignoring Slaughter's accusations, Myerson unflinchingly continued to link her antiracist homilies to the ideals of the Pageant and to authentic beauty: "You can't be beautiful and hate," one speech began. "Miss America represents all America. It makes no difference who she is, or who her parents are. Side by side, Catholic, Protestant, and Jew stand together . . . [I]f we want a strong, united America pushing on toward its unlimited horizons, there can be no place for prejudice in our nation . . . or in our hearts."[108]

It was exactly this spirited stance against prejudice that led to the initiation of her television career. Walt Framer heard Myerson speak at an Anti-Defamation League meeting and contacted her when he launched *Payoff* in 1951. According to Myerson, Framer, a Jew himself, believed television needed people from different ethnic backgrounds "to support the variety and diversity of America."[109]

As Cold War tensions heightened during the early 1950s, the paranoia McCarthyism had aroused in regard to media celebrities curbed the expression of sentiments like Myerson's. By mid-decade Myerson, now a single mother, keenly feared the loss of her career: "I was working in a business that regularly replaced on-camera people like me. During the early 1950s, dozens of my colleagues had been whisked into oblivion for holding political opinions not far different from those I had been raised on."[110] Mindful of these risks, Framer and his producers on *Payoff* downplayed Myerson's past reputation for frank speaking and, instead, relegated her to the role of a permanent Miss America—"Miss Bess," the royal lady in mink. The luxurious coat she modeled with such flair each day represented a reassuring mantle of femininity that mitigated any latent threat from her earlier powers of speech.

The image of Myerson as erotic object was especially promoted by her longtime cohost Randy Merriman. On one program, Merriman said, "Ladies love fashions . . . [and you men like] such beautiful things as Bess Myerson." Later, when Mr. McPherson was about to answer the final quiz question to win the mink coat and a trip to Paris, Merriman said to Myerson as she delivered the game envelope, "Bess, a little kiss for luck at a big moment like this?" As Myerson drew the envelope to her lips, McPherson leaned over and kissed *her*. Chagrined, Myerson turned to the camera and said, "We got our cues mixed," and Merriman joked to McPherson, "I must remind you, you answer the question first before you get *paid off*!"[111]

The elegance of Myerson's body, her height (almost six feet), her flawless complexion and features, her graceful carriage,[112] the eroticism of the fur coat, and her position at the pinnacle of the staircase, all signified a "woman on a pedestal," a sexualized spectacle. Treasured as a coveted object adorned to please men, Myerson was allowed to speak on television, but only as a subordinate. Daytime television effectively inhibited her outspoken ways, and Myerson found herself trapped again in the disguise of beauty she had agreed to wear. Like all the other women who populated the daytime airwaves, Myerson was tossed between utterance and display.

Watching, Listening

Overshadowed by the language of men, women on 1950s daytime television were obliged to speak, as Bess Myerson was, but their voices were constrained within disciplining frames. The tear-making strictures of *Queen for a Day*, overproduced vignettes on *It Could Be You*, *Who Do You Trust?*'s tomfoolery, and *The Big Payoff*'s obsession with glamour— all served to compromise a woman's enunciative power. In contrast to the "perfect listener" Kozloff finds in hosts who deferentially interview celebrities,[113] Jack Bailey, Bill Leyden, Johnny Carson, Randy Merriman, and Bob Paige all diverted women's words to their own ends. At the same time, the camera work on these programs focused a constant attention on women's bodies, recording them as variously distraught, overexcited, embarrassed, passive, amused, or merely ornamental.

This conflictual portrait of the female subject implicated home viewers as well, catching them in the same double bind. On the one hand, they were cast as voyeurs and eavesdroppers. Day by day, half hour after half hour, homemakers were encouraged to listen in on the intimate experiences of other women, overhearing their reprocessed stories and furtively studying facial muscles, unguarded gestures, and nervous smiles for secret clues to the woman's true feelings. In this regard, daytime television inevitably positioned home viewers as voiceless observers, much as the women on the shows were treated. Yet audience participation programs also promised housewives that someday they, too, might get "dolled up" and join the fun in a television studio or appear as a hopeful contestant under the searching eye of the TV camera. Viewers, too, were invited to experience the conundrum of televised femininity.

Was this incessant foregrounding of the schism in female subjectivity repressive, or did it open up a site for what second-wave feminists in the next decade would call "consciousness raising"? Surely the overuse of the pronoun "you" in the telling of women's stories (by men) offered viewers "a subjectivity that is held by no one, or may be filled by anyone," in White's terms,[114] thereby granting viewers a space for identification. Certainly a televisual flow that so consistently perpetuated the repression of women's speech served at a deeper level to expose and censure patriarchal dominance. Daytime programs of the 1950s that embarrassed women on a regular basis or drubbed them into silence uncovered the predicaments of gender inequities in postwar America.

As hundreds of women spoke and appeared on television every day, millions of women around the country were drawn to their sets to watch and listen. During the course of the 1950s, the nation's newest apparatus for feminine leisure successfully lured women both to the television studio and to America's living room sofas. Yet participation in this new enjoyment ironically obliged women to reexperience on a daily basis the subjugation of the female subject and the frustrations of repressed speech.

Daytime television of the 1950s beamed into domestic life a fresh paradox, one that celebrated the medium's promise for female expressivity, empathy, and fun, but at the same time demanded women's compliance with a femininity that was split between access to liberating speech and a retreat to spectacle and display.

9

Conclusion
Visions of Femininity

Well before soap opera's plotlines dominated daytime schedules, women's voices, women's bodies, and women's stories were already populating the new small screen. In the industry's effort to cajole women to turn their TV sets on during the day, television offered up an array of feminine possibilities. Attempts to embody an idealized television hostess—in the outmoded figure of Kate Smith, the ambiguous but promising persona of Arlene Francis, or the silenced perfection of Bess Myerson—were augmented by the camera's eager focus on the "ordinary" homemaker in all her emotional swings. From the smiling figures on shows like *Art Linkletter's House Party* and *Who Do You Trust?* to images of misery on *Strike It Rich*, *Glamour Girl*, and *Queen for a Day*, visions of everyday femininity swept across daytime broadcasting, projecting a full range of affect, from gaiety to despair. In these multifarious representations, daytime television performed and negotiated the hopes and disappointments of 1950s womanhood. From breakfast time to dinnertime, television exhorted viewers "to be women, remain women, become women," to paraphrase Simone de Beauvoir in 1949.[1]

As a portal to the future, 1950s daytime television was ambiguously Janus-like. While programmers turned to radio greats from the past to attract audiences—stars like Kate Smith, Arlene Francis, the charm boys, and all of misery's adjudicators—television simultaneously introduced new talent and fresh faces. Likewise, while daytime television glanced back at the virtues demanded of strong women during a time of war, the new medium also celebrated the decade's newest hopes for the forward-looking woman—domestic bliss, the gratifications of consumerism, and appealing new possibilities for personal glamour, beauty, and charm.

In the quest to establish the television habit as a new form of leisure during the day, programmers also looked to both the past and the future. Copying radio, the decade's many audience participation shows effectively promoted a circular interplay between public and domestic entertainment, sanctioning the pleasures of the woman traveler in a newly formulated space of leisure in the studio and a homemaker's parallel satisfactions at home. With *The Kate Smith Hour* and *Home*, NBC also turned to familiar radio staples, but both programs transformed the variety and homemaking formats into spectacular daytime enterprises, striving to attract the isolated housewife to her TV set with extravagant televisual appeals. The lavish *Matinee Theater* promoted the joys of watching daytime television with an additional lure. Because the series exemplified a valued new genre, one that was heralded as ushering in television's future, the series positioned "sofa time" as a well-earned hour of relaxation and uplift for the discerning homemaker. The guile of Janus succeeded in drawing viewers to their sets. By 1959, countless women were "held captive by a normal, healthy addiction to TV in the daytime," as *TV Guide* expressed it.[2]

Overarching this revolution in feminine leisure were the decade's rigid notions of taste values. Ongoing discourse debated whether daytime television was to be a mere extension of radio's denigrated feminine sphere, replicating soap opera, audience participation shows, game shows, and sob shows, or a site for superior programming that offered women cultural uplift. *Home* designated itself as an enlightened version of the country's more lackluster homemaking shows; and it was in opposition to the stigma already attached to soap opera that NBC cultivated *Matinee Theater*. At the antipode, *Strike It Rich, Glamour Girl*, and *Queen for a Day* were snarled in a series of ongoing controversies about exploitation and bad taste. When these formats are considered in retrospect, however, their "bad taste" can be attributed to a double bias: not only did they appear to violate what now seem arbitrary aesthetic principles associated with upper-middlebrow "quality," they also dared to expose feminine discontentment.

For the children who grew up with television during the 1950s and for their mothers, the programs at the center of this book have not been forgotten. In casual conversation about these shows, I have often witnessed a sudden flash of memory, as friends recall vivid details about programs they viewed as children almost 50 years ago. One woman remembered watching *The Kate Smith Hour* with a beloved aunt, who adored Smith in part because she was a large woman like herself. Another was able to mimic with precision Jack Bailey's opening line, "Would *you* like to be *queen* for a *day*?" Many friends associated watching daytime television with staying home sick from school, their mothers nursing them with Bayer aspirin and Campbell's soup. Others recalled the exact musical phrasings of Smith's "God Bless America" or the awe they felt when Myerson modeled the much-admired but seemingly unattainable mink coat. Arthur Godfrey's intonations, the well-modulated voice of Arlene Francis, the mesmerizing tales of woe on *Strike It Rich*, the vision of a young boy tearfully reunited with a lost dog on *It Could Be You*, and even the theme song from *Art Linkletter's House Party* were among the indelible recollections brought into consciousness in an instant. During the casual routines of everyday life in the 1950s, television left a firm imprint.

Many of the women who would remember these programs most warmly are present now only in the hearts of others: my mother-in-law, who once plotted (unsuccessfully) to become a contestant on *Queen for a Day*; my own mother, who told me years ago she didn't know why, but she sometimes felt guilty watching TV during the day (yet often enjoyed *Arthur Godfrey Time, House Party, Queen for a Day,* and *It Could Be You*). Ostensibly, television was a trivial part of their lives, providing a mere backdrop for the genuinely vital activities of mothering and home-making. Yet every day the texts of daytime television and the omnipresence of hundreds of women on the small screen offered the postwar generation new answers to the question, What does it mean to be a woman in America? My purpose has been to ask this question within the context of the decade's historical shifts in ideology and to unravel the ways in which industry forces, the genres of broadcasting, and a woman's revised position within American patriarchy all came together on 1950s daytime television.

If one adopts what Joanne Meyerowitz calls the "victim" approach to 1950s feminist history,[3] which considers the era a dark age for women's progress, daytime television can be dismissed as yet another disseminator of regressive thinking, a force that simply sought to retrain women as domestic workers and to position them anew as glamorous dolls and voracious consumers. Yet a close reading of daytime's diverse modes and texts supports the view that "1950s television was not based on a simple consensus ideology," in Lynn Spigel's words.[4] Daytime programming's volatility, ongoing contentions over feminine representations, and ambiguities attached to the speaking female subject destabilized postwar dogma and made hegemony unachievable. In the inescapable connection between women's private lives and the public world of gendered politics as seen on television, patriarchy and the dissatisfactions it generated were broadcast every day.[5] As Gloria Jean Masciarotte observed about early *Oprah*, there was "no area of politics that [was] not personal and no space where the personal [was] exempt from politics."[6] Within this context, daytime television can be understood as part of a modified history that reclaims the "backlash" epoch of the 1950s as a necessarily conflictual prelude to the raising of women's consciousness and to the advent of second-wave feminism in the 1970s.[7]

"Women's History is a new vantage point," Gerda Lerner wrote in 1979, "a stance, a way of looking at traditional material with new questions."[8] Applying this approach, Lerner not only advocated telling the stories of notable women who had been omitted from official (male) histories but also encouraged addressing women's history as "the study of a separate women's culture."[9] By approaching daytime television as a designated repository for women's culture, this volume has sought to retrieve not only the traces of TV's female celebrities but also the phantasms of those everyday women who spoke, laughed, sighed, and wept on the decade's luminescent screen.

Notes

The following abbreviations are used in the notes:

AMP "The Albert McCleery Papers," Arts Library Special Collections, Collection 98, University of California at Los Angeles
JFM Collection of J. Fred MacDonald and Associates, Chicago, IL
KSC The Kate Smith Collection, Howard Gotlieb Archival Research Center, Boston University, Boston, MA
MBC Museum of Broadcast Communications, Chicago, IL
MTR Museum of Television and Radio, Beverly Hills, CA
NBCR The National Broadcasting Company, Inc. Records, 1921–1969, Wisconsin Historical Society, Madison, WI
UCLA Radio and Television Archives, University of California at Los Angeles

Chapter 1

1. Sterling and Kittross, 656–657.
2. McCarthy, *Ambient Television*, 29–62. *Variety* estimated that in the spring of 1948 each television in a tavern drew an average of 25 viewers. See "Tele's Growth in Key Cities," *Variety*, 12 May 1948: 31.
3. "Sports Crowd Drama in May's Listing of New York Audience Pull," *Variety*, 23 June 1948: 25.
4. In September (Sterling and Kittross, 295).
5. "Radio Index—Top Night and Day Shows," *Variety*, 31 March 1948: 38; see George Rosen, "Radio Split on Video Future," *Variety*, 31 March 1948: 1, which measures radio households at 40 million in 1948.
6. "Taverns in Lead Only at Start," *Variety*, 12 May 1948: 31; McCarthy, *Ambient Television*, 53.
7. Boddy, 51.
8. Sterling and Kittross, 658.
9. Ibid., 633.
10. "The Broadcast Audience in 1959," *Broadcasting*, 9 Feb. 1959: 101.
11. See Friedan, 9, 15, 43.
12. Ryan, 41–42.
13. See Rupp and Taylor, vii; Ryan, 9–51.
14. "Radio Index—Top Shows."
15. By 1971, 42 percent of the overall daytime schedule belonged to the serials (Sterling and Kittross, 653).

16. These numbers are derived from Sterling and Kittross, 652–653.

17. Gilbert Seldes, "New Bubbles for Soap Opera," *New York Times Magazine*, 12 Sept. 1954: 25. The number of serials shot up significantly in 1965 (Sterling and Kittross, 653).

18. These figures are derived from the statistics compiled by Sterling and Kittross, 652–653. Children's programs have been subtracted from totals.

19. Allen, 125.

20. Ibid., 124.

21. Quoted in ibid., 123.

22. Kristen Hatch, "Constructing the '50s Housewife," paper presented at Console-ing Passions, 28 April 1996, Madison, WI.

23. "These Are My Children," *Variety*, 9 Feb. 1949: 34.

24. Hyatt, 469.

25. Ibid., 156.

26. Seldes, 25.

27. Allen, 125.

28. "Rating Histories, CBS Daytime TV Programs," 1953, NBCR, Box 377, Folder 6.

29. "Katz Pitches Daytime for Cigarettes," *Broadcasting/Telecasting*, 28 May 1956: 46.

30. "Wednesday Television Programs," *Chicago Daily Tribune*, 2 March 1955, Sec. 2: 2.

31. See Cassidy, "Sob Stories."

32. Beadle, 206.

33. See Chap. 2; Fink, 82; *Chicago's Very Own at 40.*

34. See Cassidy and White.

35. Brunsdon, 1. Brunsdon records the groundbreaking criticism contributed by Robert Allen, Ien Ang, Christine Geraghty, Dorothy Hobson, Carol Lopate, Terry Lovell, Michele Mattelart, Tania Modleski, and Ellen Seiter, while her extensive bibliography documents the contributions of dozens of other scholars.

36. Brooks, 4.

37. See White; Joyrich; Kozloff, *Invisible Storytellers*; Ang.

38. See Haralovich; White, 9–10, 14–15.

39. Haralovich, 61–62.

40. May, 173–174.

41. "Moore for Housewives," *Time*, 2 Feb 1953: 47.

42. Spigel, *Make Room for TV*, 95–96.

43. Boddy, 20–21; Spigel, *Make Room for TV*, 75, 78.

44. *The Bob Crosby Show*, 16 Nov. 1953.

45. Bogart, 111.

46. Carl Lindemann Jr., attachment to memo to Mort Werner, 4 Apr. 1957; text of Rod Erickson's "Speech before the Canadian Association of Radio and Television Broadcasters, 27 March 1957": 2, NBCR, Box 400, Folder 8.

47. Ripley's work is cited in Bogart, 113.

48. "Success Story," 25 Oct. 1956, NBCR, Box 400, Folder 9.

49. *Arthur Godfrey Time*, with guest host Peter Lind Hayes, circa 1952.

50. *It Could Be You*, 8 Nov. 1956.

51. NBC-TV Promotion for *Matinee Theater*, Jan. 1956, NBCR, Box 400, Folder 9.

52. Thomas E. Coffin, memo to H. M. Beville Jr., "Attention in Viewing Matinee Theater," 8 June 1956, NBCR, Box 400, Folder 9.

53. "Queen for a Day: Housewives' Schedule Wrecker," *Look*, 1 Apr. 1958: 120.

54. Gordon Cotler, "That Strange TV Studio Audience," *New York Times Magazine*, 16 May 1954: 39.

55. Quoted in Boddy, 80.

56. Boddy, 80.

57. See Munson for a discussion of virtual neighborhoods in later talk shows.

58. Brown, 190.

59. Hansen, 118.

60. 21 May 1957.

61. Interview with the author, 16 July 2001, Beverly Hills, CA.

62. See Cotler, 19; Milton Bracker, "No Question about Quiz Shows," *New York Times Magazine*, 26 July 1953: 17.

63. Cotler, 39.

64. *It Could Be You*, 3 April 1956; 8 Nov. 1956; 21 May 1957.

65. McCarthy, "Outer Spaces," 89.

66. See Cassidy, "Sob Shows," for a fuller discussion.

67. Macdonald.

68. Ibid., 62.

69. Ibid., 63–64.

70. Lynes.

71. Macdonald, 72.

72. Lynes, 23, 25.

73. "High-brow, Low-brow, Middle-brow."

74. Sargeant, "In Defense of the High-Brow," *Life*, 11 April 1949: 102.

75. Macdonald, 71.

76. See Spigel, *Welcome to the Dreamhouse*, 287 and Boddy, 80.

77. Bourdieu, 325–326.

78. Ibid., 323.

79. Lynes, 28.

80. Quoted in Boddy, 149.

81. Quoted in Jon Bruce, "How Daytime TV Can Change Your Life," 2 March 1956: 46, clipping in AMP, Box 1, Folder 4.

82. Bourdieu, 327.

83. Ibid., 294. Spigel documents the process of this refusal during the 1960s, when critics directed their aesthetic gaze at television afresh to admire a blurring of the high and low in a new postmodern imaginary (*Welcome to the Dreamhouse*, 267, 284–297).

84. Spigel, *Welcome to the Dreamhouse*, 290.

85. See Boddy, 65–92.

86. Marling, 9.

87. May, 75.

88. Marling, 10, 15.

89. Quoted in ibid., 9.

90. Marling, 15.

91. Fashions received 646 mentions. "Cooking" (617) and "Household Hints" (615) were close behind. Cited in Sternberg, 124–125.

92. Peiss, 242, 244–245.

93. Ibid., 245, 248.

94. Ibid., 245–246.

95. Marling, 15.

96. "Fashions on Parade," *Variety*, 14 April 1948: 26.

97. Runyon, 364–365.

98. "Individually Yours," *Variety Review Book*, 9 March 1949.

99. Weinstein, 10, 17–19.

100. Mann, 47.

101. Ibid., 49–59.

102. *Queen for a Day*, 19 Oct. 1960.

103. Ganas.

104. *It Could Be You*, 26 March 1960.

105. "Tele Visions: Some Beauty Contest Winners You See on TV," *TV Guide*, 10 March 1956: 20–21.

106. "Glamor May Soon Outdazzle Hollywood," *TV Guide*, 10 April 1953: 11–12.

107. "The 'Miss America' Everybody Knows," *TV Guide*, 26 March 1955: 15.

108. Ibid., 17.

109. "The Charm Boys," *Time*, 15 Feb. 1954: 78.

110. Francis, *That Certain Something*.

111. Francis, "Just Be Yourself," 6.

112. Ibid.

113. Boddy, 81.

114. S. Murray, 196.

115. Ibid., 192.

116. See Mann, 55; Spigel, *Make Room for TV*, 84; S. Murray, 197–198.

117. "Profits and Lassies," *TV Guide*, 15 Dec. 1956: 4–5.

118. Ganas.

119. White includes daytime's "couples" shows, Shop-at-Home television, televangelism, and the plots of primetime drama.

120. White, 8, 10.

121. Ibid., 67.

122. Cassidy, "Visible Storytellers."

123. Kozloff, *Overhearing Film Dialogue*, 247.

124. Ibid., 240.

125. Ibid., 244.

126. Doane, 54.

127. Elsaesser, 88–89.

128. See Joyrich, 136, 140.

129. The year 1948 saw the debut of this enormously popular format in primetime, beginning with DuMont's *Major Bowes' Amateur Hour* in March, followed by Milton Berle's *Texaco Star Theatre* on NBC and Ed Sullivan's *Toast of the Town* on CBS. See George Rosen, "'Vaudeo' Comes of Age in Texaco Show: Seen Outlet

to Vast Talent Pool," *Variety*, 16 June 1948: 30; "Tale of 2 Cities," *Variety*, 20 Oct. 1948: 27.

130. The straightforward quiz show, which reduced or omitted the element of personal confession and chiefly featured a sequence of questions and answers, is mentioned in this volume only in passing. See the work of Thomas DeLong, John Fiske, and Morris Holbrook for discussions of these games of knowledge.

Chapter 2

1. Programming for children during the day encompasses a vital but separate field of scholarly inquiry.

2. For a full discussion of network formation, see Boddy, 42–62; Schwoch; Auter and Boyd.

3. Boddy, 51, 115.

4. "Webs in Race for Affiliates," *Variety*, 24 March 1948: 31.

5. Boddy, 115.

6. "Teles' 'Illegitimate Networks,'" *Variety*, 15 Sept. 1948: 29.

7. Boddy, 115.

8. See Weinstein, 8.

9. Fink, 82; *Chicago's Very Own at 40*.

10. Sternberg, 124.

11. See Marshall and Frazier, 14.

12. Sternberg, 211. *Woman's World*, on the other hand, was canceled just six months after its debut for lack of sponsorship ("WBKB Drops Daytimer," *Variety*, 27 Oct. 1948: 27).

13. Hardenbergh, 27.

14. Margaret McKeegan's study is quoted in Pennell, 107.

15. Pennell, 107.

16. Runyon, 365.

17. Spigel, *Make Room for TV*, 80.

18. Weinstein, 4–23.

19. Halper, 141.

20. Williams.

21. O'Dell, 208.

22. Author's telephone interview with a former WCCO staff member, 11 Jan. 1996.

23. Matera, 109–110.

24. Beadle.

25. Gloria and David Rosenberg provided this information.

26. Halper, 148.

27. M. Murray.

28. See Cassidy and White.

29. "I Remember Ruth" response forms, collected as part of the exhibit "Ruth Lyons, Cincinnati's First Lady of Broadcasting," held at the Cincinnati History Museum, 4 Oct. 1995 to 1 Jan. 1996, in Ruth Lyons Project Box, Cincinnati Historical Society, Cincinnati, OH.

30. See Cassidy and White.

31. The original show aired twice a week and was hosted by Claude Kirchner. See Sternberg, 213.

32. "Hi Ladies," *Variety Review Book*, 22 Nov 1950.

33. "Bob and Kay," *Variety*, 26 July 1950: 37.

34. "Ransom Sherman Show," *Variety*, 12 July 1950: 26.

35. "Ransom Sherman Show," *Variety*, 18 Oct. 1950: 29.

36. Ibid.

37. A year later it reappeared on rival station WBKB in a truncated 15-minute format three days a week. "Ransom Sherman Show," *Variety*, 24 Oct. 1951: 43.

38. "Bob and Kay Show," *Variety*, 29 April 1953: 33.

39. "Bob and Kay with Eddie Doucette," *Variety*, 9 Feb. 1955: 36.

40. Tommy Bartlett gained such esteem as emcee that he left *Hi Ladies* to host the popular network program *Welcome Travelers*, which attracted audiences in the afternoons for another four years—on NBC, then CBS (Hyatt, 457–458).

41. See "Where to Dial Today," *Chicago Daily Tribune*, 19 March 1954: 16; Hyatt, 291–292. Douglas graduated in 1961 to host the nation's top syndicated daytime talk show from Cleveland.

42. See Boddy; Schwoch; Auter and Boyd.

43. Boddy, 50–51; Schwoch; Auter and Boyd.

44. George Rosen, "'Protect Radio' vs. Television," *Variety*, 29 Sept. 1948: 1.

45. "ABC, CBS, NBC Cold to Full Daytime Schedule; DuMont to Go It Alone," *Variety*, 6 Oct. 1948: 27; Rosen, "'Protect Radio' vs. Television."

46. "ABC, CBS, NBC Cold."

47. "Boston U.S.A.," *Variety*, 28 Jan. 1948: 31, 38.

48. "This Is the Missus," *Variety*, 24 Nov. 1948: 28.

49. Hyatt, 294.

50. Ibid., 254.

51. "Video Schedule on Co-ax Time," *Variety*, 12 Jan. 1949: 27.

52. Bob Stahl, "Daytime Tele as Profit-Maker, Key to Break Even—DuMont," *Variety*, 27 Oct. 1948: 25.

53. "Round-Clock Schedule Here to Stay as DuMont Programming Makes Good," *Variety*, 10 Nov. 1948: 29, 38.

54. In *Variety*, "Video Schedule on Co-ax Time," 27; "WTTG Gives Washington Regular Daytime Video with New Program Setup," 19 Jan. 1949: 30.

55. "DuMont Skeds 7 A.M. to 11 P.M." *Variety*, 22 Sept. 1948: 25, 34.

56. Quoted in "Inside Television," *Variety*, 30 March 1949: 32.

57. "DuMont's 'Mother' Goes Network in Daytime Spread," *Variety*, 30 Nov. 1949: 27.

58. Examples from this section appear in *Okay, Mother*, 1947.

59. These bothersome traits notwithstanding, *Okay, Mother* helped launch James's long career as a game show emcee. He went on to host *High Finance, People Will Talk*, and *Name That Tune*, and Thomas DeLong calls him "the dean of audience-participation shows" (DeLong, 224).

60. Bob Stahl, "WNBT's Daytime Preem Has Hausfrau Pull but Is Otherwise below Par," *Variety*, 9 Feb. 1949: 34. The final two shows in the afternoon were directed at children.

61. "Kathi Norris Switch to WNBT Cues Daytime Expansion for Flagship," *Variety*, 1 March 1950: 36.

62. "WNBT, N.Y., Swinging into Line as Daytime Video Airing Gains Momentum," *Variety*, 19 Jan. 1949: 24; "CBS's All-Day Programming," *Variety*, 26 Jan. 1949: 34; "Full CBS Day Airing Soon," *Variety*, 2 March 1949: 29.

63. See Schwoch, 10.

64. "Ted Steele Show," *Variety Review Book*, 1 June 1949.

65. "Kathi Norris Switch to WNBT," 31.

66. Hyatt, 122.

67. Auter and Boyd, 71.

68. Ibid., 70, 73.

69. See Auter and Boyd; Schwoch; Hess.

70. Auter and Boyd, 75–76.

71. Boddy, 51; Schwoch, 3.

72. A close reading of *Queen for a Day* follows in Chap. 8.

73. Schwoch, 7–8.

74. Ibid., 3.

75. Ibid., 7.

76. Hyatt, 353–354.

77. "'Queen for a Day,' May, 1952, Television ARB Ratings," NBCR, Box 370, Folder 18; see also Ed Hitz, "NBC Telegram" to Norman Blackburn, 21 May 1952, NBCR, Box 571, Folder 9.

78. Robert C. Temple, letter to Charles A. Barry, 17 April 1953, NBCR, Box 370, Folder 18.

79. Charles C. Barry, letter to Robert C. Temple, 27 Aug. 1953, NBCR, Box 370, Folder 18.

80. "ABC-TV Ready to Pull Out the Stops," *Broadcasting/Telecasting*, 28 Jan. 1957: 27.

81. Boddy, 56–57.

82. Goldenson, with Wolf, 168.

83. Quoted in ibid. Even in 1955, ABC was earning only 5 percent of total network revenues (Boddy, 115).

84. Quoted in Goldenson, 168.

85. Notwithstanding these successes, ABC's first full schedule of programs between 11 a.m. and 3 p.m. in 1958 resulted in widespread cancellations.

86. *Don McNeill's Breakfast Club*, Feb. 1954. This was a practice kinescope in preparation for the 1954 season of TV simulcasts and exemplifies McNeill's long-established performance style.

87. "Don McNeill's Breakfast Club," *Variety*, 14 July 1948: 42.

88. Hyatt, 69.

89. Ibid.

90. Ibid., 122.

91. Ibid., 165.

92. *Frances Langford–Don Ameche Show*, 2 Nov. 1951.

93. Hyatt, 165.

94. Ibid.

95. Ibid., 337.

96. Sterling and Kittross, 350.

97. Goldenson, 272.

98. "Daytime TV," *Broadcasting/Telecasting*, 11 Dec. 1950: 74; see also Spigel, *Make Room for TV*, 74.

99. "Daytime TV."

100. Ibid.

101. Ibid.

102. See Spigel, *Make Room for TV*, 77–86.

103. Art Woodstone, "New Data Bares TV's Whopping Success Story on Daytime," *Variety*, 12 Sept. 1956: 24, 42.

Chapter 3

1. "Kate Smith Speaks," CBS Radio, 10 Nov. 1938, quoted in Hayes, 53. In fact, Berlin gave Smith a revised version of a song he had written many years earlier.

2. Newspaper clipping, 27 Dec. 1949, *Atlanta Constitution*, in KSC, "Kate Smith Scrapbook 20," Package 18.

3. Robert W. McFadyen, memo to Sales Staff, 2 Nov. 1950: 2, NBCR, Box 567B, Folder 2; see also McFadyen, memo to Sales Staff, 7 Nov. 1950, NBCR, Box 567B, Folder 2.

4. McFadyen, memo to Sales Staff, 6 Dec. 1950, NBCR, Box 567B, Folder 1.

5. Stole, "'The Kate Smith Hour,'" 554.

6. Clipping in "Kate Smith Scrapbook, 1953–60," KSC, Package 19.

7. Sylvester L. Weaver, memo to McConnell, Wile, Madden, Sarnoff, Margraf, 27 March 1952, NBCR, Box 121, Folder 43.

8. Robert W. McFadyen, memo to Walter Scott, 23 March 1953, NBCR, Box 397, Folder 48.

9. Sam Boal, "Why Kate Smith Sings to Millions," *Coronet* (June 1952): 88; Smith repeats this story in her memoirs, *Upon My Lips a Song*, 104. While this account may be apocryphal, its wide circulation in the popular press served to strengthen Smith's patriotic aura for decades to follow.

10. Rowe, 31.

11. Eve Kosofsky Sedgwick, *Tendencies*. Durham, NC: Duke University Press, 1993, 230.

12. Feuer, "Averting the Male Gaze," 192.

13. Quoted in Boal, 89.

14. Quoted in Hayes, 98.

15. "Kate Smith: TV's Richest Woman," *Look*, 6 April 1954: 37.

16. Dowling even wrote a clause into that contract that required Smith to maintain her weight of over 200 pounds during the play's two-year run (Hayes, 9–10).

17. Smith, *Upon My Lips a Song*, 56–65.

18. Quoted in Hayes, 12.

19. Ibid., 17. Smith remembered Collins saying, "All you've got to do is sing" (*Living*, 28).

20. "Kate Smith: America's First Lady of Radio and Television," *Leisure Time*, 25 Oct. 1953, clipping in "Kate Smith Scrapbook, 1953–60," KSC, Package 19.

21. Smith, *Living*, 25–26.

22. See Feuer, "Averting the Male Gaze," 192.

23. Smith, *Living*, 174.

24. Hayes, 239–246, 267–268.

25. Quotations from these reviews appear in Hayes, 33.

26. Smith, *Living*, 171.

27. Hayes, 79.

28. Quoted in ibid., 112.

29. See Hayes, 103–104.

30. Hilmes, 261.

31. Merton.

32. Review of *Hello Everybody*, quoted in Hayes, 33.

33. Lyrics quoted in Hayes, 238.

34. "Kate Smith Clippings 1948–53," KSC, Package 18, 768.

35. "Citation," 23 Oct. 1949, KSC, Package 18.

36. Weaver, memo, 22 June 1950: 1.

37. See also in NBCR, "Showletter," 18 July 1950, Box 593, Folder 26; "A Lady Named Smith," Box 567B, Folder 2; Barry Wood to Rud Lawrence, 2 Aug. 1950, Box 567B, Folder 2; George H. Frey, letter to Ed Madden dated 3 Aug. 1950, Box 567B, Folder 2; "There IS something new about *women*," Box 567B, Folder 2.

38. Weaver, memo, 22 June 1950: 1.

39. Ibid.

40. Wood to Lawrence, 2 Aug. 1950.

41. Frey to Madden, 3 Aug. 1950: 1–2.

42. Ibid., 2.

43. "Telegram," 18 Sept. 1950, NBCR, Box 567B, Folder 1.

44. McFadyen to Sales Staff, 2 Nov. 1950.

45. Frey to Madden, 3 Aug. 1950: 1, 2–3.

46. *The Kate Smith Hour*, 3 Oct. 1950.

47. "Something new about *women*."

48. McFadyen to Sales Staff, 6 Dec. 1950.

49. Bert Briller, "Kate Smith Hits $29,000,000 Gross Jackpot on Anni in Broadcasting," *Variety*, 2 May 1951, clipping in KSC, Package 18.

50. McFadyen to Sales Staff, 7 Nov. 1950.

51. "Important Facts about THE KATE SMITH REVUE," NBCR, Box 567B, Folder 2.

52. Fred Wile Jr., memo to Robert W. Sarnoff, 5 April 1951, NBCR, Box 120, Folder 39.

53. Weaver to McConnell, 27 March 1952.

54. Mitchell Benson, memo to C. C. Barry, 2 Dec. 1952, and Benson, memo to Charles C. Barry, 12 Dec. 1952, NBCR, Box 369, Folder 10.

55. McFadyen to Scott, 23 March 1953.

56. Charles C. Barry, memo to John K. Herbert, 12 May 1953: 1, NBCR, Box 397, Folder 48.

57. See Stole, "'The Kate Smith Hour,'" 557; Weaver to McConnell, 27 March 1952.

58. Barry to Herbert, 12 May 1953: 1; also McFadyen to Scott, 23 March 1953.

59. John K. Herbert, "Kate Smith Ratings," 26 Oct. 1953, NBCR, Box 397, Folder 48.

60. Barry to Herbert, 12 May 1953: 2.

61. Robert W. McFadyen, memo to George Frey, 1 April 1953, NBCR, Box 369, Folder 10.

62. Walter D. Scott, note to Bud Barry, 2 April 1953, NBCR, Box 369, Folder 10.

63. Stole, "'The Kate Smith Hour,'" 552–561.

64. "Kate Won't Sell, NBC Isn't Buying [an inside story]," *Variety*, 30 June 1954: 25.

65. See Samuel, 119–120; Spigel, *Make Room for TV*, 81; Boddy, 159; Stole, "'The Kate Smith Hour.'"

66. Rud Lawrence, "Kate Smith Show Commercial Policy," 25 Aug. 1950, NBCR, Box 567B, Folder 3.

67. "NBC TV Sales Facts Bulletin #1: Kate Smith Show," 14 Aug. 1950, NBCR, Box 593, Folder 26.

68. Frey to Madden, 3 Aug. 1950: 2.

69. "The New Kate Smith Hour," 19 June 1953, NBCR, Box 397, Folder 48.

70. See Stole, "'The Kate Smith Hour,'" for a discussion of these issues and other production disputes.

71. Jose di Donato, letter to Herbert Hobler, 2 Feb. 1951, NBCR, Box 120, Folder 39.

72. Fred Wile, Jr., memo to Sylvester L. Weaver, Jr., 18 June 1951, NBCR, Box 120, Folder 39.

73. Gould, "Kate Smith Starts Daytime" 62. Boal dismissed the view that Collins exercised "a sinister, Svengali-Trilby influence" on Smith, writing, "Collins is not her father, nor her boy friend, nor her brother. He is her partner in business" (Boal, 91).

74. Kate Smith, "Behind the Scenes on My Show," clipping fragment in KSC, Package 18, 1950–1951: 21.

75. Wile to Sarnoff, 5 April 1951.

76. Richard A. R. Pinkham, memo to Sylvester L. Weaver Jr., 27 Sept. 1951, NBCR, Box 120, Folder 39.

77. Thomas A. McAvity, memo to Charles C. Barry, 18 March 1953, NBCR, Box 369, Folder 10.

78. McFadyen to Scott, 23 March 1953; see also Jacob A. Evans, memo to Frank Chizini, 26 Jan. 1953, NBCR, Box 392, Folder 36, regarding the Gerber complaints.

79. Stole, "'The Kate Smith Hour,'" n. 62.

80. Barry Wood, confidential memo to Charles E. Barry, 18 March 1953, NBCR, Box 369, Folder 10.

81. McAvity to Barry, 18 March 1953.

82. George H. Frey, memo to John K. Herbert, 31 March 1953, NBCR, Box 397, Folder 48.

83. Charles C. Barry, letter to Ted Collins, 30 March 1953, NBCR, Box 369, Folder 10.

84. David A. Werblin, letter to Bud Barry, NBCR, Box 369, Folder 10.

85. John B. Lanigan, memo to George H. Frey, 14 April 1953, NBCR, Box 397, Folder 48.

86. Adrian Samish, memo to Chas. C. Barry, 2 Sept. 1953, NBCR, Box 369, Folder 10.

87. See Sam Schiff, memo to Gustav Margraf, 1 Sept. 1953, NBCR, Box 397, Folder 48; John K. Herbert, letter to Ted Collins, 2 Sept. 1953, NBCR, Box 397, Folder 48.

88. Smith's enthusiasm for Borden's instant coffee, Linit, and Saran Wrap on 28 and 29 Dec. 1953 seemed perfunctory and stilted.

89. Herbert to Collins, 2 Sept. 1953.

90. Adrian Samish, memo to Charles C. Barry, 1 Sept. 1953, NBCR, Box 369, Folder 10.

91. Samish to Barry, 2 Sept. 1953.

92. Marling, 9.

93. See Feuer, "Averting the Male Gaze," 181–182, and her n. 16 regarding body size and nonwhite women.

94. Boal, 88.

95. Gould, "Kate Smith Starts Daytime," 62. Gould did, however, praise Smith's "considerable amount of personality on the screen."

96. Briller.

97. See photographs in Shulman and Youman, 55, 62, 67, 95, 330.

98. *Variety*, 2 May 1951: 39–40.

99. Like Mary Margaret McBride (Hilmes, 282)—and unlike Cincinnati's Ruth Lyons, who slimmed down for the television cameras, losing 60 pounds (Halper, 140–141).

100. Quoted in Hayes, 132.

101. Ibid.

102. *The Kate Smith Hour*, 27 Oct. 1953.

103. *The Kate Smith Hour*, 3 Oct. 1950; also 28, 29 Dec. 1953.

104. *The Kate Smith Hour*, 3 Oct. 1950; 20 Nov. 1950; 27 Oct. 1953.

105. A full list of the "dramatic segments" McCleery produced for *The Kate Smith Hour* can be found in AMP, Box 7, Folder 10; see also Boxes 69 and 70.

106. Wood to Barry, 18 March 1953.

107. Smith, "Behind the Scenes," 20.

108. Weaver, memo, 22 June 1950: 2.

109. 20 Nov. 1950.

110. 3 Oct. 1950.

111. 28 Dec. 1950.

112. 20 Nov. 1950.

113. 20 Nov. 1950.

114. 28 Dec. 1953.

115. 10 March 1953, Fragment.

116. 29 Dec. 1953.

117. *The New Kate Smith Hour*, Sept. 1953, NBCR, Box 397, Folder 48.

118. Smith, *Living*, 176–177.

119. Samish to Barry, 1 Sept. 1953.

120. Hayes, 157–160.

121. See ibid., 181–182, 193–197, 227.

122. Ibid., 225.

123. Ibid., 237.

Chapter 4

1. Hyatt, 35–36.

2. "The Charm Boys," *Time*, 15 Feb. 1954: 78.

3. Cassidy, "Sob Stories."

4. "Oceans of Empathy," *Time*, 27 Feb. 1950: 72.

5. Quoted in "Arthur Godfrey Is TV-Proof but Television May Not Be," *Newsweek*, 19 May 1952: 62; see also S. Murray, 190.

6. Jon Whitcomb, "Boy from Baltimore," *Cosmopolitan*, Oct. 1955: 49.

7. Pope, "Why Women Love Garry," 143.

8. Interview with the author, 16 July 2001, Beverly Hills, CA.

9. Garry Moore, "Introduction" to Sanford, 9.

10. Sanford, 18–19.

11. Stanley Frank, "The Host with the Most," *TV Guide*, 29 April 1961: 21; Sanford, 21.

12. In 1955 (Whitcomb, 49).

13. Whitcomb, 49.

14. Sanford, 22.

15. Whitcomb, 50.

16. Sanford, 23–25, 27–28.

17. Ibid., 36–40.

18. Ibid., 154–163.

19. See ibid., 42–48, 83, 96–99.

20. Val Adams, "About Garry Moore: The Perennial Playboy," *New York Times*, 7 March 1954, Sec. 2: 11.

21. J. P. Shanley, "TV Personalities in the News," *New York Times*, 26 June 1955, Sec. 2: 11; "Garry Moore: Commuting Comedian," *TV Guide*, 17 April 1953: 5.

22. Bill Demling and Vinnie Bogert were cited in the *Encyclopaedia Britannica Year Book*. See Sanford, 144.

23. Sanford, 22.

24. Ibid., 29.

25. Lyrics quoted in Sanford, 103–104.

26. Quoted in V. Adams.

27. Quoted in Pope, 141; Sanford, 22.

28. Quoted in Pope, 143.

29. "Moore for Housewives," *Time*, 2 Feb. 1953: 47.

30. *The Garry Moore Show*, 3 Nov. 1953.

31. "Moore for Housewives."

32. Pope, 143–144.

33. Whitcomb, 49–50.

34. Sanford, 28.

35. Ibid., 31, 37.

36. *The Garry Moore Show*, 3 Nov. 1953.

37. Schimmel is quoted in Sanford, 26–27.

38. "Moore for Housewives."

39. "The Craziest Thing," *Time*, 27 Sept. 1954: 71.

40. Bureau of the Census, *Current Population Reports: Consumer Income*, April 1956: 2.

41. Sanford, 173–175.

42. Whitcomb, 49.

43. Pope, 43.

44. *Arthur Godfrey Time*, Practice Show, 23 Nov. 1948.

45. Ibid.

46. During the summer of 1950, *Arthur Godfrey and His Ukulele* was broadcast for 15 minutes every Tuesday night as well.

47. "Arthur Godfrey Is TV-Proof," 62.

48. Ibid.

49. Hyatt, 37.

50. Edward H. Weiss, "Why Is Arthur Godfrey?" *Broadcasting/Telecasting*, 24 May 1954: 104.

51. Isabella Taves, "Why Women Love Arthur Godfrey," *McCall's*, Oct. 1953: 49.

52. Weiss, 104.

53. Bill Davidson, "Arthur Godfrey and His Fan Mail," *Collier's*, 2 May 1953: 15.

54. *Arthur Godfrey Time*, undated.

55. O'Brian, 50. Godfrey often spoke of himself as "a cripple," although he was frequently shown ice-skating, swimming, and riding horses in primetime and in publicity photos. In June 1953, he underwent hip-replacement surgery to improve his health.

56. See Hyatt, 36; Singer; *Arthur Godfrey Time*, 22 April 1953.

57. *Arthur Godfrey Time*, 14 June 1956.

58. "Arthur Godfrey Is TV-Proof," 63.

59. O'Brian.

60. S. Murray, 201.

61. Andrew A. Rooney, "The Godfrey You Don't Know," *Look*, 22 Dec. 1959: 84.

62. Lichty.

63. Hyatt, 37.

64. See S. Murray.

65. Davidson, 15.

66. Rooney, 91.

67. S. Murray 198.

68. See Weiss, 104.

69. Henry La Cossitt, "They Say He's a Funny Man," *Saturday Evening Post*, 17 May 1952: 77.

70. Author interview.

71. La Cossitt, 77; author interview.

72. Author interview.

73. Ibid.

74. La Cossitt, 72.

75. Ibid.

76. Ibid., 70.

77. Author interview.

78. Ibid.

79. Carroll O'Meara, *Television Program Production* (New York: Ronald Press, 1955), fig. 13.

80. *Art Linkletter's House Party*, circa 1957.

81. See Munson, 52.

82. *Art Linkletter's House Party*, dated 14 Dec. 1961 (probably 1960).

83. Linkletter, *Confessions of a Happy Man*, 246.

84. Ibid., 213.

85. *Art Linkletter's House Party*, 21 Feb. 1961.

86. Author interview.

87. Linkletter, *Confessions of a Happy Man*, 246.

88. La Cossitt, 69–70.

89. Ibid.; author interview.

90. *Art Linkletter's House Party*, circa 1958.

91. Author interview.

92. Linkletter, *Confessions of a Happy Man*, 190.

93. *Art Linkletter's House Party*, 14 Dec. 1961.

94. *Art Linkletter's House Party*, 7 March 1961.

95. *Art Linkletter's House Party*, 21 Feb. 1961.

96. Linkletter, *Confessions of a Happy Man*, 190.

97. Author interview.

98. Linkletter, *Confessions of a Happy Man*, 190.

99. This franchise supported two best-selling books, *Kids Say the Darndest Things!* (1957) and *The Secret World of Kids* (1959); and a more recent television revival, *Kids Say the Darndest Things*, hosted by Bill Cosby.

100. Author interview.

101. Linkletter, *Confessions of a Happy Man*, 217.

102. Author interview.

103. Linkletter, *Confessions of a Happy Man*, 228.

104. Author interview.

105. Ibid.

106. *Art Linkletter's House Party*, 21 Feb. 1961.

107. Art Linkletter, "Only Children Tell the Truth," *American Magazine* (April 1956): 120.

108. Linkletter, *Kids Say the Darndest Things!* 8.

109. Linkletter, "Only Children Tell the Truth," 120.

110. Author interview.

111. Linkletter, "Only Children Tell the Truth," 118, 120.

112. Author interview.

113. Linkletter, "Only Children Tell the Truth," 120.

114. Author interview.

115. After more than 70 years in broadcasting, Linkletter continues to travel the lecture circuit as a popular speaker in the new millennium, and his many career iterations have kept him viable in the public memory.

116. Garry Moore, "Why I'm Folding My Morning Show," *TV Guide*, 11 Jan. 1958: 6.

117. Frank, "The Host with the Most," second of three parts, 20.

118. *The Garry Moore Show*, 3 Nov. 1953.

119. Moore, "Why I'm Folding My Morning Show," 6.

120. Quoted in Singer, 119, from a WNET transcript.

121. S. Murray, 192.

122. See S. Murray, 188, and her sources.

123. *Arthur Godfrey Time*, 23 Nov. 1948.

124. *Arthur Godfrey Time*, 22 April 1953.

125. *Arthur Godfrey Time*, undated.

126. Rooney, 84.

127. Author interview.

128. Ibid.

129. *Art Linkletter's House Party*, circa 1957; 21 Feb. 1961; 7 March 1961.

130. *A&E Biography: Art Linkletter*, 2000, videotape, Art Linkletter's private collection.

131. Author interview.

132. Samuel, 99–100.

133. Pope; Carl Winston, "They'll Do Anything for Art," *Coronet* (June 1956): 60–64; Taves, 47–49.

134. Pope, 143.

135. Whitcomb, 49–50.

136. Sanford, 155.

137. Ibid., 155–156.

138. Taves, 48.

139. O'Brian, 60, 62.

140. See Singer, 42.

141. O'Brian, 62.

142. Quoted in O'Brian, 62.

143. Quoted in Singer, 119.

144. Author interview.

145. Ibid.

146. Winston, 61.

147. Author interview.

148. Segal, 294.

Chapter 5

1. See also Cassidy, "Sob Shows" and "Visible Storytellers."

2. Other examples include *Turn to a Friend* (1953), *On Your Account* (1953–1956), *Welcome Travelers* (1955–1956), *Stand Up and Be Counted* (1956–1957), and *Queen for a Day* (1956–1964).

3. Gould, "Look at 'Strike It Rich.'"

4. "Giveaways . . . Are Legal," *Business Week*, 10 April 1954: 128.

5. "Look at 'Strike It Rich.'"

6. Masciarotte, 83, 103.

7. White, 67, 181.

8. "Winning Ways," *Newsweek*, 17 Aug. 1953: 61.

9. Quoted in DeLong, 150.

10. Cox, 151.

11. Ibid., 151, 158.

12. Castleman and Podrazik, 85.

13. "Winning Ways."

14. *Strike It Rich*, 28 Nov. 1956.

15. *Strike It Rich*, 18 Nov. 1953.

16. *Strike It Rich*, 28 Nov. 1956.

17. See DeLong, 151–152.

18. Cox, 159.

19. Martin Cohen, "Strike It Rich, Please Do!" *Radio TV Mirror* (Jan. 1954): 22.

20. *Strike It Rich*, 18 Nov. 1953.

21. See especially Cassidy, "Visible Storytellers," and Chap. 8.

22. *Strike It Rich*, Summer (after 2 June) 1952.

23. Commonly, war veterans—particularly injured war veterans—and their families received privileged attention on the series.

24. Quoted in Heldenfels, 142–143.

25. See Rosemarie Garland-Thomson, "Toward a Poetics of the Disabled Body" and "Feminist Theory, the Body, and the Disabled Figure," 279–292.

26. On two extant episodes of the Wednesday evening show, *Strike It Rich* featured the Lighthouse of the Blind Choir, a 16-year-old burn victim who required plastic surgery on his hands, and a woman whose hearing aid was broken (undated).

27. *Strike It Rich*, Evening Version, undated.

28. *Strike It Rich*, Summer (after 2 June) 1952.

29. "Look at 'Strike It Rich.'"

30. Ibid.

31. Cited in DeLong, 153.

32. "Ratings Histories, CBS Daytime TV Programs," NBCR, 1953, Box 377, Folder 6.

33. "Misery Shows, TV's Disgrace," *America*, 20 Feb. 1954: 528.

34. Quoted in "Winning Ways."

35. "Ex-convict Strikes It Rich Briefly on TV, but Fame Proves a Give-away to Police," *New York Times*, 27 Jan. 1954: 19.

36. "Then the House Burned," *Time*, 15 Feb. 1954: 78.

37. "Family of 11 Fails to 'Strike it Rich,'" *New York Times*, 9 March 1954: 29; Gould, "TV's Misery Shows," 11.

38. "Family of 11."

39. Quoted in DeLong, 154.

40. "Family of 11."

41. "Then the House Burned." Walt Framer countered McCarthy's legal action with a declaratory suit of his own, claiming that *Strike It Rich* did not solicit money "within the meaning of the legal statute," but this complaint was denied, opening the way for McCarthy's case to be tried. See "Strike It Rich Loses," *New York Times*, 4 May 1954: 41.

42. "Court Sets Curb on *Strike It Rich*," *New York Times*, 29 Dec. 1954: 25.

43. "Giveaway-Takeaway," *Newsweek*, 15 March 1954: 94.

44. Ibid.

45. "Giveaway Shows Raise Ethical Question," *Christian Century*, 24 Feb. 1954: 227; "Giveaways . . . Are Legal," 128.

46. Quotations in "Giveaways . . . Are Legal,"128.

47. "Giveaway Shows Raise Ethical Question," 227–228.

48. "'Misery Shows': TV's Disgrace," 528.

49. "Stop the Misery!" *America*, 13 March 1954: 625–626. He singled out the following shows as "misery shows," programs that are "a total violation of the letter and spirit of Christian charity," and accused them all of serving communist ends: *Strike It Rich, The Big Payoff, Welcome Travelers, This Is Your Life, Wheel of Fortune, Turn to a Friend, The Ern Westmore Show*, and *Glamour Girl*.

50. Barrett, 626.

51. Quoted in Gould, "TV's Misery Shows."

52. "As We See It," *TV Guide*, 8 Jan. 1954: 3 and 26 March 1954: 2.

53. Gould, "TV's Misery Shows."

54. "Court Sets Curb."

55. Hyatt, 412.

56. Adrian Samish, memo to Frederic Wile, 4 June 1953, NBCR, Box 368, Folder 60; Ernest Theiss, memo to "List Below," 11 June 1953, NBCR, Box 368, Folder 60.

57. Peiss, 25, 144–145. Peiss notes that in 1936, *Mademoiselle* featured a "Made Over Girl," nurse Barbara Phillips, and with this article "the metamorphosis known as the *makeover* was born" (144).

58. Peiss, 144.

59. Ibid., 155, 166.

60. *Glamour Girl*, 1 Oct. 1953. The three episodes of *Glamour Girl* that exist on videotape at UCLA's Film and Television Archive were recorded on three consecutive days during October 1953, when Jack McCoy first replaced Harry Babbitt as the program's host.

61. Ibid.

62. Desjardins.

63. *Glamour Girl*, NBC, 2 Oct. 1953.

64. See Desjardins; Mellencamp. Barbara Klinger, for example, cites a major media tie-in between Universal Pictures and the Colgate Palmolive Company in October 1956. For five weeks, Douglas Sirk's *Written on the Wind* was promoted on *Strike It Rich*, in part through a beauty contest called "Miss Strike It Lovely" (63).

65. Adrian Samish, letter A to Jack McCoy, 21 Aug. 1953, NBCR, Box 368, Folder 60.

66. Adrian Samish, telegram to Jack McCoy, 26 Aug. 1953, NBCR, Box 368, Folder 60.

67. *Glamour Girl*, 1 Oct. 1953.

68. *Glamour Girl*, 3 Oct. 1953.

69. Adrian Samish, memo to Sydney Eigers, 31 July 1953, NBCR, Box 368, Folder 60.

70. Jacob A. Evans, memo to Adrian Samish, 5 Aug. 1953, NBCR, Box 368, Folder 60.

71. Clippings of these reviews are found in NBCR, Box 368, Folder 60.

72. "Glamour Girl" pamphlet, attached to John Porter, memo to "All Salesmen," 27 July 1953, NBCR, Box 397, Folder 40.

73. "NBC's Morning Show, 'Glamour Girl,' Called a New Twist in Exploiting Human Misery," *New York Times*, 21 Aug 1953. Clipping in NBCR, Box 368, Folder 60.

74. "Outlook: Sarnoff to Steer NBC for Remainder of Year," *Broadcasting/Telecasting*, 3 Aug. 1953: 71.

75. Sarnoff to Herbert, 21 Aug. 1953, NBCR, Box 368, Folder 60.

76. Adrian Samish, letter B to Jack McCoy, 21 Aug. 1953, NBCR, Box 368, Folder 60.

77. "Barry returns to Samish," 28 Aug. 1953 (note typed onto copy of Samish to McCoy B, 21 Aug. 1953), NBCR, Box 368, Folder 60.

78. Adrian Samish, memo to Chas. Barry, 24 Aug. 1953: 1–2 NBCR, Box 368, Folder 60.

79. Samish to McCoy B, 21 Aug. 1953.

80. Ibid.

81. Ibid.; Samish to Barry, 24 Aug. 1953.

82. Samish to Barry, 24 Aug. 1953: 1.

83. Ibid.

84. Ibid., 1–2.

85. Adrian Samish, letter to Jack McCoy, 24 Aug. 1953, NBCR, Box 368, Folder 60.

86. Adrian Samish, telegram to Jack McCoy, 26 Aug. 1953, NBCR, Box 368, Folder 60.

87. Fred Shawn, memo to Charles C. Barry, 28 Aug. 1953: 2, NBCR, Box 368, Folder 60.

88. Ibid.

89. Adrian Samish, letter to Jack McCoy, 2 Sept. 1953, NBCR, Box 368, Folder 60.

90. Charles C. Barry, memo to General Sarnoff, 27 Aug. 1953, NBCR, Box 368, Folder 60.

91. John K. Herbert, memo to General David Sarnoff, 1 Sept. 1953, NBCR, Box 397, Folder 40.

92. "D.S." (David Sarnoff), note written on memo, Barry to Sarnoff, 27 Aug. 1953.

93. Sid Shalit, "Glamour Girl Gets Glad Hand," *New York Daily News*, 1 Sept. 1953: 52, clipping in NBCR, Box 368, Folder 60.

94. Adrian Samish, telegram to Jack McCoy, 3 Sept. 1953, NBCR, Box 368, Folder 60.

95. Frank Cooper, letter to Charles C. Barry, 6 Oct. 1953, NBCR, Box 368, Folder 60.

96. Frank Cooper, letter to Charles C. Barry, 19 Oct. 1953, NBCR, Box 368, Folder 60.

97. Frank Cooper, letter to Adrian Samish, 23 Oct. 1953, NBCR, Box 368, Folder 60.

98. "'Glamour Girl' Draws 30,000 Letters in One Week," Television Sales Promotion, 16 Oct. 1953, NBCR, Box 397, Folder 40.

99. "Second Week Mail Response," Television Sales Promotion, 23 Oct. 1953, NBCR, Box 397, Folder 40.

100. All that remains of this final correspondence is a one-page summary of the Herbert-Barry-Samish communication, marked "751," NBCR, Box 368, Folder 60.

101. Shawn to Barry, 28 Aug. 1953: 2.

102. See Masciarotte, 97–98.

103. Wendell, 266.

104. "Look at 'Strike It Rich.'"

105. Masciarotte, 96.

106. Peiss, 55.

107. *Glamour Girl*, 1 Oct. 1953.

108. *Glamour Girl*, 2 Oct. 1953.

109. *Glamour Girl*, 3 Oct. 1953.

110. *Glamour Girl*, 1 Oct. 1953.

Chapter 6

1. The original version of this chapter won third prize at the Broadcast Education Association conference in 1997, entitled "NBC's 'Home' Show: 1950s Femininity and the Network Construction of Daytime Television." Modified sections also appear in Cassidy and White, where Mimi White and I compare the *Home* show to Ruth Lyons's *Fifty-Fifty Club* and more broadly connect consumption appeals to issues of class, taste, and region. My collaboration with Mimi White enhanced my thinking about Francis in important ways.

2. See Jezer; Lynn; and Meyerowitz, "Beyond the Feminine Mystique."

3. Lynn, 116.

4. See Spigel, *Make Room for TV*, 83–84, and Cassidy and White.

5. See the work of Spigel, *Make Room for TV*, 81–85; Stole, "There Is No Place"; Hilmes, 275–287; and Cassidy and White, for this reassessment.

6. See Lichty; James C. G. Conniff, "Arlene Francis: The Lady Is a Wit," *Coronet* (Feb. 1956): 55; Francis, *Arlene Francis*, 136.

7. Bob Chandler, "Decline and Fall of 'T-H-T,'" *Variety*, 14 Aug. 1957: 25.

8. *Variety*, 24 Feb. 1954: 32–33.

9. Figured into this amount is the cost of TV promotions on NBC itself. See George Rosen, "'Home' as Odds-on Favorite to Pay Off NBC-TV's $1,200,000 Mortgage," *Variety*, 3 March 1954: 35; Spigel, *Make Room for TV*, 208, n. 33.

10. "The Tall Gambler," *Time*, 10 Dec. 1954: 45.

11. As Spigel points out, three local programs from the late 1940s even overtly mimicked the format of the women's magazine well before it was promoted by Pat Weaver—Chicago's "Women's Magazine of the Air," Seattle's "Women's Page," and "Vanity Fair" in New York City (*Make Room for TV*, 80). See also Weinstein; Hilmes, 276; and Williams.

12. Gould, "'Home.'"

13. Margaret McKeegan's study is quoted in Pennell, 107.

14. Pennell, 109.

15. May, 87, 141–142.

16. Marshall and Frazier, 14.

17. Haralovich, 61.

18. May, 167.

19. Quoted in Marshall and Frazier, 14.

20. Rosen, "'Home' as Odds-on Favorite," 35; Spigel, *Make Room for TV*, 81.

21. Gould, "'Home'"; see also Stole, "There Is No Place," 145.

22. Weaver, with Coffey, 250; Spigel, *Make Room for TV*, 82; Stole, "There Is No Place," 145.

23. "For the Girls at Home," *Newsweek*, 15 March 1954: 93.

24. R. A. R. Pinkham, "Report on 'Home' to the NBC Affiliates," 9 April 1954, NBCR, Box 123, Folder 26.

25. Spigel, *Make Room for TV*, 85–87.

26. Stole, "There Is No Place," 141.

27. Bride, 12.

28. Lawrence, 15.

29. Ibid.

30. Quoted in Pennell, 114.

31. Quoted in Stole, "There Is No Place," 148.

32. Lawrence, 46.

33. Wilson, 83–105.

34. Quoted in Boddy, 105.

35. Quoted in Stole, "There Is No Place," 141.

36. "For the Girls at Home," 92.

37. See Wilson; Cassidy and White.

38. "For the Girls at Home," 92.

39. Meyerowitz, "Beyond the Feminine Mystique," 230.

40. Meyerowitz, "Introduction," 2.

41. Meyerowitz, "Beyond the Feminine Mystique," 231.

42. In the report prepared for Pat Weaver to present at the April 1954 meeting of NBC affiliates, R. A. R. Pinkham wrote that *Home* "is dedicated to the proposition that whatever the service magazines can do well in print, we can do better with sight and sound and demonstration on TV" (Pinkham, "Report on 'Home'").

43. Quoted in Stole, "There Is No Place," 148.

44. Spigel, *Make Room for TV*, 82–83.

45. Quoted in Stole, "There Is No Place," 147.

46. *Home*, 21 Sept. 1954.

47. *Home*, 20 May 1954.

48. Gould, "'Home.'"

49. Shayon, "The Hurry of 'Home,'" 38.

50. Ibid.

51. Alfred Bester, "Antic Arts: At Home with Arlene Francis," *Holiday* (Oct. 1956): 82.

52. Interview with the author, 1996, Santa Monica, CA. Jenkins was one of television's female pioneers; in 1951, she produced WNBT's highly acclaimed day-

time program *What's the Problem?* in New York City and continued her career as a writer/producer/director until the 1960s.

53. "Arlene Francis," *Newsweek*, 52.

54. Correspondence with the author, 1996. See also Phyllis Adams, "Program Topics," *Home*, 1954–1955, Private Collection of Phyllis Adams Jenkins.

55. Francis, *Arlene Francis*, 149.

56. Quoted in Bester, 82.

57. See script for *Home*, "The Final Show," 9 Aug. 1957.

58. "TV Hits the Road," *Newsweek*, 2 May 1955: 88.

59. Francis, *Arlene Francis*, 141–159.

60. *Home*, Dickie segment, 10 Feb. 1956.

61. *Home*, 12 Nov. 1956.

62. Meyerowitz, "Beyond the Feminine Mystique," 240.

63. "American Women's Clubs Cite Radio, TV Programs," *Broadcasting/Telecasting*, 11 June 1956: 98.

64. *Home*, "Portrait of a Lady" script, 3.

65. "Arlene Francis," *Newsweek*, 50.

66. "Arlene Francis: TV's Busiest Woman," *Look*, 4 May 1954: 52; Katherine Pedell, "What's HER Line?" *TV Guide*, 9–16 July 1954: 4–6.

67. Francis, *Arlene Francis*, 21–27.

68. For a fuller biography see Cassidy and White, 37–41, 57.

69. Quoted in Richard Gehman, "The Amazing Armenian," Part 1, *TV Guide*, 23 June 1962: 19.

70. See "The 'Miss America' Everybody Knows," *TV Guide*, 26 March 1955: 17.

71. See Francis, *That Certain Something*, and Chap. 1.

72. Francis, "Just Be Yourself," 6.

73. Pedell, 4.

74. See Bester; Stole, "There Is No Place," 143–144.

75. Pennell, 111.

76. "Arlene Francis," *Newsweek*, 54.

77. Bester, 80.

78. Francis, *Arlene Francis*, 136; "Demonstrating for Dow," AMP, Box 2, Folder 1.

79. Roul Tunley, "You Don't Have to Be Beautiful," *American Magazine* (Oct. 1954): 117.

80. See "Portrait of a Professional: Arlene Francis," *Look*, 24 Nov. 1959.

81. Pedell, 5.

82. Bester, 80.

83. Rowe, 50–91.

84. "Arlene Francis," *Newsweek*, 50.

85. Ibid., and cover.

86. Bester, 80.

87. "For the Girls at Home," 93.

88. Tunley, 114.

89. Francis, *Arlene Francis*, 11.

90. Peter was born 28 January 1947.

91. May, 6.

92. Gatlin, 55.

93. Katz and Lazarsfeld, 223–224.

94. Kaledin, 212.

95. Bolt, 95–96.

96. Kaledin, 64.

97. See Rowe, 31.

98. "Arlene Francis," *Newsweek*, 50.

99. Rowe, 31.

100. *What's My Line?*, CBS, 21 Feb. 1954, MBC.

101. Conniff, 54.

102. "Arlene Francis," *Newsweek*, 54.

103. Conniff, 56.

104. *Home*, 11 April 1957.

105. "Arlene Francis," *Look*, 52.

106. Meyerowitz, "Beyond the Feminine Mystique," 234.

107. Ibid., 237.

108. "Arlene Francis," *Look*, 54.

109. E-mail correspondence with the author, 23 Dec. 2003.

110. E-mail correspondence with the author, 19 June 2000.

111. Pedell, 4.

112. "A $200,000 Home," *Television Age* (April 1954), clipping in NBCR, Box 280, Folder 21.

113. Rosen, "'Home' as Odds-on Favorite," 35.

114. "Be It Never So Humble," *Life*, 29 March 1954: 50–51.

115. See "For the Girls at Home"; Gould, "'Home'"; "Be It Never So Humble"; "A $200,000 Home."

116. "A $200,000 Home."

117. Philip Hamburger, "Television for the Ladies," *New Yorker*, 3 April 1954, attachment to John H. Porter, "Memo to Network Sales Staff," NBCR, 14 April 1954, Box 280, Folder 21.

118. Spigel, *Make Room for TV*, 83.

119. Charles C. Barry, memo to Richard Pinkham Report #2, 2 March 1954: 2, NBCR, Box 369, Folder 5.

120. Barry to Pinkham, 2 March 1954, and Charles C. Barry, memo to Richard Pinkham, 3 March 1954: 2, NBCR, Box 369, Folder 5; Spigel, *Make Room for TV*, 84.

121. Barry to Pinkham Report #2, 2 March 1954, 2.

122. Charles C. Barry, memo to Richard Pinkham, 4 March 1954, NBCR, Box 369, Folder 5.

123. John Crosby, "Constructive and Creative," *New York Herald Tribune*, 3 March 1954, attachment to Porter, "Memo to Network Sales Staff."

124. Hamburger.

125. Interview with the author, 1996.

126. *Home*, 20 May 1954.

127. *Home*, 22 Oct. 1956.

128. See Cassidy and White, 45–46.

129. *Home*, 12 Nov. 1956.

130. Ibid.

131. These statistics are from Lichty.

132. Chandler, 42.

133. Wilson, 101.

134. By the beginning of 1956, David Sarnoff had promoted Weaver to chairman of the NBC board of directors. Although Weaver briefly influenced programming decisions after his promotion, his power at the network rapidly declined, so much so that he resigned in frustration in the fall of 1956 (Weaver, with Coffey, 267–270).

135. See Chaps. 2 and 8.

136. Francis, *Arlene Francis*, 160. While the professional life of Arlene Francis faltered briefly after *Home* was canceled, her career continued to prosper for many years. She appeared as a regular panelist on *What's My Line?* until 1975, made numerous guest appearances on television through the mid-1980s, received the Broadcasters Award for Lifetime Achievement in 1987, and was heard daily on New York City's WOR-radio until 1990, the year she turned 83. Francis retired to San Francisco, where she died on 31 May 2001.

137. Francis, *That Certain Something*, 10.

138. Francis, *Arlene Francis*, 159–160.

139. George Rosen, "Top Beefs on Daytime Airing," *Variety*, 6 May 1953: 23.

140. Timberg argues that Francis was a key historical figure in the establishment of daytime talk shows, 39–45.

141. See www.arlenefrancis.com.

142. Ryan, 41.

Chapter 7

1. Boddy, 188.

2. Eight evening anthologies were mentioned, including the *Goodyear Playhouse* and the *Kraft Television Theatre*. "The House Lights Dim," AMP, 15 Nov. 1955, Box 2, Folder 2.

3. Weaver, "Memorandum" dictated to Jane Murray.

4. See Boddy, 80–90.

5. Weaver, "Memorandum" dictated to Jane Murray, 138.

6. Gilbert Seldes, "New Bubbles for Soap Opera," *New York Times Magazine*, 12 Sept. 1954: 44.

7. "For a Better Soap," *Newsweek*, 20 Dec. 1954: 54.

8. "Soap in Your Eyes," *Newsweek*, 1 Feb. 1954: 74.

9. "For a Better Soap."

10. The number of quarter hours of serial drama climbed moderately during these years, from 55 in 1957, to 65 in 1958, and 70 in 1959. While some of these shows were among daytime's most watched programs, other women's formats collectively outnumbered soap operas during the late 1950s by more than 3 to 1 (Sterling and Kittross, 652–653). See also Allen, 122–126.

11. Weaver, "Memorandum" dictated to Jane Murray, 144.

12. McCleery, "Memorandum on NBC Matinee Theatre," 17.

13. See Chap. 1.

14. Seymour Korman, "In Hollywood: McCleery's 5 Dramas a Week," *Chicago

Daily Tribune, 4 Feb. 1956, clipping in AMP, Box 1, Folder 4; "Biography of Albert McCleery."

15. Quoted in Korman.

16. McCleery and Glick.

17. "Biography of Albert McCleery."

18. Maggy Fisher, "McCleery Outlines Plans for West Coast Theater TV," *Radio-TV Daily*, 12 Aug. 1955, clipping in NBCR, Box 151C, Folder 59.

19. "Biography of Albert McCleery."

20. Fisher; Zuma Palmer, "Big Responsibility on Shoulders of Albert McCleery," *Citizen-News*, 13 Dec. 1955, clipping in AMP, Box 1, Folder 4.

21. "'Matinee': No Dearth in the Aft," *Variety*, 17 Oct. 1956: 48.

22. Ibid.

23. Albert McCleery, letter to Kenneth McGowan, 4 Jan. 1962, AMP, Box 19, Folder 3.

24. Shayon, "Just like Radio," 23.

25. "'Matinee': No Dearth," 48.

26. Quoted in Jon Bruce, "How Daytime TV Can Change Your Life," 2 March 1956: 47, clipping in AMP, Box 1, Folder 4.

27. See Jean Corlis, "Albert McCleery—Champion of the Ladies," 24 Aug. 1956, clipping in AMP, Box 1, Folder 4.

28. Quoted on the brochure for "The 25th Anniversary Celebration of NBC Matinee Theater," AMP, Box 19, Folder 3.

29. Boddy, 191; 126–139.

30. Quoted in Bruce, 47.

31. See Boddy, 73.

32. See Bruce for the few exceptions.

33. Quoted in Corlis; see Boddy, 87, on the television playwright.

34. Albert McCleery, "Pipe Dream to Reality," after 31 Oct. 1956: 10, AMP, Box 1, Folder 4.

35. McCleery, "Five Do's and Don't's."

36. Ibid.

37. McCleery, "Pipe Dream to Reality," 10.

38. McCleery, "Five Do's and Don't's."

39. Philip Minoff, "Accent on Faces," *Cue*, 24 Aug. 1951: 34, 26, clipping in AMP, Box 1, Folder 3.

40. McCleery, "Five Do's and Don't's."

41. Boddy, 83–84.

42. Weaver, "Memorandum" dictated to Jane Murray, 140; see also "NBC-TV Gets Daytime Bug," *Variety*, 2 Nov. 1955, clipping in AMP, Box 1, Folder 4.

43. Weaver, "Memorandum" dictated to Jane Murray, 129–145.

44. McCleery, "Memorandum on NBC Matinee Theatre."

45. Ibid., 1–2.

46. McCleery, "Memorandum on NBC Matinee Theatre."

47. Ibid., 11.

48. Weaver also urged McCleery to integrate NBC stars into the series.

49. McCleery, "Memorandum on NBC Matinee Theatre," 6–7.

50. Palmer.

51. Quoted in Fisher.

52. Weaver, "Memorandum" dictated to Jane Murray, 133.

53. "You Are Invited to the *COLOR* Programs," "Televisionotes," 31 Oct. 1955, NBCR, Box 391C, Folder 25.

54. Sterling and Kittross, 657; Brochure, "Matinee Theater," attached to William G. Thompson Jr., memo to sales presentations department, "TV Co-op Program Sales," 2 Feb. 1956, "In Color," NBCR, Box 400, Folder 9; see "Daytime Television Program Has Taken a Big Stride Forward," story by the Associated Press after premiere, clipping in AMP, Box 1, Folder 4.

55. Harriet Van Horne, "How Ya Gonna Get Any Cookin' Done?" *New York Telegraph and Sun*, 18 Oct. 1955, clipping in NBCR, Box 151C, Folder 59.

56. Lucia Carter, "Now Housewife Has Intelligence!" *Chicago Sun-Times*, 14 Aug. 1955, clipping in AMP, Box 1, Folder 4.

57. Weaver, "Memorandum" dictated to Jane Murray, 140.

58. "'NBC's Matinee Theatre' Set to Break Record for Advance Participating Sales Now Held by 'Home,'" press release, 22 Sept. 1955, NBCR, Box 151C, Folder 59.

59. Joe Culligan, memo to Robert W. Sarnoff, 2 Nov. 1955, NBCR, Box 391C, Folder 25.

60. "'Matinee Theatre' to Break Record."

61. "Matinee Schedule, Days Positions Sold," 16 Dec. 1955, NBCR, Box 391C, Folder 25.

62. "'Matinee': No Dearth," 26; Bruce.

63. Fisher; Palmer.

64. "Drama Factory," *Time*, 20 Aug. 1956: 72.

65. "The NBC Matinee Theater, Devised and Produced by Albert McCleery, Presents '200 Hours of Color-Plus,'" attachment to Morris Rittenberg, sales memo, 20 Aug. 1956, NBCR, Box 400, Folder 8.

66. "Drama Factory."

67. McCleery, "Pipe Dream to Reality."

68. The Albert McCleery Papers contain dozens of reviews gathered from around the country in Box 1, Folder 4. I have presented representative samples here.

69. John Crosby, "Afternoon Show in Large Brackets," *New York Herald Tribune*; Jack Gould, "TV: 'Matinee Theatre,'" *New York Times*, 1 Nov. 1955, reprinted in "Accolades from the New York Critics . . . ," AMP, Box 1, Folder 4. See also NBCR, Box 151C, Folder 59.

70. In *Variety*, "NBC Matinee Theatre" and "Tele Reviews," 1 Nov. 1955, AMP, Box 1, Folder 4.

71. Donald Freeman, "'Matinee' Future Is Up to Women," *San Diego Union*, 3 Nov. 1955, AMP, Box 1, Folder 4.

72. "NBC Matinee Theatre," 1 Nov. 1955: 15.

73. Roland E. Lindbloom, "NBC Bids for Daytime TV Audience," *Newark New Jersey News*, 1 Nov. 1955, AMP, Box 1, Folder 4.

74. Anthony LaCamera, "First Matinee Theatre Show 'Sudsy,'" *Boston American*, 1 Nov. 1955, AMP, Box 1, Folder 4.

75. "Matinee Theater," *Broadcasting/Telecasting*, 7 Nov. 1955, AMP, Box 1, Folder 4.

76. Larry Wolters, "Bad Show No Better in Color," *Chicago Daily Tribune*, 2 Nov. 1955, AMP, Box 1, Folder 4.

77. Quoted in Bill Weber, "Matinee for 10 Million," *TV-Radio Life*, 14 Oct. 1955: 3, clipping in AMP, Box 1, Folder 4, and Bruce.

78. "Drama Factory."

79. "The NBC Matinee Theater," attachment to Morris Rittenberg, sales memo, 20 Aug. 1956.

80. "'Matinee': No Dearth," 26.

81. Quoted in Bruce.

82. "Drama Factory."

83. Quoted in Bruce.

84. See UCLA collection.

85. Quoted in "Drama Factory."

86. "Drama Factory."

87. Ibid.

88. Bill Moseley, "Summary of NBC Matinee Theater Audience Analysis 3/17/56," memo to Albert McCleery, 5 April 1956: 1, NBCR, Box 400, Folder 9.

89. Lucia Carter, "The 'Heights' Stymie Video," *Chicago Sun-Times*, 1 Dec. 1955, AMP, Box 1, Folder 4.

90. "Drama Factory."

91. Quoted in Bruce, 46.

92. Carter, "The 'Heights.' Stymie Video."

93. "NBC Matinee Theater, Sales Kinescope, Success Story," script, Final Version, 25 Oct. 1956: 2, NBCR, Box 400, Folder 9.

94. Weber, "Matinee for 10 Million."

95. "NBC-TV Promotion," Jan. 1956, NBCR, Box 400, Folder 9.

96. "Afternoon TV Gets Dramatic Lift," *Chicago Sun-Times*, 1 Nov. 1955, clipping in AMP, Box 1, Folder 4.

97. Freeman.

98. "NBC-TV Gets Daytime Bug as Full Hour Dramas Bow in Tint," *Variety*, 2 Nov. 1955, clipping in AMP, Box 1, Folder 4.

99. Moseley, 1.

100. Ibid.

101. Thomas E. Coffin, memo to H. M. Beville Jr., "Attention in Viewing Matinee Theater," 8 June 1956, NBCR, Box 400, Folder 9.

102. "A Cloud for Jeni," NBC, UCLA, Videotape: T38924.

103. "Give Me a Wand," NBC, UCLA, Videotape: T5663.

104. "NBC Matinee Theater, Sales Kinescope," 8, 9, 6.

105. "'Matinee': No Dearth," 48.

106. Another prominent woman on the staff was one of television's few female directors, Livia Granito.

107. "Ethel Frank, Supervising Story Producer of 'Matinee Theater,' Sees Exciting Opportunities for Writers in the Series," press release, 20 Dec. 1955: 1–2, NBCR, Box 151C, Folder 59.

108. "NBC's Albert McCleery," press release, 9 Nov. 1955: 2, NBCR, Box 151C, Folder 59.

109. "'Matinee': No Dearth," 48.

110. Ibid.

111. Shayon, "Sex in the Afternoon," 32.

112. Minoff.

113. "It Takes a Good Man to Woo and Win a Million Hearts," attachment to Donald Foley, memo to TV Network Sales Staff, 21 Aug. 1956, NBCR, Box 400, Folder 9.

114. Quoted in Thomas E. Coffin, memo to H. M. Beville Jr., "John Conte," 6 June 1956: 1, NBCR, Box 400, Folder 9.

115. "It Takes a Good Man."

116. "Matinee Idol," *TV Radio Mirror*, clipping in AMP, Box 1, Folder 4.

117. Robert Wood, memo to Stockton Helffrich, "Re: Matinee," 1 Nov. 1955, AMP, Box 1, Folder 9.

118. Among them were the use of "damn" and "hell," mental illness, suicide, and even the competence of the FBI.

119. The booklet *NBC Radio and Television Broadcast Standards* can be found in AMP, Box 16, Folder 9.

120. John Graves, script review form, 13 June 1956, NBCR, Box 151C, Folder 60.

121. Robert A. Wood, memo to Albert McCleery, "Open-mouthed Kissing," 5 July 1956, NBCR, Box 151C, Folder 60.

122. Moseley, 1.

123. Mrs. A. H. Kemp Jr., letter to NBC TV Program Department, 2 April 1956, and Stockton Helffrich letter to Mrs. A. H. Kemp Jr., NBCR, Box 151C, Folder 59.

124. Robert Wood, memo to Stockton Helffrich, "NBC Matinee Theater, 'Eye of the Storm,'" 14 Nov. 1956, NBCR, Box 151C, Folder 61.

125. See correspondence in NBCR, Box 151C, Folder 61.

126. Robert Wood, memo to Stockton Helffrich, "Matinee Theater," 25 Oct. 1956, NBCR, Box 151C, Folder 61.

127. Boddy, 147–149.

128. *Matinee Theater*, "This One Is Different."

129. *Matinee Theater*, "Two Picture Deal."

130. Boddy, 148–149.

131. Ibid., 188.

132. John B. Lanigan, memo to Pinkham, Frey, Culligan, McAvity, Marcy, Chester, McCleery, 4 Jan. 1956, NBCR, Box 400, Folder 9.

133. "Matinee Theater Facts and Figures," 7 March 1956: 4, NBCR, Box 400, Folder 9.

134. Joe Culligan, memo to Sylvester L. Weaver, 27 March 1956, NBCR, Box 126, Folder 20.

135. Lanigan to Pinkham et al., 4 Jan. 1956.

136. Culligan to Weaver, 27 March 1956.

137. Jerry Chester, memo to Mort Werner, 12 March 1956, NBCR, Box 126, Folder 20.

138. Bill Rubens, memo to Lew Marcy, "NBC Matinee: Local Ratings," 26 June 1956, NBCR, Box 400, Folder 9.

139. Chester to Werner, 12 March 1956.

140. Mitch Lipman, "Matinee 5 to 1 over Film Festival," attachment to Joe Culligan, memo to Sylvester L. Weaver, 26 March 1956, NBCR, Box 126, Folder 20.

141. Ben Gross, "NBC Should Pause before Dropping 'Matinee' Show," 2 March 1956, clipping in NBCR, Box 151C, Folder 59.

142. Mitch Lipman, "*Matinee Theatre* Reaches New ARB Rating 'High,'" 31 Aug. 1956, NBCR, Box 400, Folder 8.

143. Culligan to Weaver, 27 March 1956.

144. Dwight Whitney, "Exit 'Matinee Theater,'" *TV Guide*, 21 June 1958: 26, clipping in NBCR, Box 151C, Folder 65.

145. "The Ghost of 'Matinee Theater,'" *TV Guide*, 25 April–1 May 1959: 27, clipping in NBCR, Box 151C, Folder 65.

146. Oscar Godbout, "Drama on Crisis in '68 Scheduled," NBCR, Box 151C, Folder 65.

147. Stockton Helffrich, memo to Bob Wood, 12 June 1958, NBCR, Box 151C, Folder 65.

148. Helffrich to Wood, 12 June 1958.

149. Ben Gross, "Matinee Theatre Fans Have Raised $110,000," *Daily News*, 19 June 1958, clipping in NBCR, Box 151C, Folder 65.

150. "The Ghost of 'Matinee Theater.'"

151. Ibid.

152. Quoted in Gross, "Matinee Theatre Fans."

153. "Suggested copy for Matinee Theater Foundation Commercial," NBCR, Box 151C, Folder 65.

154. "NBC Refuses Ads Urging Net Keep Matinee Theatre," *Hollywood Reporter*, 23 June 1958, clipping in NBCR, Box 151C, Folder 65.

155. "The Ghost of 'Matinee Theater.'"

156. Stockton Helffrich, memo to Continuity Acceptance Personnel, O&O Stations, Radio & Television Program Personnel, 12 Jan. 1956: 4, AMP, Box 1, Folder 9.

157. Hyatt, 334.

158. "Biography of Albert McCleery."

159. McCleery, "Theater's Debt to Television."

160. Ibid.

161. See Bourdieu, 294; Spigel, *Welcome to the Dreamhouse*, 297.

162. See Blake.

163. Robert F. Lewine, letter to Albin Zobel, 3 July 1958, NBCR, Box 151C, Folder 65.

164. See Brown.

165. Hyatt, 282.

Chapter 8

1. Doane, 54.

2. Kepley, 52–53.

3. "NBC-TV's Major Daytime Advances; Forge Ahead on Sales, Ratings," *Variety*, 6 Feb. 1957: 27+.

4. Goldenson, with Wolf, 168.

5. Ibid., 163.

6. Hyatt, xiii.

7. The Daybreak plan also required the establishment of a "D rate," which reduced the daytime revenues ABC delivered to affiliates from one-half to one-third of nighttime rates, and which was called "Ollie's folly" by vocal opponents (Goldenson, 168–169).

8. Hyatt, xiii.

9. Goldenson, 169.

10. See DeLong, Chap. 22 and p. 228.

11. Seldes, "New Bubbles for Soap Opera," *New York Times Magazine*, 12 Sept. 1954: 44.

12. "Soap in Your Eyes," *Newsweek*, 1 Feb. 1954: 74.

13. Kozloff, *Overhearing Film Dialogue*, 247.

14. Ibid., 240, 242.

15. See Cassidy, "Visible Storytellers," for a more detailed discussion of the misery show's affiliation with melodrama and TV's confessional mode.

16. Charles C. Barry, memo to Robert Sarnoff, 12 Feb. 1954, NBCR, Box 370, Folder 18.

17. William H. Fineshriber, memo to Robert W. Sarnoff, 15 Feb. 1954, NBCR, Box 582, Folder 72.

18. Tom McAvity, memo to Fred Wile Jr., received by Michael Dann, 28 Jan. 1955, NBCR, Box 378, Folder 1.

19. George F. McGarrett, memo to Sam Fuller, 4 March 1955, NBCR, Box 378, Folder 1.

20. "NBC Figures Show Record-Topping '56," *Broadcasting/Telecasting*, 7 Jan. 1957: 62.

21. "NBC-TV's Major Daytime Advances," 46, 27.

22. "NBC-TV Cites Advance in Afternoon Audience," *Broadcasting/Telecasting*, 11 Feb. 1957: 91.

23. "Troubles and Bubbles," *Time*, 15 April 1957: 76.

24. Chuck Barris, memo to Daytime Sales Specialists, 28 Aug. 1956, NBCR, Box 400, Folder 8.

25. "In Review: *Queen for a Day*," *Broadcasting and Telecasting*, 9 Jan. 1956: 14.

26. Carl Lindemann Jr., memo to Kenneth Bilby, 1 Oct. 1957, NBCR, Box 143, Folder 12. *Queen for a Day* stabilized NBC's afternoon lineup for three years; in the middle of 1960, ABC announced that it had acquired rights to the program. NBC disputed the transaction, claiming it retained a five-year option to renew *Queen*'s contract. Ultimately, the networks settled the legal disagreement out of court, and *Queen for a Day* aired on the ABC network 28 Sept. 1960 to 2 Oct. 1964 (Hyatt, 352–354).

27. Quoted in Blake, 416.

28. Interviews in Ganas.

29. Ganas.

30. "*Queen for a Day* Reunion Excerpt."

31. Blake, 417.

32. "Troubles and Bubbles."

33. Blake, 416.

34. Ganas.

35. Blake, 417.

36. See Ganas.

37. Ibid.

38. Blake, 418.

39. Kellman on Ganas.

40. *Queen for a Day*, 19 Oct. 1960.

41. Doane, 56.

42. "Troubles and Bubbles."

43. *Queen for a Day*, 19 Oct. 1960.

44. *Queen for a Day*, Undated Fragments.

45. Blake, 417.

46. Ibid., 416.

47. *Queen for a Day*, 1960.

48. *Queen for a Day*, 19 Oct. 1960; March 1956.

49. Ganas.

50. Interviews in Ganas.

51. *It Could Be You*, 21 May 1957.

52. *It Could Be You*, 3 April 1956.

53. *It Could Be You*, 21 May 1957.

54. *It Could Be You*, 8 Nov. 1956.

55. Hyatt, 230.

56. Correspondence with the author, 28 Aug. 2000; see also "Secret Agents X-9, 10, 11, 12, Etc.," *TV Guide*, 10 Nov. 1956: 14–15.

57. *It Could Be You*, 3 April 1956.

58. *It Could Be You*, 8 Nov. 1956.

59. *It Could Be You*, 11 Sept. 1957.

60. *It Could Be You*, 19 March 1954.

61. *It Could Be You*, 21 May 1957.

62. Ibid.

63. *It Could Be You*, 8 Nov. 1956.

64. Correspondence with the author, 28 Aug. 2000.

65. *It Could Be You*, 19 March 1954.

66. *It Could Be You*, 11 Sept. 1957.

67. *It Could Be You*, 24 Feb. 1959.

68. *It Could Be You*, 11 Sept. 1957.

69. *It Could Be You*, 19 March 1954.

70. *It Could Be You*, 24 Feb. 1959; see "'Dr. Livingstone, I Presume,'" *TV Guide*, 18 July 1959: 22–23.

71. *It Could Be You*, 24 Feb. 1959.

72. *It Could Be You*, 11 Sept. 1957.

73. *It Could Be You*, 26 March 1960.

74. *It Could Be You*, 3 March 1960.

75. Kozloff, *Overhearing Film Dialogue*, 11.

76. Correspondence with the author, 11 Dec. 2003.

77. Correspondence with the author, 28 Aug. 2000.

78. *It Could Be You*, 11 Sept. 1957.

79. *It Could Be You*, 24 Feb. 1959; 11 Sept. 1957; 3 April 1956; 8 Nov. 1956.

80. *It Could Be You*, 26 March 1960.

81. Hyatt, 464.

82. E-mail correspondence with the author, 10 Sept. 2002.

83. *Do You Trust Your Wife?*, 1958.

84. Ibid.

85. Ibid.

86. *Who Do You Trust?*, after 1958.

87. Ibid.

88. *Do You Trust Your Wife?*, 1958.

89. Ibid.

90. Ibid.

91. Ibid.

92. *Who Do You Trust?* after 1958. When Carson left daytime television to host the *Tonight* show in 1962, his successor, Woody Woodbury, failed to replicate Carson's popularity, and *Who Do You Trust?* was canceled in December 1963 (Hyatt, 464).

93. Kozloff, *Overhearing Film Dialogue*, 11.

94. Hyatt, 59; DeLong, 225.

95. "*The Big Payoff*'s Third Anniversary," ad in *Variety*, 5 Jan. 1955: 195.

96. "Framer Strikes a Rich Big Payoff," *Variety*, 5 Dec. 1956: 35.

97. "Winning Ways," *Newsweek*, 17 Aug. 1953: 61.

98. *The Big Payoff*, undated (before March 1953, with Randy Merriman).

99. *The Big Payoff*, undated (before 10 March 1958, with Bob Paige).

100. Ibid.

101. *The Big Payoff*, undated (before March 1953).

102. Ibid.

103. *The Big Payoff*, undated (before 10 March 1958).

104. Ibid.

105. Ibid.

106. Quoted in Dworkin, 182, 189.

107. Dworkin, 189–190, 203.

108. Quoted in ibid., 196–197.

109. See Dworkin, 205–206.

110. Quoted in ibid., 215.

111. *The Big Payoff*, undated, before March 1953.

112. Alexander, 53–54.

113. Kozloff, *Invisible Storytellers*, 8.

114. White, 146, in her discussion of "That was then; this is now."

Chapter 9

1. Beauvoir, xix.

2. "Everything under the Sun," *TV Guide*, 19–25 Sept. 1959: 38.

3. Meyerowitz, "Introduction," 4.

4. Spigel, *Welcome to the Dreamhouse*, 362.

5. See Feuer, "Melodrama, Serial Form, and Television Today"; Elsaesser; Masciarotte, 96.

6. Masciarotte, 96.

7. Rupp and Taylor.

8. Lerner, 174.

9. Ibid., 158.

Works Cited

Alexander, Shana. *When She Was Bad: The Story of Bess, Hortense, Sukhreet, and Nancy*. New York: Random House, 1990.

Allen, Robert C. *Speaking of Soap Operas*. Chapel Hill: University of North Carolina Press, 1985.

Ang, Ien. *Watching Dallas: Soap Opera and the Melodramatic Imagination*. Translated by Della Couling. New York: Methuen, 1985.

"Arlene Francis: The Quick Queen of Television." *Newsweek*, 19 July 1954: 50+.

Art Linkletter's House Party. CBS, circa 1957. UCLA. Videotape: VA7063T.

———. CBS, circa 1958. UCLA. Videotape: VA7757T.

———. CBS, 21 Feb. 1961. MTR. Videotape: B:11487-2.

———. CBS, 7 March 1961. MTR. Videotape: T87:0506.

———. CBS, dated 14 Dec. 1961 (probably 1960). UCLA. Videotape: VA7757T.

Arthur Godfrey Time, Practice Show. 23 Nov. 1948. MTR. Videotape: T76:0044.

———. CBS, 22 April 1953. MTR. Videotape: T76: 0044.

———. CBS, 14 June 1956. JFM. Kinescope.

———. CBS, undated. Kinevideo. Videotape.

Arthur Godfrey Time, with guest host Peter Lind Hayes. CBS, circa 1952. MBC. Videotape: 4010.3.

Auter, Philip J., and Douglas A. Boyd. "DuMont: The Original Fourth Television Network." *Journal of Popular Culture* (winter 1996): 63–83.

Barrett, Alfred J. "Stop the Misery!" *America*, 13 March 1954: 625–26.

Beadle, Mary E. "Alice Weston: Cleveland's 'First Lady of Television.'" In *Indelible Images: Women of Local Television*, edited by Mary E. Beadle and Michael D. Murray, 203–213. Ames: Iowa State University Press, 2001.

Beauvoir, Simone de. *The Second Sex*. 1953. Translated and edited by H. M. Parshley. New York: Vintage Books, 1989.

The Big Payoff. NBC, undated (after 31 Dec. 1951 and before March 1953, with host Randy Merriman). MTR. Videotape: B02975.

———. CBS, undated (after 30 Dec. 1957 and before 10 March 1958, with Bob Paige). UCLA. Videotape: VA5949T.

"Biography of Albert McCleery." AMP, Box 19, Folder 3.

Blake, Howard. "An Apologia from the Man Who Produced the Worst Program in TV History." In *American Broadcasting: A Source Book on the History of Radio and Television*, edited by Lawrence W. Lichty and Malachi C. Topping, 415–420. New York: Hastings House, 1975.

The Bob Crosby Show. CBS, 16 Nov. 1953. MTR. Videotape: T78:0137.

Boddy, William. *Fifties Television: The Industry and Its Critics*. Chicago: University of Illinois Press, 1990.

Bogart, Leo. *The Age of Television: A Study of Viewing Habits and the Impact of Television on American Life*. 3rd ed. New York: Frederick Ungar Publishing Co., 1972.

Bolt, Christine. *Feminist Ferment: The Woman Question in the USA and England, 1870–1940.* London: University College of London Press, 1995.

Bourdieu, Pierre. *Distinctions: A Social Critique of the Judgement of Taste.* Translated by Richard Nice. Cambridge: Harvard University Press, 1984.

Bride, Esther Lee. "Building Daytime Television Shows to Sell." *Practical Home Economics*, Oct. 1952: 12–13+.

Brooks, Peter. *The Melodramatic Imagination: Balzac, Henry James, Melodrama, and the Mode of Excess.* New Haven: Yale University Press, 1976.

Brown, Mary Ellen. "Motley Moments: Soap Operas, Carnival, Gossip, and the Power of the Utterance." In *Television and Women's Culture: The Politics of the Popular*, edited by Mary Ellen Brown, 183–198. London: Sage, 1990.

Brunsdon, Charlotte. *The Feminist, the Housewife, and the Soap Opera.* Oxford: Oxford University Press, 2000.

Cassidy, Marsha. "Sob Stories, Merriment, and Surprises: The 1950s Audience Participation Show on Network Television and Women's Daytime Reception." *Velvet Light Trap* 42 (fall 1998): 48–61.

———. "Visible Storytellers: Women Narrators on 1950s Daytime Television." *Style* 35, no. 2 (summer 2001): 354–374.

Cassidy, Marsha, and Mimi White. "Innovating Women's Television in Local and National Networks: Ruth Lyons and Arlene Francis." *Camera Obscura* 51 (2002): 30–69.

Castleman, Harry, and Walter J. Podrazik. *Watching TV: Four Decades of American Television.* New York: McGraw-Hill Book Company, 1982.

Chicago's Very Own at 40. WGN-TV, 1988. Kinevideo. Videotape.

Cox, Jim. *The Great Radio Audience Participation Shows: Seventeen Programs from the 1940s and 1950s.* Jefferson, NC: McFarland & Co., Inc., Publishers, 1999.

DeLong, Thomas A. *Quiz Craze: America's Infatuation with Game Shows.* New York: Praeger, 1991.

Desjardins, Mary. "Maureen O'Hara's 'Confidential' Life: Recycling Stars through Gossip and Moral Biography." In *Small Screens, Big Ideas: Television in the 1950s*, edited by Janet Thumim, 118–130. London: I. B. Tauris, 2002.

Do You Trust Your Wife? ABC, 1958. "Game Show Program X." Shokus Video. Videotape: 314.

Doane, Mary Ann. *The Desire to Desire: The Woman's Film of the 1940s.* Bloomington: Indiana University Press, 1987.

Don McNeill's Breakfast Club. ABC, Feb. 1954. Kinevideo. Videotape.

Dworkin, Susan. *Miss America, 1945: Bess Myerson's Own Story.* New York: Newmarket Press, 1987.

Elsaesser, Thomas. "Tales of Sound and Fury: Observations on the Family Melodrama." In *Imitations of Life: A Reader on Film and Television Melodrama*, edited by Marcia Landy, 68–91. Detroit: Wayne State University Press, 1991.

Feuer, Jane. "Averting the Male Gaze: Visual Pleasure and Images of Fat Women." In *Television, History, and American Culture: Feminist Critical Essays*, edited by Mary Beth Haralovich and Lauren Rabinovitz, 181–200. Durham, NC: Duke University Press, 1999.

———. "Melodrama, Serial Form, and Television Today." *Screen* 25 (1984): 4–16.

Fink, John. *WGN, A Pictorial History.* Chicago: WGN, Inc., 1961.

Fiske, John. "Women and Quiz Shows: Consumerism, Patriarchy, and Resisting Pleasures." In *Television and Women's Culture: The Politics of the Popular*, edited by Mary Ellen Brown, 134–143. London: Sage, 1990.

Frances Langford–Don Ameche Show. ABC, 2 Nov. 1951. Kinevideo. Videotape.

Francis, Arlene. *Arlene Francis: A Memoir*. New York: Simon and Schuster, 1978.

———. "Just Be Yourself." *TV Guide*, 3 Sept. 1960: 4–7.

———. *That Certain Something: The Magic of Charm*. New York: Julian Messner, Inc., 1960.

Friedan, Betty. *The Feminine Mystique*. New York: Norton, 1963.

Ganas, Monica, producer. "*Queen for a Day*: The Cinderella Story." Master's thesis, University of Kentucky, 1996. Videotape.

Garland-Thomson, Rosemarie. "Feminist Theory, The Body, and the Disabled Figure." In *The Disability Studies Reader*, edited by Lennard J. Davis, 279–292. New York: Routledge, 1997.

———. "Toward a Poetics of the Disabled Body." In *Marginal Groups and Mainstream American Culture*, edited by Yolanda Estes, Arnold Lorenzo Farr, Patricia Smith, and Clelia Smyth, 208–225. University Press of Kansas, 2000.

The Garry Moore Show. CBS, 3 Nov. 1953. JFM. Kinescope.

Gatlin, Rochelle. *American Women since 1945*. Jackson: University Press of Mississippi, 1987.

Glamour Girl. NBC, 1, 2, 3 Oct. 1953. UCLA. Videotape: VA6095T.

Goldenson, Leonard H., with Marvin J. Wolf. *Beating the Odds: The Untold Story behind the Rise of ABC: The Stars, Struggles, and Egos That Transformed Network Television by the Man Who Made It Happen*. New York: Charles Scribner's Sons, 1991.

Gould, Jack. "'Home,' Daytime Show for Women on NBC, Starts Ambitiously." *New York Times*, 5 March 1954: 26.

———. "Kate Smith Starts Daytime Video Program over WNBT." *New York Times*, 26 Sept. 1950: 62.

———. "A Look at 'Strike It Rich' as Video Entertainment: Human Emotions and Commercial Appeal." *New York Times*, 9 Nov. 1951: 34.

———. "TV's Misery Shows," *Sunday New York Times*, 7 Feb. 1954: X11.

Halper, Donna L. *Invisible Stars: A Social History of Women in American Broadcasting*. Armonk, NY: M. E. Sharpe, 2001.

Hansen, Miriam. *Babel and Babylon: Spectatorship in American Silent Film*. Cambridge: Harvard University Press, 1991.

Haralovich, Mary Beth. "Sitcoms and Suburbs: Positioning the 1950s Homemaker." *Quarterly Review of Film and Video* 11 (May 1989): 61–84.

Hardenbergh, Margot. "The Hustler: WTNH-TV, New Haven." In *Television in America: Local Station History from across the Nation*, edited by Michael D. Murray and Donald G. Godfrey, 19–38. Ames: Iowa State University Press, 1997.

Hayes, Richard K. *Kate Smith: A Biography, with a Discography, Filmography, and List of Stage Appearances*. Jefferson, NC: McFarland & Co., Inc., Publishers, 1995.

Heldenfels, Richard D. *Television's Greatest Year: 1954*. New York: Continuum, 1994.

Hess, Gary N. *An Historical Study of the DuMont Television Network*. New York: Arno, 1979.

"High-brow, Low-brow, Middle-brow." *Life*, 11 April 1949: 99–102.

Hilmes, Michele. *Radio Voices: American Broadcasting, 1922–1952*. Minneapolis: University of Minnesota Press, 1997.

Holbrook, Morris B. *Daytime Television Game Shows and the Celebration of Merchandise: The Price Is Right*. Bowling Green: Bowling Green State University Popular Press, 1993.

Home. NBC, 20 May 1954. JFM. Kinescope.

———. NBC, 21 Sept. 1954. MTR. "Home 1954," Videotape: 13376.

———. NBC, 22 Oct. 1956. MTR. "*Home* Show with Arlene Francis: *Home* in Philadelphia," 686th ed. Videotape: B:20626.

———. NBC, 12 Nov. 1956. MBC. Videotape: 4010.3.

———. NBC, 11 April 1957. MTR. "*Home* Show with Hugh Downs: April in Paris Ball," 807th ed. Videotape: B:03679.

Home, Dickie Segment. NBC, 10 Feb. 1956. Private Collection of Phyllis Adams Jenkins, Santa Monica, CA. Videotape.

Home, "The Final Show." Script for *Home*'s last show, 9 Aug. 1957. Private Collection of Phyllis Adams Jenkins, Santa Monica, CA.

Home, "Portrait of a Lady." Script of *Home*'s interview with Margaret Chase Smith, 7 March 1957. Private Collection of Phyllis Adams Jenkins, Santa Monica, CA.

Hyatt, Wesley. *The Encyclopedia of Daytime Television*. New York: Billboard Books, 1997.

It Could Be You. NBC, 19 March 1954. MTR, 207. Videotape: B:26974.

———. NBC, 3 Apr. 1956; 8 Nov. 1956; 21 May 1957. JFM. Kinescopes.

———. NBC, 11 Sept. 1957. UCLA. Videotape: VA1476T.

———. NBC, 24 Feb. 1959. UCLA. Videotape: 9556T.

———. NBC, 3 March 1960, MTR. Videotape: B:45656.

———. NBC, 26 March 1960. MTR. Videotape: B:03112.

Jezer, Marty. *The Dark Ages: Life in the United States, 1945–1960*. Boston: South End Press, 1982.

Joyrich, Lynne. "All That Television Allows: Television Melodrama, Postmodernism, and Consumer Culture." *Camera Obscura* 16 (Jan. 1988): 129–153.

Kaledin, Eugenia. *Mothers and More: American Women in the 1950s*. Boston: Twayne Publishing, 1984.

The Kate Smith Hour. NBC, 3 Oct. 1950. MTR. Videotape: T81:0843.

———. NBC, 20 Nov. 1950. MTR. Videotape: T:02209.

———. NBC, 10 March 1953. MTR. Fragment. Videotape: B:07207.

———. NBC, 27 Oct. 1953. UCLA. Videotape: T3055.

———. NBC, 28 and 29 Dec. 1953. Shokus Video. Videotape: 517.

Katz, Elihu, and Paul F. Lazarsfeld. *Personal Influence: The Part Played by People in the Flow of Mass Communications*. Glencoe, IL: The Free Press, 1955.

Kepley, Vance, Jr. "From 'Frontal Lobes' to the 'Bob-and-Bob' Show: NBC Management and Programming Strategies, 1949–65." In *Hollywood in the Age of Television*, edited by Tino Balio, 41–61. Boston: Unwin Hyman, 1990.

Klinger, Barbara. *Melodrama and Meaning: History, Culture, and the Films of Douglas Sirk*. Bloomington: Indiana University Press, 1994.

Kozloff, Sarah. *Invisible Storytellers: Voice-over Narration in American Fiction Film*. Berkeley: University of California Press, 1988.

———. *Overhearing Film Dialogue*. Berkeley: University of California Press, 2000.

Lawrence, Ruddick C. "The Networks' View of Homemaker Shows." *Practical Home Economics*, Oct. 1952: 15+.

Lerner, Gerda. *The Majority Finds Its Past: Placing Women in History*. New York: Oxford University Press, 1979.

Lichty, Lawrence W. Unpublished Database. Northwestern University, Evanston, IL.

Linkletter, Art. Interview with the author. 16 July 2001, Beverly Hills, CA.

———. *Kids Say the Darndest Things!* Englewood Cliffs, NJ: Prentice-Hall, 1957.

Linkletter, Art, with Dean Jennings. *Confessions of a Happy Man*. New York: Bernard Geis Associates, 1960.

Lynes, Russell. "High-brow, Low-brow, Middle-brow." *Harper's*, Feb. 1949: 19–28.

Lynn, Susan. *Progressive Women in Conservative Times: Racial Justice, Peace, and Feminism, 1945 to the 1960s*. New Brunswick, NJ: Rutgers University Press, 1992.

Macdonald, Dwight. "A Theory of Mass Culture." In *Mass Culture: The Popular Arts in America*, edited by Bernard Rosenberg and David Manning White, 59–73. Glencoe, IL: The Free Press, 1959.

Mann, Denise. "The Spectacularization of Everyday Life: Recycling Hollywood Stars and Fans in Early Television Variety Shows." In *Private Screenings: Television and the Female Consumer*, edited by Lynn Spigel and Denise Mann, 40–69. Minneapolis: University of Minnesota Press, 1992.

Marling, Karal Ann. *As Seen on TV: The Visual Culture of Everyday Life in the 1950s*. Cambridge: Harvard University Press, 1994.

Marshall, Jane, and Louise Frazier. "The Homemakers' View of Television." *Practical Home Economics*, Oct. 1952: 14–15+.

Masciarotte, Gloria Jean. "C'mon, Girl: Oprah Winfrey and the Discourse of Feminine Talk." *Genders* 11 (1991): 81–110.

Matera, Fran. "WTVJ, Miami: Wolfson, Renick, and 'May the Good News Be Yours.'" In *Television in America: Local Station History from across the Nation*, edited by Michael D. Murray and Donald G. Godfrey, 106–127. Ames: Iowa State University Press, 1997.

Matinee Theater. NBC. "This One Is Different." UCLA. Videotape: T5666.

———. NBC. "Two Picture Deal." UCLA. Videotape: T3892.

May, Elaine Tyler. *Homeward Bound: American Families in the Cold War Era*. New York: Basic Books, 1988.

McCarthy, Anna. *Ambient Television: Visual Culture and Public Space*. Durham, NC: Duke University Press, 2001.

———. "Outer Spaces: Public Viewing in American Television History." Ph.D. diss., Northwestern University, 1995.

McCleery, Albert. "Five Do's and Don't's for Television Production," drafted 24 Nov. 1952. AMP, Box 6, Folder 2.

———. "Memorandum on NBC Matinee Theatre," 12 Sept. 1955. AMP, Box 1, Folder 7.

———. "Theater's Debt to Television," 12 Sept. 1960. AMP, Box 4, Folder 1.

McCleery, Albert, and Carl Glick. *Curtains Going Up*. New York: Pitman Pub. Co., 1939.

Mellencamp, Patricia. "Situation Comedy, Feminism, and Freud: Discourse of Gracie and Lucy." In *Studies in Entertainment: Critical Approaches to Mass Culture*, edited by Tania Modleski, 80–95. Bloomington: Indiana University Press, 1986.

Merton, Robert K. "Effectiveness of the Kate Smith Bond Drive." Columbia University Consulting Report, Jan. 1944, KSC, Box 2.

Meyerowitz, Joanne. "Beyond the Feminine Mystique: A Reassessment of Postwar Mass Culture, 1946–1958." In *Not June Cleaver: Women and Gender in Postwar America, 1945–1960*, edited by Joanne Meyerowitz, 229–262. Philadelphia: Temple University Press, 1994.

———. "Introduction." In *Not June Cleaver: Women and Gender in Postwar America, 1945–1960*, edited by Joanne Meyerowitz, 1–16. Philadelphia: Temple University Press, 1994.

Modleski, Tania. *Loving with a Vengeance: Mass-Produced Fantasies for Women*. New York: Routledge, 1990.

Munson, Wayne. *All-Talk: The Talkshow in Media Culture*. Philadelphia: Temple University Press, 1993.

Murray, Michael D. "Charlotte Peters: One of a Kind." In *Indelible Images: Women of Local Television*, edited by Mary E. Beadle and Michael D. Murray, 143–154. Ames: Iowa State University Press, 2001.

Murray, Susan. "Our Man Godfrey: Arthur Godfrey and the Selling of Stardom in Early Television." *Television and New Media* 2, no. 3 (Aug. 2001): 187–204.

NBC Radio and Television Broadcast Standards. AMP, Box 16, Folder 9.

"NBC-TV's Major Daytime Advances; Forge Ahead on Sales, Ratings." *Variety*, 6 Feb. 1957: 27+.

O'Brian, Jack. *Godfrey the Great*. New York: Cross Publications, Inc., 1951.

O'Dell, Cary. *Women Pioneers in Television: Biographies of Fifteen Industry Leaders*. Jefferson, NC: McFarland & Co., Inc., Publishers, 1997.

Okay, Mother. DuMont, dated 1947. "Game Show Programs X." Skokus Video. Videotape: 314.

Peiss, Kathy. *Hope in a Jar: The Making of America's Beauty Culture*. New York: Metropolitan Books, Henry Holt and Co., 1998.

Pennell, Ellen LaVerne. *Women on Television*. Minneapolis: Burgess Publishing Company, 1954.

Pope, Elizabeth. "Why Women Love Garry." *Women's Home Companion*, Sept. 1953: 42–43, 141–144.

Queen for a Day. NBC, March 1956. MTR. Videotape: T85:0679.

———. ABC, 1960. Shokus Video. Videotape: 314.

———. ABC, 19 Oct. 1960. UCLA. Videotape: VA14028T.

———. Undated fragments. MTR. Videotape: 02399.

"*Queen for a Day* Reunion Excerpt." *Good Morning America*, 1 March 2000. UCLA. Videotape: T79431.

Rowe, Kathleen. *The Unruly Woman: Gender and the Genres of Laughter*. Austin: University of Texas Press, 1995.

Runyon, Steven C. "San Francisco's First Television Station: KPIX." In *Television in America: Local Station History from across the Nation*, edited by Michael D. Murray and Donald G. Godfrey, 353–366. Ames: Iowa State University Press, 1997.

Rupp, Leila, and Verta Taylor. *Survival in the Doldrums: The American Women's Rights Movement, 1945 to the 1960s*. New York: Oxford University Press, 1987.

Ryan, Barbara. *Feminism and the Women's Movement: Dynamics of Change in Social Movement, Ideology, and Activism*. New York: Routledge, 1992.

Samuel, Lawrence R. *Brought to You By: Postwar Television and the American Dream*. Austin: University of Texas Press, 2001.

Sanford, Herb. *Ladies and Gentlemen, The Garry Moore Show: Behind the Scenes When TV Was New*. New York: Stein and Day Publishers, 1976.

Sarnoff, David. Memo to John K. Herbert, 21 Aug. 1953. NBCR, Box 368, Folder 60.

Schwoch, James. "A Failed Vision: The Mutual Television Network." *Velvet Light Trap* 33 (spring 1994): 3–13.

Segal, Lynne. *Slow Motion: Changing Masculinities, Changing Men*. London: Virago Press, 1990.

Shayon, Robert Lewis. "The Hurry of 'Home.'" *Saturday Review*, 10 April 1954: 37–38.

———. "Just like Radio." *Saturday Review*, 28 July 1956: 23.

———. "Sex in the Afternoon." *Saturday Review*, 17 Nov. 1956: 32.

Shulman, Arthur, and Roger Youman. *How Sweet It Was: Television, a Pictorial Commentary*. New York: Bonanza Books, 1966.

Singer, Arthur J. *Arthur Godfrey: The Adventures of an American Broadcaster*. Jefferson, NC: McFarland & Co. Inc., Publishers, 2000.

Smith, Kate. *Living in a Great Big Way*. New York: Blue Ribbon Books, 1938.

———. *Upon My Lips a Song*. New York: Funk & Wagnalls, 1960.

Spigel, Lynn. *Make Room for TV: Television and the Family Ideal in Postwar America*. Chicago: University of Chicago Press, 1992.

———. *Welcome to the Dreamhouse: Popular Media and Postwar Suburbs*. Durham, NC: Duke University Press, 2001.

Sterling, Christopher H., and John M. Kittross. *Stay Tuned: A Concise History of American Broadcasting*. 2nd ed. Belmont, CA: Wadsworth Publishing Company, 1990.

Sternberg, Joel. "A Descriptive History and Critical Analysis of the Chicago School of Television: Chicago Network Programming in the Chicago Style from 1948 to 1954." Ph.D. diss., Northwestern University, 1973.

Stole, Inger L. "'The Kate Smith Hour' and the Struggle for Control of Television Programming in the Early 1950s." *Historical Journal of Film, Radio, and Television* 20 (2000): 549–564.

———. "There Is No Place like *Home*: NBC's Search for a Daytime Audience, 1954–1957." *Communication Review* 2, no. 2 (1997): 135–161.

Strike It Rich. CBS, Summer (after 2 June) 1952. MTR. Videotape: B:33062.

———. CBS, 18 Nov. 1953. UCLA. Videotape: VA2645T.

———. CBS. 28 Nov. 1956. JFM. Kinescope.

Strike It Rich, Evening Version. CBS, undated. UCLA. Videotape: VA5949T.

Sturcken, Frank. *Live Television: The Golden Age of 1946–1958 in New York.* Jefferson, NC: McFarland & Co., Inc., Publishers, 1990.

Timberg, Bernard M. *Television Talk: A History of the TV Talk Show.* Austin: University of Texas Press, 2002.

Weaver, Sylvester L. "Memorandum from NBC's Pat Weaver, 1955," regarding *Matinee Theater.* Appendix I, dictated to Jane Murray, 4 July 1955. In Sturcken, 129–145. Jefferson, NC: McFarland & Co., Inc., Publishers, 1990.

———. "Memo subject 'Kate Smith.'" 22 June 1950. NBCR, Box 119, Folder 35.

Weaver, [Sylvester L.] Pat, with Thomas M. Coffey. *The Best Seat in the House: The Golden Years of Radio and Television.* New York: Knopf, 1994.

Weinstein, David. "Women's Shows and the Selling of Television to Washington, D.C." *Washington History* 11, no. 1 (spring/summer 1999): 4–23.

Wendell, Susan. "Toward a Feminist Theory of Disability." In *The Disability Studies Reader*, edited by Lennard J. Davis, 260–278. New York: Routledge, 1997.

White, Mimi. *Tele-Advising: Therapeutic Discourse in American Television.* Chapel Hill: University of North Carolina Press, 1992.

Who Do You Trust? ABC, after 1958. Bruce Simon Video. Videotape.

Williams, Mark. "Considering Monty Margetts's *Cooks Corner*: Oral History and Television History." In *Television, History, and American Culture: Feminist Critical Essays*, edited by Mary Beth Haralovich and Lauren Rabinovitz, 36–55. Durham, NC: Duke University Press, 1999.

Wilson, Pamela. "NBC TV's 'Operation Frontal Lobes': Cultural Hegemony and 50s Program Planning." *Historical Journal of Film, Radio, and Television* 15 (March 1995): 83–105.

Index

confessional game shows, 23–24, 104–106; and female subjects, 24, 184–185, 187, 189–194, 213; and home viewers, 213; and public censure, 105. *See also* misery shows

confessional modes, 7, 23–24. *See also* confessional game shows; misery shows

Conte, John, 165, 171, *173*, 175–176, 180; as matinee idol, 172

Conte, Ruth, 180–181

cosmetics, 19. *See also* glamour, postwar

Crane, Ruth, 30

Crosby, Bob, 76

Crosby, John: review of *Glamour Girl*, 128; review of *Matinee Theater*, 162, 166

Culligan, Joe, 178, 179

Curtains Going Up, 160

Davis, Mary Webb, 118, 130

daytime television programming: competition in, earliest, 27–28, 39–40; competition in, mid-decade, 185–187; debates over "quality," 7, 157–158; delay by major radio networks, 33–34; early local, 28–33; sample lineup in 1955, 5. *See also names of specific networks and stations*

daytime television viewing: advertiser concerns about, 9–10; and *The Fifty-Fifty Club*, 30–31; growth of, 2, 46–47; leisure and home reception of, 7, 8–11, 136; and soap opera, 4; and women, 5–6

Dennis James Show, 45

Dior, Christian, 7, 19, 66

Don McNeill's Breakfast Club, 44–45

Downs, Hugh, 137, 139, 152

Do You Trust Your Wife? See Who Do You Trust?

DuMont Television: daytime programming on, 19, 34–39; demise of, 39–40

Edwards, Ralph, 186, 194

fashion, 18–20. *See also* glamour, postwar

Fashions on Parade, 19

Fedderson, Don, 203

"femcee," 21

feminist history, 3, 132–133

The Fifty-Fifty Club, 12, *30–31*

The First Hundred Years, 4

Flying High, 52

Foch, Nina, *168*

Framer, Walt, 106, 112–113, *113*, 206, 211

The Frances Langford-Don Ameche Show, 45

Francis, Arlene, 6, 17–18, *132*, *140*; career of, 144, 241n136; as first "femcee," 21; as "homemaker," 145–147; persona of, on television, 144–148; as saleswoman, 22, 145; verbal skills of, 147–148; views of, on charm, 21–22, 145

Frank, Ethel, 165, 171

Freed, Fred, 139–140

Frey, George H., and *The Kate Smith Hour*, 59, 64

Friedan, Betty, 2–3

Gabel, Martin, 145

Gabel, Peter, 147, 149

The Garry Moore Show, 78–80; audience participation in, 82–84; leisure and home reception of, 80–81; sponsors of, 97

General Federation of Women's Clubs, 141

"giveaway shows," 104; legal action against, 115

glamour, postwar, 7–8; and consumer products, 19–20; and cosmetics, 19; and fashion, 18–20; on *Glamour Girl*, 117–122; and Hollywood, 20–21, 118–119; on *Queen for a Day*, 194; and studio audiences, 23; and television commercials, 22–23

Glamour Girl, 7, 18, 20; and confessing subjects, 24, 119–121; promotion of, 121–122, 128; and public censure, 105, 122–129; ratings of, 128; and the therapeutic makeover, 117–122, 130

Lyons, Ruth, 6, 30–31; as saleswoman, 22

Macdonald, Dwight, 14–18
"the makeover," 117–118; on *Glamour Girl*, 130
male hosts ("charm boys"), 6, 25, 38
Margetts, Monty, 30
Market Melodies, 39
Matinee Theater, 11, 16–17; censorship and "adult" themes on, 171–175; budget for, 189; color broadcasting of, 164; and "Course for Collision," 179; demise of, 178–181; and the Foundation for the Preservation of *Matinee Theater*, 180; Hollywood production site for, 163–165; leisure and home reception of, 10, 169–171; promotion of, 157, 164–165; ratings of, 178–179; reviews of, 166–167; and sample dramas, 167–168; and soap opera, 25, 158–159, 165–169, 182; sponsors of, 165, 177–178; and "This One is Different," 175–176; and "Two-Picture Deal," 176–177
McAvity, Thomas A.: and *The Kate Smith Hour*, 64; and *Queen for a Day*, 187
McCarthy, Henry, 114–115
McCleery, Albert, 17–18, *161*; and arena/populist theater, 160–161, 165; and the "cameo shot," 160; career of, 159–160, 181; founding memo on *Matinee Theater* by, 163–164; on the "upbeat ending," 168; on "quality" television, 166–167, 179; on sexual themes on television, 171–175; on televisual style, 161–163; on theater vs. television, 181–183; vignettes of, on *The Kate Smith Hour*, 69
McCoy, Jack, 117–120, 124
McFadyen, Robert, and *The Kate Smith Hour*, 59–60, 64
McMahon, Ed, 202
Meade, Julia, 23, 37–39, 72
melodrama, on television, 7; misery shows, 24, 187–194

Merriman, Randy, 185, 207, 212
Merton, Robert K., 56–57
The Mickey Mouse Club, 43, 186
Mills, Ted, 136, 138
misery shows: and confession, 23–24, 186; and melodrama, 186–193; NBC discussion of, 124–127; and public censure, 105, 115–116, 235n49
Moore, Garry, *79*: camera rapport of, 77–78, 83; on housewives, 8, 81–82; as salesman, 22, 97; and sex appeal, 100–101
Morfit, Thomas Garrison. *See* Moore, Garry
Morgan, Louise, 30
Moseley, Bill, and *Matinee Theater*, 170
Much Ado About Nothing, 168
Mutual Broadcasting System, 40–43
Myerson, Bess, 6, 21, 67, 72, *206*, *208*; and anti-Semitism, 211; and conflicts as Miss America, 210–212; persona of, on *The Big Payoff*, 206–212; as saleswoman, 23

NBC Television: daytime programming on, 15–17, *33–34*, 39–40, 154–156, 185–186
Niles, Wendell, 195–196, 199

Okay, Mother, 10, 35–39; leisure and home reception of, 36
O'Keefe, Winston, 165
"Operation Daybreak," 43–44, 186
"Operation Frontal Lobes," 16, 137

Paige, Bob, 185, 207, 208
Paley, William, 78, 106
Paradise Bay, 181
Paul, Ralph, 106, 107
Payne, Ed, 189–190
People Are Funny, 89
Peters, Charlotte, 30
Phillips, Irna, 4
Pinkham, Richard A. R.: and *Home*, 137, 145, 150–151; and *The Kate Smith Hour*, 64
Procter & Gamble, 5, 43, 60, 165, 189